My Struggle for Self-Realization

(An Autobiography)

Swami Satchidananda Giri

Sri Sri Yogoda Ashram

SHIPRA

(First Published in India in 2015)

Rs. 1250; US$ 50

ISBN: 978-81-7541-799-1

2023

My Struggle for Self-Realization: An Autobiography

Sri Sri Yogoda Ashram, Village: Golkunda,
P.O.: Mamurjor, District: Purulia, W.B.

Published by:
SHIPRA PUBLICATIONS
LG 18-19, Pankaj Central Market
I.P. Ext., Patparganj, Delhi 110092, Ind
Tel.: +91 11 2223 5152; 96500 28065
E-mail: info@shiprapublication.com
www.shiprapublication.com

Contents

Preface

'My Struggle for Self-Realization' is the autobiography of Swami Satchidananda Giri. Swamiji was the direct disciple of Sri Sri Paramhansa Yoganandaji, founder of Yogoda Satsanga Society of India and Self-Realization Fellowship.

Swamiji maintained diary meticulously since 1945. These diaries contained two types of writings — essays on a variety of themes of spiritual and social issues, incidences, and episodes with which Swamiji was directly associated. Narrations of these incidences are genuine, intense and very personal. Every episode provides glimpses of important spiritual experience. Each episode is a mile stone on the way to Swamiji's Self-realization; indeed, a vivid description of His 'Struggle for Self-Realization'. Each episode is a beacon light for the meditating minds of his young disciples who have begun their inspired journey for understanding the self.

This book, hence, does not read like one of the many autobiographies. It is something unique, something that touches the deeper chords of our very being. We are grateful to Swamiji for sharing His wealth of spiritual experience with us through this book.

A few words of acknowledgement are due.

The entire manuscript was earlier composed and produced in book form, but only limited number of copies. Swami Krishnananda Giri of **Paramahansa Yogananda Ashrama in Purulia** gave the impetus for the full-scale publication of this autobiography; Swami Krishnandaji reviewed the entire manuscript and edited it meticulously. Swami Abhayananda Giri, a direct disciple of Swami Satchidananda Giri and his caregiver till the last moment provided good input to fill the gaps between 1969 and 2005 when Swamiji breathed his last.

Sri Soumen Panja computerized the handwritten manuscript – noting in diaries by Swami Satchidananda Giri; Sri Sabyasachi Panja produced the cover design. Sri D. Kumar of Shipra Publications graciously undertook the responsibility of printing, production and publication of this book.

On behalf of all the disciples of Swami Satchidananda Giri, I express my heartfelt thanks to all those who either directly or indirectly helped 'My Struggle for Self-Realization' see the light of the day.

I feel blessed and grateful to Swamiji for entrusting the work to me.

Marmar Mukhopadhyay

Chapter 1

My Parents and Early Struggle for Meditation

I was born in June 1915 at Kalagachhi in the District of Jessore, in the then Bengal, India. After the division of Bengal (in 1947), it came to be known as East Pakistan, and later (in 1971) as Bangladesh. My mother's maternal uncle's house was at Kalagachhi. My own maternal uncle's house was at Joypur, six miles away from Kalagachhi. Joypur was a lovely village situated on the banks of New Ganges. I have vivid recollections of the place, where in my early years, I would sit on the banks of the New Ganges and enjoy seeing the fish play in the river. My maternal uncle used to catch fish and I would sit by his side. We were three children - two boys and one girl, I, Anil Kumar Basu being the eldest son. My father and mother were Bengalees, belonging to the Kshatriya caste. Both, endowed with saintly nature, were keen worshippers of Lord Vishnu, the preserver of the cosmos. Vishnu is the second God of the trinity, the first being Brahma, the creator, and the third, Shiva, the destroyer. My parents were independent in their own ways, but there was intense mutual love and affection between them. They were serene, pure and dignified.

My father, Nagendra Nath Basu, was disciplined and at times very stern. Though he had great affection for us, we always observed some reverential distance. I never saw him going to a Cinema Hall or Theatre. He never took any kind of intoxication such as cigarette, tea, coffee or the like, what to speak of alcoholic drinks. His innate nature was soft and affectionate. He worked as a Police Inspector under the then State Government in Orissa. He could easily conquer the hearts of the public while he was in service. Years later, I had witnessed a unique scene while he was leaving the service for good from Bhuban Police Station under the State Government of Dhenkanal. The villagers of Bhuban and the neighbouring locality followed him for miles together. Some were lamenting, "We have lost our father for good". My mother was also a queen of hearts who taught and guided us through her love. She influenced me through her devotional songs and prayers which came from her heart's love for Lord Krishna. She used to play Kartal along with the songs in the shrine during her daily puja ceremony. I had also learnt from her the Mantras and the process of puja of different gods and goddesses, especially the Divine Mother.

My parents were given mantras by the family Guru. My father received the sacred thread from the Guru of Kayastha Sabha. He used to do Japa of 'Gayatri', which is the essential spiritual duty of all Brahmins and Kshatriyas, who had got the sacred thread.

I received my sacred thread from a Guru from Orissa, selected by my parents at Bhuban. From time to time, my father changed his place of service from one State Government to another as a Police Inspector, for reasons best known to him. When my father was in the Kashipore Estate in Orissa as a Police Inspector, I was then 5 or 6 years old. I have vivid recollections of the place where I used to play with the boys of the neighbouring locality. Our quarter was encircled with bamboo sticks 10 to 12 feet high. Facing our quarter, there was a small hill covered with dense forest, at the top of which, sometimes a tiger could be seen roaming freely. From the very infancy I had a fascination for nature. At the age of six, I was sent to the doctor of the State Charitable Hospital for my early education. The doctor was one of my father's friends. My parents used to send me there not only for study but to keep me confined so that I might not meet with any accident on the street while playing with boys.

My first tutor was my mother herself. I vividly remember the first day of my study under her guidance. She gave me Tal leaves, 4 to 5 feet in length and 2 to 2.5 inches in breadth, one pen made of a sort of reed used in India and an inkpot with washable black ink. My mother told me to write and instantly I began writing an alphabet with my pen without any help from my mother. The alphabet was a mathematical figure. My mother encouraged me saying, "my child writes very well". "Being encouraged thus, I filled up the whole page with that alphabet. At the end, my mother took me in her lap and showered kisses on my face, very common for a child of that age".

My second tutor, the said doctor, was a surgeon. The sight of any small operation caused me pain at heart. Hence, I used to leave the place at the time of operation. At the age of seven, I was sent to the school of Jangalbadhal for education under the care of my uncle (elder brother of my father), Debendra Nath Basu. Jangalbadal was a small village in the district of Jessore, nearly a mile away from the Singia Railway Station. It was my native village where I was brought up along with my cousin brothers. My high school was situated by the side of the river Bhairab, very near the Singia Station. It was 84 miles away from Sealdah Railway Station, Calcutta.

I used to fly kites with my cousin brothers. Though generally we used to play kites of smaller size with very thin cotton threads, still sometimes we would play with special type of kites, six to eight square feet in size with strings made of jute. There were very thin cane strips attached to their top; which in contact with the gentle breeze, used to produce a very peculiar sound audible from a great distance. I had a fascination for such big kites due to their melodious sound.

At the age of eight or nine, I found a small note book in post card size by the side of the path leading to our house, on the front cover of which there were very beautiful pictures of Lord Krishna and Radha. As there was no address written on the notebook, it was not possible for me to find out its owner. I kept the note book on my table in the reading room and offered flowers at their feet in the way puja is performed, which I had learned from my mother.

I used to play various kinds of games with my friends at School and also with my village mates. I learnt the art of swimming and rowing and could easily climb a 40 to 50 feet high coconut or beatlenut tree.

There was a big banyan tree by the side of our bathing ghat. We would generally climb up the tree and jump into the river. This tree also had a long thick branch which had grown parallel to the ground. Along with my friends, I used to ride this branch (It is also a type of game for the children. Some boys used to ride like the riding of a horse and others used to swing the branch with a rope attached to it). At school, I learnt to play football, cricket, badminton, volleyball, ring, marble top and also mastered the arts of long jump, high jump, pole jump and such other games and sports.

Among my classmates, four boys were my best friends - Shyamapada, Sivakrishna, Hemchandra and Haripada. There was a spirit of competition among us which was mainly in the fields of study and play, which afterwards extended to the spiritual field also. Shivakrishna was a poet, who could compose poems instantly on any subject. Once our class teacher ordered him to compose a poem on an umbrella. He forthwith composed a beautiful poem in his mother tongue within a very short time and placed the same before the teacher. Shyampada was a mathematician. Sometimes he would secure cent per cent marks in mathematics. Generally, Shivakrishna would secure the highest marks in vernacular. Shyampada generally secured the highest marks in Mathematics. But in aggregate either Shyamapada or myself used to get the highest marks. Our Mathematician Shyamapada Singha had a very good knowledge in Geography of the world. Once, I had examined his knowledge in Geography. He could easily point out the cities, rivers, mountains, or any other places of interest in different countries of the World. I have a clear memory regarding keen competition between Shyamapada and myself. I once secured 86% marks in History while he secured 85%, I secured 85% marks in Geography while he secured 86%. This way we both stood first, securing equal number of marks in aggregate.

As regards competition in the spiritual field, I headed the list. None of my friends could perform Yogasans like me. We all used to read religious books, notable works of Acharya Shankara (the founder of our Swami order), Paramahansa Nigamanada, the Kathamrita of Paramahansa Ramakrishna and the lives of great Yogis of India. I was regular in the practise of yogic exercises. Years later, Hemchandra learnt the preliminary Kriya Yoga techniques from me. I had learnt various kinds of Hatha Yoga, Laya Yoga and eight varieties of Pranayama, besides the Japa of Brahma 'Gayatri'.

Recalling my very early realization, I clearly remember that during the night when I went to bed, I would see a dazzling light, enveloping the whole room, and myself floating in the light. Sometimes in that blaze of light, I could see the whole room, with all the things around me and hear the astral music like the divine concert of the play of different musical instruments. As I was very young, I could not understand that this symphony of musical sounds actually emanated from my own inner soul. I thought that at a distant place, the puja of the Divine Father was going on always. I could smell the perfume of different scented flowers even while working in the deserted land or in meadows and would search for the flower tree from which such sweet fragrance came. Once, I was puzzled when I saw nothing except grass within the range of a mile from which perfume could hardly have spread all over the land. Afterwards, I came to know that the origin of the perfume was within me. From my early boyhood I used to strictly follow the rules and regulations of the Brahmacharya. While walking my attention or gaze was on the toes so that my mind may not be diverted to the nearby objects of sight and that no diversion may cause a break in my japa of the divine name.

I used to practice the yogic techniques three times a day regularly and on many occasions I could perform it five times a day. Initially, I could not sit for more than twenty minutes at a time in one sitting. At leisure, I would sit for meditation five times a day - 2 to 3 a.m.; 4 to 5 a.m.; 9-30 a.m.; 5 p.m. and lastly at 7 p.m. We had one reading room where I had to study with my cousin brothers. Hence, it was difficult for me to practise the yoga techniques among so many people of the family. In order to avoid their attention I used to take my bath half an hour earlier than the scheduled time. My cousins would go for bath after me. It was between 9 a.m. to 9.30 a.m. when the study room was empty and other members of the family were engaged in their respective duties at home. Then I used to meditate. As regards late night and early morning Sadhana, there was no difficulty as everyone else of our family would be asleep. As I slept in one room on the eastern side of the building, I could perform the yoga techniques at night and in the morning. For my afternoon sadhana, I selected the empty school building where no one came to disturb me.

The village school was situated nearly a mile away from my home. I could not manage to come back in time for the evening study as the family members expected. Everyday they used to scold me for my late presence for the evening study. I prayed to God to find out a suitable solitary place for my meditation very near to my house. God responded in a way to test the depth of my love for him. I got the direction from inside to enter into the jungle for my solitary meditation. There was a jungle very near to our house known to all as the residence of ghosts. The villagers used to discuss about abodes of the ghosts. They used to say that there were seven ghosts that were living in the seven different banyan trees in the jungle. A tributary of the river Bhairab was flowing by the side of jungle. Sometime a tiger would come in that forest and reside there temporarily. I had come to know from my relatives that no ghost would dare to come to a devotee of God. So, mentally chanting the name of God, I visited the jungle with a fearful heart. I saw the jungle was not as thick as it was thought to be. In the middle of the jungle, beautiful green grass had grown. My fear went away as neither ghost nor ferocious beast came to me. I thanked God from the core of my heart as He had guided me to find a very suitable place for meditation.

Daily I started to meditate in the jungle after coming back from the school. I would recite or chant some of the famous verses of Acharya Shankara, specially Mohamudgara and Kawpin Panchaka before meditation.

After a few days I selected another place for my afternoon meditation. It was nearer than the jungle. There was an old orchard very near to our house, also concealed in a jungle. One day as I was absorbed in my daily afternoon meditation, my mind was drawn outside by the characteristic noise of a number of wild boars passing by my side. From the next day, I changed the place of meditation. There was a burning ghat near our bathing place. It was a very lonely spot. No one would go there due to the fear of ghosts and wild animals because it was situated by the side of a forest. In the evening, I had seen, on many occasions, wild foxes roaming in search of food. In the cremation ground, we used to bury the dead bodies of young children instead of burning them. The foxes would dig the places to devour them. For several days, I had gone there for meditation, but due to the quarrel of the foxes which caused much disturbance, I left that place too.

In that way I changed several places for meditation. One day I tried to meditate on a margosa tree (neem) in the jungle but it proved to be impracticable. One of the best solitary places which I had discovered for my meditation was the roof of my house which had neither the staircase nor the stairs, hence no one could climb on the roof of the house. With the help of a bamboo I used to go to the roof of the building and would meditate as long as I wished to do so. There were balconies on all sides of the roof. Hence, no one could see me from outside what I was doing. Behind the building there was an orchard partly covered with jungle. I had kept one bamboo on the back of the building near the jungle. Because of the jungle, no one could visit that side of the building. I could meditate there anytime without any disturbance. In the morning, after my Yogic exercises, I used to go out for a stroll, when I used to perform "Kaki Mudra" (Long inhalation and exhalation through the mouth following some rules and regulations of breathing) in the open air.

As regards my spiritual progress, I would always feel new joy and bliss in my heart. Sometimes, I could get an inkling of the intuitive hearing which ordinarily could not be heard with the physical ears. My memory became sharper and I had no difficulty in my study. I could memorise my lessons only by reading the same once or twice. Due to this reason, my private tutor liked me very much. All teachers of the school also loved me dearly for my sweet behaviour and keen intellect.

I would prepare my lessons perfectly. The teachers generally did not ask me any questions pertaining to my lessons. When other children of the class could not answer a very difficult question I was asked to explain the same to them. I would, forthwith satisfy the teachers as well as the students with my perfect answers.

Though I received ever new joy and bliss in meditation, still my heart was always ailing for self-realisation. I was always thinking seriously about my future flight from home in search of a true Guru for self-realisation. My mind had changed to a great extent, without my knowing how. I was thinking as to how I could become a Swami like Vivekananda. My relatives noticed the change of attitude in me, but no one could guess what I was thinking and for what my heart was longing. Sometimes they used to tease me with sarcastic words, but I took them lightly, though wounded at heart, as I knew that no good effect would be produced by harsh and prompt reply. At that time, early marriage was the order of the day. Sometimes, female members among my kinsmen or relatives would advise to select a bride for me even in my presence. In their opinion, all my other worldly thoughts would vanish if I could get a suitable bride as my life companion. They would often come to test me by a volley of questions. They would ask me, whether I wished to get married. One of them said that she knew a very beautiful girl, as a prospective bride. Inwardly, I could feel that she had come to test me; in reality, she had not the least intention to get me betrothed. Though the very word of marriage would produce wrath in me, still, suppressing my feelings, I would give instant reply in a witty way, "No, I would not like to have a bride now, as I want to complete my studies first. If you give me a beautiful wife, she will draw my entire attention towards her. Further, when young ones will come by dozen who will maintain them? After finishing my studies when I shall be able to stand on my own feet, with my own earnings, I can easily select a girl of my own choice". Inwardly, she became very pleased with the reply and being unable to put any counter-question, went away laughingly.

From my early childhood, I had no attachment for meat, fish or eggs. One day my uncle came to me and asked, "Why are you not taking meat and fish? What is your intention? Are you going to be a 'Sadhu' (Sadhu is a term generally used for a saint, monk or a swami)? What ashram are you going to join? Those, who have nothing to eat at home, or who have not the least capacity to earn their own living, generally take shelter under a religious institution or become a Sadhu. Most of the thieves, murderers, or criminals put on the saffron or ochre coloured dress to live in disguise. If you go to a Math or Ashram, the policemen will arrest you, thinking you to be one of these culprits". Though such remarks against the character of the saints would easily produce wrath in me, still, somehow suppressing my inner feelings, I replied, "No, I have not the least intention to be a Sadhu. Further, if those who have nothing to eat generally go to the religious institutions, then for what shall I be a monk? I have no sorrow, nor any want. I have enough to eat. I have no taste for meat or fish, rather I dislike them. There is no other reason for not taking meat, fish or egg.

This uncle and aunt did not allow me to read religious books lest my mind should be diverted towards religion and I might flee from the house in search of God; but my heart's craving overcame the ban and I began to read the spiritual interpretation of the Holy Bhagavad Gita in my mother tongue written by Kumar Nath Mukherjee who had received the title "Sudhakar" i.e., mine of nectar of his spiritual power and knowledge. I would sit on a woollen blanket and read the Holy scriptures loudly. There arose a vehement protest from the uncle and aunt, but I was firm in my resolution. For a number of days, they tried to dissuade me from the study of that Holy book but in vain. I was adamant not to pay any heed to their protest. After a few days, the discontentment subsided from both the sides. They, too, came to realise that the bullets of words would not hurt me. Besides the reading of the Holy text, all other religious duties were performed in strict secrecy.

My Daily Routine

I would get up at about 4 a.m. in the morning. After the morning rituals, I would sit on a deer skin for my meditation. I would practice in the morning Mahamudra pranayama and meditation on the six 'Chakras' (plexuses) and on five 'Tatwas'. I would perform the type of pranayama, which was followed by all the Brahmins who had got the sacred thread. It was not the same kind of pranayama which I had got from Paramahansa Yoganandaji afterwards. It was a typical kind of pranayama with which japa i.e., counting of "Om" goes simultaneously. It includes first inhalation and holding the breath in the lung and exhalation in the ratio of 1:4:2; i.e., if the time period of inhalation is for 15 seconds, the time period for holding the breath will be one minute and that of exhalation will be for 30 seconds. My japa of "Om" with this pranayama was between ten to eleven thousands. I used to practice the above techniques up to any time between 5 to 5-30 a.m., then walk for half an hour. At about 6 a.m. in the morning, I would do physical exercise which included long jump, high jump and some free hand exercises. Six to seven boys used to do their exercises along with me. At about 6-30 a.m., I would come back from my exercises and, after a wash and breakfast, study up to 9-30 a.m., devoting myself to the daily task of the school. At 9-30 a.m. I would go for a bath which lasted for 10 to 15 minutes. From 9-45 a.m. to 10-15 a.m. would do Mahamudra and Pranayama; 10-15 a.m. to 10-30 a.m. take meal; and after 5 to 10 minutes rest I would start for the school. Our school was at a distance of fifteen minutes walk, where I had to spend my valuable time from 11 a.m. to 4 p.m. with the teachers. I would come back home at about 4-15 p.m. and after a wash and tiffin, I would study religious books, specially the Holy Bhagavad Gita for some time. At about 5-30 p.m. I would go to the jungle for yogic exercises. The inmates of my house would think that I had gone out for a stroll. During summer season, I would practice the Kriya exercises from 6 p.m. in the abode of the so called ghosts. The Kriya exercises included Mahamudra, Pranayama with 10 to 11 thousand japa of 'Om' and meditation. I then study from 7-15 p.m. to 9-15 p.m.; meal 9-15 p.m. to 9-30 p.m. After meal, I would read Bhagavad Gita for sometime. At times, instead of reading Gita I would go out for a walk for 10 to 15 minutes. At about 10 p.m., I would go to bed. Though I would get up at about 2 a.m. in the night for meditation, I could not sit for more than 15 to 20 minutes as sleep would overpower me. Total number of 'Japa' of 'Om' was between 20,000 to 25,000 in 24 hours. Whenever I would get leisure time, I would be doing japa of 'Om'. In that way, I completed one year.

I thought that, within one or two years, I would be able to acquire much spiritual power but no sign of such improvement was perceptible. The only thing I felt was peace of mind and heart. At that tender age, my aim of life was the acquisition of supernatural yogic powers, to see the astral kingdom and awakening the coiled force (Kulakundalini) at the base of the spine. I had more love for supernatural power than for God. Not being able to get the desired result within two years and a half, I was somewhat depressed, but I used to follow the daily routine as before.

I was promoted to Class I, which is the same as Class X of the School final standard of the present system of education. I stood first in the said examination. There was a little change in the daily routine. It was the omission of reading Holy Bhagavad Gita in the morning. I used to recite the same at night after my meal at about 9-45 p.m. to 10 p.m., when all members of the family were in their respective rooms. I would close the doors in order to avoid sudden intrusion of anyone in my room while I would be reciting the verses of the Bhagavad Gita mentally. The above routine was followed while I would attend the school. During long vacations, the said routine was changed as the time of our midday meal changed to 12-30 p.m. Hence, the time for meditation before meal was changed to 11-30 a.m. I could devote much more time during vacations, as I had no anxiety for going to school. I generally used to go to take my bath in the river that was flowing by the side of the jungle, the abode of the ghosts. After finishing my bath, I would pluck variety of flowers and worship divine Parents sitting under a banyan tree, on which the so-called ghosts were supposed to be living. Then I used to sit for meditation in forest as before.

Days passed by, and so did weeks and months, still no perception of the desired result was visible and hence, a doubt naturally crept into my mind, whether I was following the yogic techniques correctly. My heart was longing for a true Guru. The world, with its versatile beauty, hundred and one varieties of enjoyment and thousand and one kinds of allurements and temptations, was powerless to attract me. My mind was so much overwhelmed with the thought of renunciation that I had no attraction even towards my own relatives. I had a strong desire to go to Kakilamukh, Jorhat, Assam in the Saraswat Math under the feet of Paramhansa Nigamanda whom I was then mentally worshipping as a Guru and a guide, who would help me go further on such a long distance of the spiritual path. The words of my uncle had produced some influence in my mind. I thought, if without holding any University degree I became a Swami, people might think that I had taken the garb of a Swami for food. Therefore, I decided that only after taking proper education I should become a renunciate.

Somehow the message was spread that I had become a Sadhu and the villagers started coming to me for the mitigation of their sorrows. I used to give them good advice according to my ability. Some of the relatives being jealous used to address me as a 'Sadhu' in a sarcastic tone, and used to ask me: "When are you going to take the garb of a Sanyasi (Swami)? Such sarcastic tone naturally would produce wrath in me. Angrily, I used to give sharp reply, "No, I am not a Sadhu. Real saints have no anger. They are unruffled under all circumstances. No one can produce any feeling of wrath in a saint by abusing him. But you see I have in me angry feelings of wrath. This is not the sign and symptom of a saint". My opponents, bewildered, could not furnish any satisfactory reply to that. Henceforth, I meditated still more secretly so that no one could get any clue to my inner nature.

Very near to our home, there lived a widow, who was also a relative of mine. Her husband was a very religious minded man. Perhaps she was a disciple of Sri Ramakrishna Math or the admirer of that society as she had purchased all their publications and used to read the books she had with her. The Ramakrishna Kathamitra (Gospels of Sri Ramakrishna) compiled by his disciple Sri Mahendra Nath Gupta impressed me much. Those books (in 5 parts) influenced me in such a way that my strong hankering after supernatural spiritual powers became stronger. I had come to understand the truth from the sayings of Sri Ramakrishna, "That un-conditional love for God and faith in Him are the essential things for self-realisation which a devotee can acquire only through unconditional surrender to Him. Henceforth, I was trying my best to surrender myself completely at the feet of God. I had also realized that I could not get self-realization without the help of a True Guru and God's Kripa (blessings). Regular study of the Gita confirmed the said truth. The following verses of the Holy Bhagavad Gita inspired me to surrender everything at His feet.

1. "Therefore, Arjuna, think of me at all times and fight. (Do Sadhana) with mind and reason thus surrendered to me, you will doubtlessly come to me".

   Chapter VIII, Verse 7.

2. "Even if the vilest sinner worships me with exclusive devotion, he should be considered a saint; for he has rightly resolved. Specially he becomes virtuous and secures lasting peace. Know it for certain, Arjuna, that My devotee never falls. Arjuna, Womenfolk, Vaisyas (Members of the trading class), Sudras (those belonging to the labouring class), and even those that are born of the womb of a sinner (such as the pariah), by taking refuge in Me, they attain the supreme goal".

   Chapter IX, Verse 30-32.

3. "I consider them to be the best Yogis who endowed with supreme faith and ever united through meditation with Me worship Me with the mind centered on Me".

   Chapter XII, Verse 2.

4. "They who fully partake of this nectar of pious wisdom, set forth above, who are endowed with faith and are solely devoted to Me, those devotees are extremely dear to Me".

   Chapter XII, Verse 20.

I was doing all my spiritual exercises very secretly. I previously expressed that I had got a very lovely portrait of Lord Krishna and Radha fixed on the cover of a notebook which was placed on my table in my reading room. Though I used to worship the greatest Avatara and His consort in my reading room where generally no one used to visit, still at times, if any among my relatives, entered my study room, could see the flowers on my table in front of the pictures. Observing this, they would give the news to other relatives and thus this poor body became the target of their discussion.

I had come to know from the word of Lord Krishna: "Whosoever offers to me with love a leaf, a flower, a fruit or even water, I appear in person before that disinterested devotee of purified intellect and delightfully partake that article offered by him with love".
Gita Chapter IX. Verse 26.

One day while teaching and explaining some portion of our textbook, our Sanskrit teacher told us, "The Lord God sees the heart and not the language. If a person performs puja (offering flowers, sweets, fruits, and such other articles) with the utterance of correct Mantras, and the other with the wrong ones, the result in both the cases will be the same if both perform with the same devotion". Hence, without any hesitation, I used to offer flowers, tulsi leaves, water and such other things at the feet of the Lord of the Universe with the Mantras compiled by myself according to the Laws which I had learnt from the Sanskrit Class Teacher. I also used to offer water, technically as tarpan, at the feet of the fore-fathers, saints and gods and goddesses. While I used to take my bath in the river that was flowing by the side of the jungle of the ghosts, I used to perform "Tarpan", especially during long vacations (Durgapuja and Summer) when I could afford more time. At that time I would devote longer periods in meditation. I would go twice daily to that jungle, once at about 11-30 a.m. and again at about 5 p.m. to meditate. One day, while I was practicing yogic exercises in that ghost jungle at about 12 noon, one of our servants entered that jungle and saw me performing the Mahamudra. The servant used to respect me and sometimes take advice from me for the mitigation of his sorrows. He asked me, "Are you suffering from any stomach trouble? I replied in the negative and forthwith told him that I was performing some exercises, I further requested him not to disclose the fact to anyone. He respectfully agreed. The bathing ghat (Ghat - place where people take bath i.e., common bathing place) was on the northern side of our village. Sometimes, I used to take my bath (when the school was running as usual) at the common ghat on the eastern side of the village. Though the servant agreed not to divulge the secret of my life to any one, still I thought the place of my meditation must be changed.

There was another jungle by the side of the eastern ghat; it was not so thick. By the side of the public path, there was another banyan tree equally tall and big like the one on the northern side of the other jungle where I used to perform my Puja. There was a very old and tall fern tree (Himalayan type) by the side of the banyan tree. There was a raised platform at the base of the twin trees where the villagers used to perform Kali Puja yearly. Hence, on that special occasion, the villagers would clear the bushes in front of the twin trees. Clay model of Goddess Kali was placed there. The village priest, as a representative of the villagers, would worship the Goddess Kali on the day specified for Her. I used to join the ceremony along with the villagers. Nearly the whole night was spent on that occasion as the Puja ceremony lasted for five to six hours. Except on the special occasion, no one would go there. The jungle was not as dense as it looked from the road side. There was a red 'Jaba' (Malvasi order) tree behind twin trees. I selected that place for my Puja and meditation. After taking bath in the common ghat, I would pluck red jaba flowers (known in India as Jhumka Jaba) and perform my Puja as usual at the old altar.

My mother was a true devotee of God. She would get up at 3 a.m. daily and meditate for hours together. In the early morning, she would sing devotional songs melodiously. She loved Lord Krishna the most. She had collected many devotional songs which she had noted in her notebook. Whenever she became busy with her household duties, I would go stealthily to her room to collect those songs. I would learn those songs and I sang them while walking. I had learnt the Puja Mantras and process from her as already told before. In one sense, she was my first Guru. Afterwards I collected the Puja book in which detailed instructions were available for the Puja process of different gods and goddesses. From that book I learnt various kinds of prayers, hymns and invoking mantras for different gods and goddesses and the Shastric Mandates for their Pujas.

My mother came to understand that I was adamant as regards Puja of gods and goddesses. No one could dissuade me from my noble purpose, however rude or harsh words one might inflict on me. My mother observed the tremendous pain I underwent due to the ill-treatment, for the sake of God, from the relatives. She came forward and saved me. She instructed me to worship the Lord in her Puja room.

She used to keep aside various kinds of scented flowers, scandal paste, tulsi leaves ('Tulsi' is a kind of pungent smelling leaf of the Bilabiatae order recognised as a very sacred leaf for Puja purposes, used in all the temples throughout India) and incense for the purpose of worshipping God. My mother had to suffer much for that act of kindness towards me. The female members, specially the two aunts, would abuse her on the charge of spoiling me. She would hear all those insults calmly without speaking a word. In their opinion, I was spoiled by my mother and would not be able to do any service to the family. Besides puja, all other religious works were performed confidentially.

Now I can humbly say that I have been amply rewarded by God for the sufferings I had to endure during my early life from the relatives who used to rebuke me and pass harsh remarks that I was spoiled by my mother and would not be able to do any service to the society. These relatives later came to me for initiation. The two aunts, including my parents and all other family members, had taken kriya yoga initiation from me.

I had got special instruction from my Guru Paramhansa Yoganandaji to give initiation to my parents. My mother first took the kriya yoga initiation from me. She and my younger sister Shrimati Renukabala Mitra had got their kriya yoga initiation from me on 25th September 1947 at 6, Umesh Dutta Lane, Calcutta. Shrimati Purnima Guha, daughter of my sister also got (she was then unmarried) kriya-yoga initiation from me along with her mother. Shrimati Puspa Rani Basu, younger sister of my mother, took kriya yoga initiation from me on 2nd October 1947 at her own residence at Dighalia, Jessore, now in Bangladesh. Her daughter Shrimati Gitarani too, got her initiation along with her mother on the same day.

Smt. Basanta Kumari Sarkar, the eldest sister of my father (one of the said aunts) took kriya yoga initiation from me on 16th October 1953. At the time of Durga puja Mahaastami day, my mother acted as an assistant during kriya initiation at Kakdwip, 24 Parganas, West Bengal. Kanak Chandra Basu (maternal uncle and aunt), maternal uncle of my brother-in-law P.K. Mitra took kriya initiation from me on 30th January 1952 at Yogoda Ashram, Ranchi. Another aunt who tortured me and my mother the most (wife of Shri Debendra Nath Basu, the eldest brother of my father) took kriya yoga initiation from me at her residence Subhas Colony, Dum Dum, Cantt. Calcutta -28, on 12th July 1951. Shriman Saroj Kumar Basu, son of the said aunt and wife of

Saraj Kumar had also got Kriya initiation from me along with their mother on the same date and time. Shri Prafulla Cumar Mitra and his daughter Anima Mitra got their Kriya initiation on 25th October, 1950. (P.K. Mitra is the husband of my sister). Shri Sudhir Kumar Chakrabarty, my family priest who is the in-charge of our temple at my village Jangalbadhal, Jessore, took Kriya initiation from me at 4B Umesh Dutta Lane Calcutta 6 on 9th October, 1954. I have only mentioned some of the names of my relatives who got kriya initiation from me. Nearly all my relatives had got kriya-yoga initiation from me.

Chapter 2
My University Degree and Meeting My Guru

After the school final examination, I had gone to visit my maternal uncle's house at Joypur, Jessore, for a change. It took three month time to get the result of the first University Examination. Previously the School Final Examination was under the University. Now- a –day's, it is under the Board of Secondary Education. It was the first time that I had the taste of freedom. I was completely released from the anxieties of studies and examination at least for three months. No one would ask me to study. I would swim in the Ganges (Naba Ganga) thrice daily as it was the summer season (April and May). My routine for physical exercises was as follows - wrestling, some free hand exercises, some instrumental exercises including some exercises on the parallel bars. I got a separate room for myself, where I used to sleep but for my meditation I could use the attic. This attic was engaged on every Thursday when the house womenfolk would worship the Goddess of wealth, Lakshmi. On that day, I would practice my Yogic exercises in my room. Members of my maternal uncle's family were all religious minded. Most of them had initiation form their Guru, Swami Yogananda of Nabdwip. Maternal uncles, Isana and Patal (they were the cousin brothers of my own maternal uncle Mantu), got their initiations at the age between 10 to 12 years. I had observed that they used to follow similar techniques that I used to do. I used to practice my spiritual exercises secretly, though there was no bar to do the same openly. My parents had also come with me. My father had to return to Jangalbadhal at his own residence after a few days. My mother, along with her two sisters, used to worship gods and goddesses. I would observe their Puja ceremony with devotion, sitting on a separate seat. In due course of time, the result of my matriculation examination was out. I got a letter from my father intimating me that I was one of the successful candidates and he further instructed me to return for higher studies immediately.

My father had sent me to one of my brother-in-laws' house (husband of my eldest cousin sister) at Senhati in the district of Khulna, now in Bangladesh for higher education, as there was no college in my village. There was a class I degree College at Daulatpur, nearly 2.5 miles away from my residence. I would go there for my study on foot, crossing the river Bhairab. The subjects I had selected for my study were Physics, Chemistry, Mathematics and Botany. Botany was my optional subject. Vernacular (Bengali) and English were compulsory subjects. The calibre of my consciousness was increasing day by day in the college. Our veteran Professor of Chemistry taught us, as though through magic. He would demonstrate various kinds of chemical reactions with the help of a demonstrator. For a couple of months, I witnessed many wonders, the explanation of which I got later. The Professor of Mathematics also came to know me as I was very much interested in Mathematics. On the very first day when I had the opportunity to use the telescope in the Physics Laboratory, I was surprised to see the distant objects distinctly.

Inwardly, I was very glad to see that, at my new residence, an attic was lying vacant. No one was using that room. Hence, I cleaned the room for the purpose of my solitary meditation. In that house of my brother- in-law, I had full freedom. My eldest cousin sister loved me very much. I got in her the heart of a mother. She was very simple with motherly affection; she used to cook and serve vegetable dishes to me. The inmates of the house used to take fish, meat and eggs. She had to prepare vegetable diet for me specially. All sorts of separate arrangements as regards utensils and cooking implements were made for me and she never uttered a single word of discontentment for the extra work she did for me.

My brother-in-law was a Kaviraj (a Bengali word used for Ayurvedic physician). He was skilled in the art of healing. He would prescribe medicines merely by feeling the pulse of the patient. He had some special knowledge of pulse reading. I had observed his art of healing. He could correctly detect the exact disease through feeling of the pulse. Many times I had witnessed his way and method of treatment. He would express all internal symptoms of the patients including the hereditary ones. At times, the patients protested as if the physician had gone wrong in detecting the true symptoms, but when he authoritatively divulged all the secrets of the disease, they would agree.

The climate of the place did not suit me. During rainy season, I had to walk on foot through muddy path. I had developed malaria and afterwards dysentery due to the unhygienic condition of the locality. My brother-in-law, after curing my diseases, advised me to go to Calcutta for a change as I had a long vacation at my disposal. He sent a letter to my father to that effect. My father was then residing at Calcutta. Before going to Calcutta, I had a mind to visit Joypur.

On the appointed date and time I started for Joypur. As far as I can recollect, I started by the 9-30 p.m. steamer. I was scheduled to change the steamer at 12-30 a.m. at the Kalia Junction to catch another steamer there. There were three other fellow passengers with me bound for the same destination. At 12 o'clock in the night I was overpowered with sleep and requested my fellow companions to intimate me when the steamer would reach the Kalia Junction. Due to the cold breeze we all went into deep slumber. The steamer reached the junction at its fixed time, waited there for an hour according to its scheduled halt and then whistled several times, starting for its destination at 1-30 a.m. The steamer was running speedily through the river Madhumati. The T.T.I. (Travelling Ticket Inspector) came to us to inspect the tickets at about 2 a.m. After examining the tickets he rebuked us for our mistake and informed us that we had gone far away from our destination. As the steamer was running not through the new Ganges but through river Madhumati, we all impatiently pleaded for some solution. After pausing for a few moments he said, "As the steamer is going through the Madhumati river, the place Kalna will be the nearest stop for your Lohagara Station (Our destination was Lohagara). However, we had to pay extra for that journey. Had we changed the steamer at Kalia Junction we would have reached the destination at 5 a.m. But it was around 7.00 a.m. when we reached the Kalna stop. Though there was no scheduled stoppage at Kalna halt, the T.T.I. had managed to stop the steamer for us at Kalna. At Kalna stop we were simply surprised to see the whole vicinity of Kalna innundated with water, as it was rainy season. River Madhumati was swollen with excessive intake of water both from the heaven and from the land. We observed that the flooded water had engulfed everything except the upper part of the bushes. Each one of us had to go to different villages and as such had to take different routes from that forlorn place. I got the necessary direction from one of my fellow companions. I had with me a bundle of college books, an umbrella, few clothes and a pair of shoes. Though the weight was not much, still it was very difficult for me to move with all those articles in that ocean of water, the average depth of which was 2' to 3'. I had to walk on foot for almost mile in order to reach Lohagara Junction, wherefrom I hired a boat for Joypur. I reached the house of my maternal uncle round 9.30 a.m. I had sent a letter to my uncle about my arrival time there. I narrated the story of my late arrival to them. They were very sorry to hear that I had an attack of dysentery on the way. Soon, their family doctor arrived with his bag. For several days I suffered from bacillary dysentery. The Doctor prescribed non-vegetarian diet. In his opinion, if I did not take non-vegetarian diet the ravage of the disease would reappear. However, obstinately, I refused to take the non-vegetarian diet. My uncle wrote about the disease to my father who in reply had requested him to send me back immediately to Calcutta.

According to my father's wishes, I left for Calcutta via Senhati in order to fetch all other belongings left there. My brother-in-law also received another letter from my father instructing to send me immediately to Calcutta. My brother-in-law selected an auspicious date and time for my journey and he escorted me up to Daulatpur station.

Early morning on the following day, I arrived at Calcutta. My father was very sorry to see my condition. He immediately sent for a doctor who advised me to take meat and fish preparations. As per the doctor's advice, my parents requested me again and again to take non-vegetarian diet. Other members of the family (one of my uncles and his wife) also fervently requested me to take the same. My uncle tried to persuade me with logic. His argument was: "If you do not live at all, how would you continue with your religious work?" The doctor said, "If you do not take at least soup of the fish preparation you will die because of relapse of the fatal bacillary dysentery." Hence, with folded hands, they requested me to take, at least for a few days, the soup only. I had already realised the truth of his words. I thought that disobedience to all my relatives, specially parents, uncles and aunts might be the cause of the repeated attack of the dysentery. I also thought that any

How I should get rid of that dreadful disease so that I might continue my religious pursuits. I, after a long mental struggle, agreed to take the soup of fish preparations only. They were very much pleased with me. I had mentally decided to exclude it from my diet as soon as I regained my health.

By that time, my father had managed to secure a Transfer Certificate from the Daulatpur College and admitted me to Vidyasagar College, Calcutta.

I was then in a completely changed environment, from a simple rural one to a town where people were not simple but stylish, pompous, proud and selfish in nature which I came to understand by mixing up with my college friends. It was very difficult for me to keep pace with them. I thought within myself, that outwardly I should be like them but inwardly I should be with my own thoughts, religious pursuits and, above all, with God. My father purchased modern clothes for me. I had to cut my hair according to the general fashion of the college students. When my relatives observed that I had adjusted myself according to the custom of the time, they became very glad and invited me to meals. I accepted the invitation for meals. Due to this change in my behaviour, the relatives thought that I had forsaken the religious path.

However, I performed my 'sadhana' regularly as before. I used to practice my yogic exercises on the roof of the three-storeyed building. At about 4 a.m., I would get up from bed though I could not get the same peace and bliss I used to get at home in my childhood. Habit had become a second nature to me. Bliss or no bliss, I continued with my 'sadhana'. The college friends were all worldly-minded. The whole atmosphere was against my nature, poisonous from head to feet. Nowhere, I could get solace. I would get good books to read. I would also read the Holy Bhagavad Gita in 'Sanskrit' but could not get the same pleasure as I used to get previously.

After a few months, I had a mild attack of fever, and became very weak. The doctors could not detect the real reason of my ailment. I was under the treatment of the best physicians in Calcutta for months together without any result. At last, the house physician of my younger sister was consulted. He too could not cure me of my ailments. My friend, Jagabandhu Das, who lived, at 46/B, Amherst Street, Calcutta who was a very good physician. He used to practice according to our Indian Ayurvedic System. He was a yogi, who had got his initiation from Swami Bholananda Giri of Hardwar. He would diagnose the disease through feeling the pulse. At last, I went to him for treatment. After careful examination he told me, "You are not suffering from any disease but from reaction of poisonous drugs; you are really over-medicated". He prescribed two medicines for me and advised me to purchase the same from a particular shop where I could get genuine medicines. He further told me, "Don't be afraid, your ailments will vanish within seven days. For the first five days, you will not get any result. On the sixth day, 75% of your ailment will go away and on the seventh day all the symptoms will vanish and you will be alright. Please do not take bread or any dry food. You must take rice, curd, vegetable soup and the like. You should also take regular bath with overnight cold water from the tank". As I was suffering from fever, I declined to take bath with overnight cold water, lest I should catch cold.

My body temperature was then 99.50F. He forthwith told me, "Well brother, follow my instruction. If you do not get any good result and if you find that on the seventh day there is any trace of your ailment, come here and throw all the pills of my medicines on the street". I purchased the two medicines from that particular shop, the cost of which amounted to Rs. 2.50. With fearful heart, I would take bath with overnight cold water and was taking medicines according to his prescription. Lo! On the sixth day, 75% of my ailment was gone and on the seventh day, I was completely cured. I went to my friend to give my hearty thanks on the seventh day.

Two years had been allotted by the University of Calcutta for the study of Intermediate course, either Art, Science or Commerce. These two years were spent either with friends, relatives or with the doctors. When the notice of the final examination came, I was amazed to realize that the whole course was practically untouched by me. Those who had deposited the examination fee to the University were allowed to sit for the exam.

As I had deposited the required fees, I was sent for the final examination. Within that short period of time, I was able to go through the science course, but literatures, namely vernacular and especially English, were untouched. My relatives, including my father, advised me not to appear at the examination as they knew that I did not got sufficient time. I took the chance. In due course of time, the result was out. I myself had gone to the Senate House (University) to see the result. Not finding my name in the list of the successful candidates, I got a great shock.

Due to this shock, practically unconsciously, I started on foot towards the Sealdah Station, and entered into the Southern Section of it. I had not a single penny in my pocket. I was unconscious about my behaviour. I saw a train that was ready to start. As I occupied a seat, the train whistled and started on its way. It was a local train. The passengers were coming in and going out at every stop. After half an hour, I regained consciousness and started thinking about what I had done and what might be the consequence. Fortunately, I remembered the address of one of my relatives (elder sister of my mother) whose residence was at Baruipur, which was on the same line through which I was passing. I visited her, who was very happy to see me.

My cousin brothers and sisters engaged me in various indoor games. For two days, no one asked about my examination result. On the third day, one of my cousin brothers, who was at that time studying in one of the colleges of Calcutta enquired about my University Registration Number in order to find out my result. Hence I had to confess the truth that I had run away from my home due to my failure in the examination. He soon informed my parents regarding my stay at their residence.

Six days after my flight, I received a letter from my father, who wrote: "I am glad to know that you are now residing with your aunt. Stay there a few days more. To be unsuccessful is a common fate to many, hence do not worry".

After 25 days I returned home. My father advised me to deposit money for fresh admission in the same college. I was re-admitted in Vidyasagar College. When I collected the marksheet of my examination, I came to know that I was unable to secure pass marks in English language only. It took a few days more to resume all the duties as before.

A great internal struggle ensued within me when I saw that I had lost my joyous state during meditation. I used to pray, "Lord, why have you brought me here? Please save me from this world, come Father, come."

In my earlier days, I used to think myself to be a yogi like the Swamis or Saints known to me at that time but alas where was I ? I had fallen from the garden of Eden, from Heaven to Hell!

I realised at heart how difficult it was to be away from the world while mixing with worldly minded friends of college and the people around me, trying my level best to balance the two diagonally opposite worlds, internal and external. I used to take vegetable diet and observe austerity on the 11th day of the moon as well as on the new and full moon days according to the Hindu custom. I would avoid the company of the college friends as far as possible. Sometimes, when I tried to avoid them, I would tell them, "I have an invitation." To speak the truth I would get some invitation from the newspapers: "There will be a public meeting on the spiritual interpretation of the scriptures or on Kali Kirtan. All are welcome to attend". I would participate in those religious meetings, by locating them in the newspapers.

Once, as I was passing through Raja Rammohan Roy Road, my attention was drawn to a religious procession headed by the Yogoda Satsanga Society of India. The members and followers of that party were singing devotional song (Kirtan) with musical instruments. One person distributed pamphlet in which I noticed "Swami Yogananda, who has uplifted thousands of Americans will deliver a lecture on 25th September 1935 at 6-30 p.m. in the Albert Hall on Pranayama". On this day, in order to know more about Pranayam, I entered the Albert Hall nearly an hour before the lecture. More than two thousand people had already occupied the Hall.

What I had heard in that meeting was really inspiring. I came to understand that what I was practising was not based on scientific method. He invited the audience: "Whosoever is desirous to know or learn the process, may come to me on the next Sunday in the evening at 4/2, Rammohan Roy Road, but do not come to me only to satisfy your curiosity".

I visited him the next day and enrolled my name as one of the candidates desirous to learn and practise his system. Two more young men were also with me, who had also enrolled their names as they too were desirous to follow the path of Pranayama. To my amazement, on the next Sunday, the 29th September, 1935, I observed that more than one hundred persons had already enrolled their names as his followers or disciples. At the entrance, our enrolment cards were checked and we were allowed to enter into the place of initiation. At the appointed time, Swamiji came. He purified our bodies with the vibrations of 'Om' and then initiated us in the art of Kriya Yoga System. His youngest brother, Sri Bishnu Charan Ghosh, demonstrated Mahamudra, according to his direction.

Swamiji used to take regular classes at least once a week and would give us various kinds of lessons regarding health, diet and yogic exercises. On the next day of our initiation i.e., on the 30th September, 1935, he imparted his first lesson. His private secretary Mr. C. Richard Wright took a series of movie pictures with the help of a movie camera. Swamiji delivered only a few lectures on the above subject at this place. Afterwards, he imparted his instructions from 48, Bechu Chatterjee Street, the then Calcutta Branch Centre of Yogoda Satsanga Society of India. I was then residing on the same street, about two minutes walk from the Ashram. It was our rented house. I do not remember exactly when we had left our former residence at 7, Williams Lane.

After a few days, while he was residing at Calcutta Centre (84, Bechu Chatterjee Street), one night I had a vivid dream. In that dream, I saw that Swamiji had appeared in a blaze of light and instructed me about the exercises. I did likewise. By that time, we had shifted from our previous residence at Bechu Chatterjee Street to Guru Prosad Chowdhury Lane at a distance of 3 minutes' walk from the Calcutta centre. The following morning I hastened to the Ashram to know the fact more clearly from the lips of Swamiji. When I entered the Ashram, he was taking rest. So I got the opportunity to practice my Kriya techniques in Guru Mandir. After finishing my spiritual exercises, I sat under the feet of my Gurudeva and asked him about the dream, whether he had actually visited. In a very grave tone, he replied in the affirmative. I could not dare to put any further question looking at his grave attitude. After a pause, I told him that I could not understand properly the new process about which he was speaking. In his grave tone, he replied, "you will get it afterwards".

On the first day of our initiation, he foretold us, "I see that many, present in this gathering, will get self-realisation in this life. And whosoever will practice the Kriya techniques devotionally twice a day devoting an hour in each sitting shall get God."

The first two days after my initiation, I could not practice my Kriya Yoga techniques but on the third day at about 5 a.m., I could perform the techniques successfully on the roof of my house. After finishing my former regular Yoga exercises, I did the Kriya only for 5 minutes which I learnt from Swami Yoganandaji. As I had done the Jyoti Mudra, to my astonishment, I beheld a very beautiful dazzling white light resembling strong lightening, in the centre of that Astral Sun appeared a deep Blue Ball with all the glory. I was filled with joy. I had tried in vain for more than 8 years to see the Astral Sun through the regular spiritual exercises. The same appeared before me without any effort whatsoever. Five minutes of Kriya practice in comparison with those long years of Sadhana, was nothing but an insignificant effort. A new hope, an inspiration and joy overwhelmed me. I thought within myself that if I could practise the Kriya technique regularly, unending joy would be the result. Henceforth, I used to perform my Kriya techniques early in the morning, daily on the roof and regularly enjoyed the same Astral light. In the evening, I used to practise the same in my own room.

After a few days, I went to the then Secretary, Sri Sailesh Mohan Majumdar of Calcutta Town Centre at 84, Bechu Chatterjee Street, and asked his permission to practice my Kriya in the Ashram premises. He gladly gave me his consent. As days rolled on, my former spiritual exercises became shorter and shorter and within a couple of months they disappeared from the regular routine of my Sadhana. Soon, I started going to the Ashram in the morning also. Besides my morning Sadhana on the roof of the house, I would practise the same in the morning at the Ashram.

I had the opportunity to attend a few night classes on my return home. On my way back, I used to think, "If my parents ask me the reason of my late return what I shall say in reply. I can neither speak false words nor can I disclose the truth. What shall I do now? But when I used to arrive at my house, they would not ask me a single question regarding my delay in returning home. I used to thank God for that".

At the end of October 1935, our Gurudeva left for Mysore. Thus, I missed his company for a few days. From Mysore, he returned to Calcutta. After a short stay at the Calcutta Centre, he went to Delhi and returned. Again after a short stay at Calcutta, he left for Madras. From Madras he returned to Calcutta and visited the Ranchi Yogoda Headquarters. From Ranchi he went to Kashmir. From Calcutta, he again went to Ranchi Yogoda Brahmacharya Vidyalaya, and after a short stay there, he came back to Calcutta. Then finally, he intended to return to America. We had the opportunity to give him a farewell with various kinds of devotional offerings. I had garlanded him with a sweet scented rose garland on behalf of the Yogoda Satsanga Society, Calcutta. But due to some reason or the other, he could not start finally. He had to come back to Calcutta from Bombay. Then after a month's stay at Calcutta Centre, on the 22nd August 1936, he started for America finally from Bombay.

Gurudeva, in one of his regular classes at Calcutta Centre, advised us to attend the Anniversary of Yogoda Satsanga at Serampore in the house of our Param Guru, Swami Sri Yukteswar Giriji Maharaj. He further informed us that his Gurudeva would be present on the occasion.

On 24th December 1935, we got the opportunity to go to Serampore to participate in the annual function of the Society. We saw that Gurudeva was sitting amidst his spiritual brothers, admirers and disciples. The Holy vibration of devotional songs in tune with various kinds of instruments such as Mridanga and Kartal and the like had turned the whole atmosphere of the room into Heaven on Earth. A very beautiful heavenly perfume was emanating from an unknown place. I looked around to find out the source of the scent, but I could not detect any such thing. I recollected my early experience and surmised it must be the Astral one coming out of the body of our Gurudeva. As I was thinking, Gurudeva opened his eyes (He was in a trance at that time) and looked at me in such a compassionate manner that I instantly got the solution of the problem regarding the source of the heavenly odour. His affectionate glance conveyed the thought in me, "You are the blessed one, who rightly has guessed the true source of the Astral perfume." I was astonished when he opened his eyes and blessed me amidst such a huge gathering. Instantaneously a thought arose in my mind, "He must be God, otherwise such heavenly odour cannot emanate from the body of a man." His look became more compassionate. I thought, "I am fortunate to receive his blessings".

At about 12-30 p.m. we were invited to take the prasad (consecrated Indian meal). I was again surprised to find that a very sweet fragrance was coming from the prasad. The taste of the meal too was extraordinary and unearthly as it was consecrated. The meal that was served was of a general type. Various kinds of chopped vegetables were boiled with rice. Due to the presence of chopped pieces of beet root in the rice, it had turned red. It was not "Khichuri" as it did not have dal (pulse). In Khichuri, dal must be one of the essential ingredients along with rice. Besides, that typical rice, there were other kinds of dishes which had been served. All of them were very delicious. Being tempted by heavenly taste and alluring fragrance, I took the "Prasad" to my heart's content.

Param Gurudeva and Gurudeva

In the last meeting with the Param Guru at about 4-30 or 5 p.m., there was a huge gathering in the courtyard of the house. The agenda of the meeting comprised religious songs with instruments and lectures. The speech of Gurudeva was short but Param Gurudeva delivered quite a lengthy lecture. His subject matter of speech was "Vishwarupadarsan Yoga (Gita Chapter eleven)". I was highly satisfied as he had solved my vital problem which was giving me trouble for a long time. At the end of his speech, he said, "I have a mind to take complete rest. I have handed over all my powers to my son, Swami Yogananda. He will look after you all". At about 10 p.m. we returned to Calcutta.

I had the good fortune of joining all the classes our Gurudeva used to take regularly. I had attended nearly all his public lectures delivered at Calcutta. I do not remember all the dates of his speeches. The following short notes might be quoted from my note book.

1. He delivered a public lecture on 'the quickest way to contact God' in the Y.M.C.A hall at Bhawanipur on the 15th February, 1936.
2. He presided over the function of the "All Bengal Physical Association" held at Senate House in the evening. He delivered his speech on "Health" which was the subject matter on that occasion. Date not recorded.
3. At about 5-30 p.m. he delivered his speech on the Art of living in the Ashutosh Hall. Date not recorded.
4. At the end of the month of February 1936, he spoke on the life of Maharshi Nagendra Nath Bhaduri at 6-30 p.m. in the Raja Rammohan Library hall, where a special meeting was held on that occasion in memory of Maharshi Nagendra Nath Bhaduri.
5. In the month of April 1936 he spoke on 'Truth' at the University Institute. Date not recorded.
6. He delivered a lecture on Religion on 5th July 1936 at Vivekananda Library, Tollygunj at 7 p.m.

In that way my days were passing happily. I could not find time to look into my college books. Sometimes I would think, "Last year due to want of preparation I got plucked in English. This year too I don't find time to go through the college books. Shall I have to face the same fate like the previous year?" A firm conviction came from within, "Through the blessings of Whom man can cross the ocean of life safely, surely, He will help me pass the coming examination". Hence, without hesitation I used to join all classes and lectures of Gurudeva.

I clearly remember the two most important incidents of my life. They were the two important lectures of Gurudeva, one was held on the night before my final examination in Mathematics and the other on the night before the final examination of Botany. The lecture that was held at Bagbazar and the physical demonstration had continued up to 12-30 a.m. I reached home at 1.00 a.m. The other lecture continued up to 10.30 p.m. When the result of my Science examination was out I was very glad to know that I was one among the successful candidates. The spiritual brothers with whom I was in close contact were also glad at the news of my success.

Swamiji's Preparation for U.S.A.

On the 2nd week of June 1936, Swamiji intended to go to Bombay in order to sail for U.S.A. On the 29th May 1936, we, the devotees and members of Y.S.S., assembled at Y.S.S. Premises (84 Bechu Chatterjee St.) for his farewell. We were very sorry to part with him. In the farewell meeting, Gurudeva told us, "I do not find my body in the ship. I do not feel I am sailing now." We could not understand exact meaning of his words at that time, the real meaning of which was revealed a few days later. His date for sailing was fixed for the 14th June 1936 from Bombay. A few days before his sea-voyage, he intimated his private Secretary Mr. C. Richard Wright, "I am not going, you better return to your motherland." At that news he (Mr. Wright) became very sorry and all his hopes for returning to his motherland vanished as his spiritual brothers and sisters in U.S.A. had repeatedly told him, "Don't come alone. If you cannot bring with you Swamiji, you will not be allowed to land." In the meantime, the American Express Company informed Swamiji that the ship could not accommodate his Ford Car in that journey, which would be possible only on the 22nd August 1936.

Hence, it was arranged with the company that his date of departure would be changed from 14th June 1936 to 22nd August 1936.

Swamiji came back to Calcutta on 3rd July 1936 morning. On 4th July 1936, there was a festival on the occasion of Guru Purnima. There was another strange coincidence on that day. It was a day of Lunar eclipse, the duration of which was 1 hour 57 minutes from 21hrs., 56 mts., and 42 secs to 23 hrs., 53mts., 42 secs. On the concurrrence of those auspicious moments on that day, we thought ourselves very blessed to have the sacred 'Darshan' of our Gurudev, who was regarded in the scriptures as the God of Gods, the Lord Himself. Hence, I hastened to all the Newspaper offices at Calcutta to arrange for circulation of the news that "on the occasion of Gurupurnima on the 4th July 1936 at 3 p.m., there will be a special meeting at Yogoda Satsanga Premises at 84, Bechu Chatterjee St. where Swami Yogananda Giri, Sister Ettie, Mr. C. Richard Wright will be present. Swamiji himself will conduct the meeting."

That day an extra-ordinarily huge gathering was entertained cordially by the Ashramites. We divided the responsibilities among ourselves according to our abilities. Swamiji delivered a lecture befitting the occasion. We were all benefited by his speech.

As the function was over, all the brothers and sisters went away. At night I saw that there were three spiritual brothers and one sister who had decided to stay in the Ashram to have the company of our Master. The sister was a nun, who had got her vow of Sannyasini from our Gurudeva. Her monastic name was sister Radharani, the mother of Sri Kshitish Chandra Ghosh. I don't remember the names of the three spiritual brothers. According to the Hindu custom, we serve our Guru in every way. I took a handmade 'tal' leaf to fan the Master. I made up my mind to fan him throughout the night and as such I prayed to him mentally to help me to execute my holy duty. However, at dead of night I felt a little sleepy. Though Gurudeva was supposed to be asleep which was apparant by his tremendous snoring sound, he silently pinched me with the help of his toes. The sleepy tendency vanished - I thanked him with gratitude silently for his instant response at my mental prayer. My spiritual brothers and sisters could not know this as he was sleeping in the dim light. We all successfully passed the test. At 3 a.m. Gurudeva ordered to sit for meditation. My spine was somewhat relaxed and inclined forward. He again, with the help of the toe, slightly pressed the spine just opposite the naval. Instantaneously, my spine became straight and the life force began to ascend quickly upward. We enjoyed the peace and bliss upto 5 a.m. when he ordered us to take rest. He told us, "I don't require any service from you. I generally don't take any service from any one. Today I have taken your service in order to loosen the knots of the matter and spirit". I too realised that he did not require any service from us. We were serving a sleeping body which had no sensation of touch.

He used to speak about various kinds of his realisation. Sometimes he would speak about manners, customs and behaviours of different races, especially of U.S.A., France and Great Britain. One day he spoke at length about the administration of different Governments and their differences which helped me much in one of my Calcutta University Final papers in Economics afterwards.

One day, in the course of our talks, he assured us, "I will lead you to such a place where there is no disease, no sorrow but eternal bliss. In that land, your body will be made of light."

After 4 days of stay at 84, Bechu Chatterjee St., he shifted his residence to 39, Raja Dinendra St., Calcutta-9.

On 17th August 1936, without informing us, he stealthily started for Bombay from where he embarked on the ship on the 22nd August for U.S.A. via London.

We came to know from the newspaper cutting that Mr. C.R. Wright sent us from London that his speech and yogic feats were highly appreciated by the people of London. He had delivered a few lectures in the huge auditorium like Caxton Hall in London. Among his yogic feats, the one that had the greatest circulation with caption in the prominent newspapers was as follows, "He was lying down on his back. A block of ice (3 feet x 2 feet x 1 feet) was placed on his open chest for half an hour. The Doctor declared him to be dead as the circulation of the blood had stopped due to the solidification of the blood. Afterwards he regained his normal circulation of blood and resumed his lecture."

When Gurudeva had left us for U.S.A., it was time for me to resume my study of the degree course. I had taken admission in the Arts Section so that I would get much more time for my spiritual search than what I would otherwise get if admitted to science section. In the science section, I should have to devote more time in the practical classes. I had a special charm for the Vedas. In order to know more about Vedas I took Honours in Sanskrit paper. In the Sanskrit Honours Class, I got the opportunity to read the Vedic Grammar and the Vedas. In the Arts Course, Vernacular (Bengali) and English were compulsory papers. Besides the above, I had Economics as one of the chosen subjects. Two years had been allotted by the Calcutta University for our Bachelor's Degree course; technically known as 3rd Year and 4th Year Course, (B.A. B.Sc. or B.Com).

While I was studying in the 3rd year, during the Puja vacation, a band of enthusiastic spiritual brothers got the opportunity to visit Y.S.S. Ashram, Ranchi. There was only one worker left at Calcutta centre. Bibhuti, Rebati, Kalidas, Krishna Chaityana and myself used to go to the Ashram regularly. At that time Rebati and Biman used to stay in the Ashram. I used to conduct the weekly meetings at that time. Sometime I used to go to the Ashram between 2 to 3 p.m. to enjoy Kirtan. Bibhuti could play Mridanga well. Krishna Chaittyana was expert in playing the string instruments. Generally, we used to sing chorus songs. I would go to the market to purchase fruits, sweets and flowers and used to perform the puja whole-heartedly. I would keep day to day notes in my note book as regards daily happenings and especially the time devoted for spiritual works and a short description of the realisation. Following lines are quotations from my own notebook - the then daily routine and some of the realisations during my meditation.

Dated the 9th November, 1936: I woke up at 4-10 a.m. After washing hands and feet I sat down for meditation, but drowsiness overpowered me. The struggle with my sleepy tendency continued for some time, when at last it conquered me and I was forced to lie down on the bed. The senses retired but I was fully conscious within. I was watching the play of light in the Kutastha i.e., third eye which was nothing but the reflection of the eternal light.

In the Ashram, I again practised Kriya from 6 a.m. to 7-10 a.m., when I had immense pleasure due to the appearance of ever new, ever increasing and ever beautiful light in the Kutstha which lasted for half an hour, the brightness of which might be imagined as the conglomeration of one hundred suns and moons. Yesterday's vision of Lord Krishna and Sri Radha repeated today. Study of Gita, domestic duties up to 10 a.m.; from 10 a.m. to 11-15 a.m. Kriya; meal at 11-30 a.m.; from 12 noon to 2 p.m. domestic duties. From 2 p.m. to 5-15 p.m. study and rest; from 5-30 p.m. to 6 p.m. physical exercises; 6 p.m. to 6-55 p.m. devotional songs (Kirtan); 7 p.m. to 8-15 p.m. prayer and Kriya; 8-30 p.m. to 10 p.m. study of College books.

Today's revelation during evening meditation was somewhat different, the description of which was as follows, "During meditation in the evening I could see strong light in Kutastha at will. During the after effect of Kriya, i.e., while I was at rest I saw in the third eye the divine couple Sri Radha and Sri Krishna, the beauty of which was beyond description. The light that was emanating from the body of Sri Krishna was ever changing, due to which I had ever new and ever increasing bliss.

The beauty and the light of the body of Sri Radha was more beautiful and stronger than that of Sri Krishna. The lights of the two bodies were playing-either they were embracing each other or playing separately. The appearance of Radha blessed me first. At first, she was alone in Kutastha. Hundreds and thousands of rays and sparks were coming out of Her body. Millions and trillions of atoms were seen to be issuing out of the rays of the body. Sometime, it was seen that the atoms conglomerated into stars. All of a sudden, the stars in their playful mood had merged into the body of Sri Radha. In that way, I was observing the eternal play of creation and destruction of that eternal power of Sri Radha. I came to understand that we were all sparks of the Supreme Being, playing for a while on the earth and then would have to be merged one day in Him.

At night, from 10-40 p.m. to 11-15 p.m., the constant revelation of a very dazzling white light; at 11-30 p.m. the usual bright white light came to escort me to the dreamland or to the subconscious state of mind.

The 7th January 1937: (Revelation-the vision of the Astral world) I woke up at about 3-30 a.m. Shortly after, I was meditating, leaning on my back. While I was meditating I had the vision of the Astral world. First, I saw a large astral fish, very beautiful to look at, all made of light. There were some known and unknown faces with me. They all tried to catch the fish when Lo! to our utter astonishment the fish had changed its form into the figure of our Paramparam Guru Sri Sri Shyama Charan Lahiri Mahasaya.

The vision changed. I saw a beautiful garden, in which there was a suitable room for meditation. I, along with two of my companions, entered into that room for meditation, when the scene shifted - all the forms vanished. Various kinds of astral sounds were heard and in the spiritual eye, astral sun appeared. The vision again changed. In place of astral sun, a very beautiful garden re-appeared with all its glory. The trees, the plants, the flowers were all made of various kinds of lights from violet to red. The display of all the seven main colours and their mixtures were seen in the petals of flowers. Was it the garden of paradise where Lord Krishna used to play with His Beloved Sri Radha? While I was enjoying the beauty of the flower garden, I was perplexed to see that all the trees had vanished from the garden and in their place stood a little blooming plant, gradually that too vanished. There remained the infinite astral sky only, the beauty of which was beyond description. Gradually, the beautiful sky disappeared. I regained consciousness at 6-40 a.m. I was refreshed and exhilarated. I went to the Ashram and there again I performed the yogic exercises for an hour from 7-15 a.m. to 8-15 a.m.; study at home upto 9-45 a.m.; then at college upto 4 p.m.; the daily round of duties; the rest were the same as before; retirement at 11 p.m.

The 16th January 1937: At about 4 a.m. I had a new revelation. I realised that I was going out of the physical body with my astral one all made of light to an unknown land, the beauty of which could not be described. When I was soaring higher and higher to that wondrous land, I was afraid to some extent, but as I realised that there was nothing to care, I was overwhelmed with Supreme joy. I realised that the whole cosmos was nothing but the ocean of condensed light. As it was astral and invisible to the ordinary eye, it was very difficult to draw a parallel description. If the beauty and strength of a full moon in the sky of autumn be multiplied thousand times, in imagination, we might approach to the nearness of that beauty. Like a piece of wood in the ocean rising up and down, I was marching on and on to the unknown land. I had no idea of time as I was floating on the ocean of light. I felt that some invisible power was directly guiding me and I was powerless to go against the current. Hence, after a while, I was afraid as there was no trace of any land. The whole cosmos was nothing but ocean of light. Being afraid, I was remembering God and was taking His name. I mentally surrendered myself to the feet of Gurudeva and to his guidance as there was no other alternative, when he placed me in Kutastha, and gradually, I regained my outward consciousness. It was 4-20 a.m.

I have narrated, how my college days were spent specially in the year 1937. I have also expressed how I used to get various kinds of realisations during meditation at that time. Sometimes I used to get vision of gods and goddesses at the time of meditation. On going through the notebook, I find that on 27/07/37 I had the vision of Lord Narayana and Shyamsundara (Lord Krishna). On 25/08/37. I had the vision of Goddess Durga sitting on her lion. On 23/10/37, I had the vision of Gurudeva Sri Sri Shyama Charan Lahiri Mahasaya. On 26/12/37, I had the vision of Pentogonal Star in Meditation. On 7/01/38, I had seen my own self, made of light at the Kutastha. On the 24th February 1938, Sri Gurudeva appeared before me at 3-30 a.m. his hand touched me on the right side of my body.

A tremendous electric current was flowing from his hand to my body, thereby charging my whole being. I could not bear the electric current for a long time. After a few seconds, when the current became unbearable, I expressed the same mentally and he withdrew his hands.

On the 13th March, 1938, the display of astral light at the Christ centre was somewhat different. After Kriya practice, when I was taking rest looking at the third eye, usual dazzling light first appeared which had entertained me with the display of various colours (I was performing Kriya at about 4 a.m.). At last just in front of me stood an astral sun spreading light all over the cosmos, very strong light but at the same time soft and soothing, engulfing my mind for a long time.

B.A. final examination was to be held from 14/03/38 to 19/04/38 with breaks. It is needless to say that I got the Calcutta University Arts

Degree in due course. Nearly three months time was required to know the result. I had not joined the university's convocation meeting in order to receive the diploma, the reasons of which were as follows:

1. At the convocation, it was a custom to wear special convocation dress which was quite different from our Indian dress. I was at that time very strict and did not like to use any other dress but the dress that Mahatma Gandhiji had advised as to wear.
2. Those who could not join the convocation meetings, could get the diploma at the cost of rupees five, which was fixed as the fees for the same.
3. I was not planning to use the diploma. The certificates were required (Degree, diploma etc.) for service only. I had a mind not to join any service but to renounce the world. My aim of life was renunciation.

20 years later, I had to collect the same from the University for official record of Ranchi Yogoda Satsanga Vidyalaya, high school. I had to pay rupees twenty for the same. Inscrutable are the ways of God!

Chapter 3

I Become a Monk of The Swami Order

I joined Yogoda Satsanga Calcutta Centre as a worker on 1st November, 1938. Later, I was selected by the authorities of the Eastern Headquarters of the Yogoda Satsanga Society (YSS) of India, Ranchi as a teacher and worker and I joined on 20th January, 1939. As a teacher, I worked in the School from 11 a.m. to 3-30 p.m.; and as worker, I looked after the boys. I had to teach the boys how to perform Shiva Puja besides conducting the general prayer in the morning and in the evening.

I was allotted one solitary cottage as my residence. It was in the midst of the jungle, where generally no one would dare to go out of fear for ghosts. It was named as Gita Kunja (Kunja means bower). I did my best and the authorities of YSS were satisfied; I was selected as a relieving Headmaster of the Yogoda Satsanga Brahmcharya Vidyalaya at Ejmalichak in Midnapur (West Bengal). Shri Janardan Sahoo, then Headmaster of the School had to join the teacher's training programme in the B.T. College. Sri Sahoo was familiar with my art of training the boys and my method of teaching; he recommended my name to Swami Satyananda Giri, the principal of the Yogoda Brahmacharya Vidyalaya as the relieving Headmaster. It was decided that after the summer vacation I would join the School.

On 20th May, 1939 the Y.S.S. Vidyalaya Ranchi was closed for the summer vacation, and I started for Y.S.S. Ashram, Puri on 21st to spend the vacation there. I had great opportunity to visit various places of interest at Puri during my stay there. On 28th June, 1939 I started for Y.S.S. Vidyalaya at Ejmalichak. I reached Panskura station at 1 (one) in the night. I spent the rest of the night there. In the morning, I went to Tamluk by bus, and from there by boat reaching the school on 29th June 1939. I joined the School as Headmaster on 4th July, 1939.

As Headmaster, I had very little work in the school. When the Assistant Headmaster came to handover the keys of the school and office to me, I told him, "I am here for a short period; besides, I do not know the office work here. Please continue to do the office work as usual. Wherever you want me to sign, please bring it up. I shall gladly do that. I am ready to help you whenever you need". He was happy; took back all the keys with him. Because of availability of time, I used to take some classes regularly.

I delivered lectures every Friday evening at the religious meetings of the Y.S.S. Ashram of the Ejmalichak Centre. On every Saturday, I used to impart religious instructions to the boys of the school. The teachers also would join my religious classes. I used to deliver regular lectures on various subjects. The subject matter of my first speech was aims and ideals of the Brachmacharya Vidyalaya, Ejmalichak; I also spoke on Gita, Upanishad, ideal of life, how to increase the intellect, character, knowledge and work, etc. I spent many happy days here before returning to Ranchi.

I took the vow of renunciation at Guru Mandir of Ranchi on 19th July, 1940 from Swami Satyananda Giri, then representative of our Gurudeva, as He was in U.S.A. It was Friday, the Guru Purnima. The whole Ashram and Vidyalaya were happy for the double event. I was re-christened as Brahmachari Animananda.

I was initiated in Brahmacharyam, the first step of renunciation in a ceremonial way, known as 'bibidisa'. The ceremony lasted for several hours. Sri Ramachandra Nath Bhattcharya, Sanskrit teacher helped me in the ceremonial Homa - the fire ceremony.

On 1st August 1942, I was appointed the Headmaster of Y.S.S. Brahmacharya Vidyalaya, Ranchi. I used to teach Yogasanas to both students and teachers, besides my daily duties in the School and the Ashram. During the Summer and Puja vacations, I used to visit different religious places in India. I visited Puri several times. I visited Hardwar for the first time in June, 1944; holy places at the heart of the Himalayas, specially Kedarnath, Badrinath, Gangotri and Jamunotri in 1947; Sri Brindaban, Mathura and such other places in the same year after my return from the Himalayas.

In the month of September, 1947, I received special instruction from Paramhansa Yoganandaji to give initiation to my relatives. His instruction to spread the teachings of Y.S.S. and initiate the public at large came on 9th March, 1948. I was appointed the Chief Administrator of Ranchi by Paramahansa Yoganandaji. This was passed by the committee on 7th August, 1951. I was, thus, appointed Secretary of all the departments of Ranchi institution including Hospital (Y.S.S. Sevanam), Ashram and Vidyalaya.

Paramahansa Yoganandaji initiated me into Swami order in a non-ceremonial (Bidwat) way. He had selected my renunciate name, Yogi Swami Satchidananda Giri. He planned to give the renunciate's robe in 1951 which I was eagerly waiting for. But he could not come to India. He left his mortal body on 7th March, 1952. I accepted the robe of renunciation officially from Swami Atmananda Giri on 25th April, 1955.

In fact, I thought of not accepting the robe from any one. But people would not recognise me as a Swami if I did not accept the renunciate robe from a Swami officially. Hence, I had to accept the robe from Swami Atmananda Giriji who was then the official representative of Paramhansa Yoganandaji. I was also influenced in my decision by my friends and others in the Y.S.S. to fulfil the silent wish of Paramahansa Yoganandaji and to receive the robe from the Chief Spiritual Director of Y.S.S. India. I quote the silent wish of my Gurudeva which really forced me to accept the robe of a renunciate officially.

"We all must make great sacrifices for God and His Works. I bear many scars, but I bear them proudly and so must you. If you love God and me, you will do so willingly" (Letter of Paramahansa Yoganandaji dated the 20th September, 1945).

"I have read your entire letter with interest and am touched when I realize how you are growing in the spirit of the Beloved and that you know as you grow in His Grace, the responsibilities will also grow. The tests will come, but never a test which you cannot pass because your faith and devotion to Divine Mother and Father of us all will help you to draw all the necessary knowledge to pass the test. I will be ever nearer you in spirit to aid you. God's children who have dedicated themselves to Him and to His service are never really alone. Their fellowmen in the world may pass them by scoff and scorn when they cannot understand, but this, as you know, is only temporary ignorance. The Divine Mother dwelling in them is the same as in you except that you have welcomed and accepted Her light, and they have rejected it.

The happiness that is growing within you, the love that is growing and the joy; all these your fellowmen want but they do not know, it will only come through God's contact. This is what we in Y.S.S. and S.R.F. have to tell them in such a way that they will want God and His blessings above everything else. I am happy that you have interested your family in the work to the extent that they care for God even as you do. And as for yourself, dear Animananda, remember that when you are doing your regular meditations and kriya practice with the love of Divine Mother in your heart, I am there with you in spirit. I will help you to interknit the Divine outside with the Divine inside yourself. Your joy will increase and the love you feel will grow until others notice it and you can help them and thereby fulfill my greatest wish, that we in Y.S.S. and S.R.F. may be able to awaken God's love in all true thirsty hearts. All my love and unceasing blessing always" - P. Yogananda 23/12/49.

"Your every letter assures me of your deep, intense devotion for God and the Gurus, and the desire to serve them unconditionally in all works. Do not be discouraged if God does not respond in the way in which you desire Him to. Often times, devotees are tested when they feel He has withdrawn His grace. During such times, one should cultivate patience, refusing to become distressed because of His seeming absence. Spiritual duties and meditation should never be neglected at any time, for then the outer environment tends to draw one away from the inner-self. As long as there are human beings on earth, there will arise misunderstandings due to the limitation of man. However, such misunderstandings bear the lessons which we are to learn in order to truly progress. It always touches my heart to see how you strive to live your life according to my advice and suggestions.

I know you are doing your utmost to aid others on the spiritual path and you must continue to do so with whole heart" (Paramhansa Yoganandaji, March 7, 1950).

Chapter 4
Spreading of the Science of Kriya Yoga

From my early childhood, my relatives used to watch my spiritual practices secretly. When they came to know that I have been authorised by my Guru to initiate, many of them approached me to learn the science of kriya and finally for initiation. My relatives were scattered all over India and specially all over Bengal. Hence, I went from place to place to initiate them.

I started to spread the Kriya Yoga technique, in 1948, from Yogoda Math, Dakshineswer (West Bengal). Many from Calcutta and its suburbs got the Kriya Yoga initiation from me in 1948. Paramahansa Yoganandaji wrote the following to me on the 27th February, 1948

"...I have something very vital to write to you, since you have asked for my direction. I want you to settle in Yogoda Math. I am writing to Prakas to that effect. From there I want you to lecture and give classes around Calcutta. Give regular lectures and classes wherein (in the classes) the concentration technique (watching the breath) and the meditation technique (listening to the Aum Sound) will be given as well as instructions in the Yogoda exercises, followed by Kriya Yoga initiation classes.

Prakas Das should give the classes in Calcutta proper, but you should give the classes in suburbs and outlying vicinities and try to convert thousands to the path of Kriya, urging them to become connected with Y.S.S. and Yogoda Math.

It is very true that you should not tell your spiritual experiences to any one else except me. By telling them to others you lose some of the truth that you experienced. The Divine Romance with God must be kept in strict secrecy".

"Please write to me once a month, or twice a month, informing me all about your activities as directed elsewhere in the letter. I want to know what you are doing at regular intervals.

"For His work you must follow me with 100% loyalty; for, God has sent you to me, and God, the Gurus and my humble self will work through you."

"Try to get some workers who are deeply interested in Y.S.S. to join our work at Yogoda Math and prospective students who might some day come to America to help with the ever-growing work here. They must be sincere, loyal and have the desire to completely dedicate their lives to God, Y.S.S. and Gurus".

"Please start at once for Yogoda Math on receipt of this letter. I am writing to Prakas Das also. This letter must not be discussed with any one except Prakas."

"Please be true to the end 100 percent loyal to the will of Gurus and you will reach your goal. All's well that ends well."

Please stick to your place, interest young men and elderly people who would feel some responsibility to develop Yogoda Math.

"Unceasing blessings and love to you" (Paramahansa Yogananda).

I was working strictly according to the above instruction. After sometime, the Board of Directors decided that Y.S.S. Ranchi urgently needed my presence there; accordingly, the General Secretary requested Paramhansa Yoganada to advise me to go to Ranchi. Hence Paramhansa Yoganandaji too advised me to go to Ranchi. I reached Ranchi, and from there I used to do the preaching throughout India.

Sri C.V. Chandappa, an advocate of Ceylon, came to me for initiation in April 1948; afterwards, he took the robe of renunciation on 16th September, 1949 from me at Ranchi Y.S.S. Paramahansaji was very glad to know that he had got his Brahmacharyam from me. His new name was Brahmachari Sivananda. Mrs. Margaret Macdonald Beaton from England came to me for initiation; she was initiated into preliminary yoga techniques on 10th August, 1952. Mr. Duke Alley and Mrs. Edith Alley came from Australia to me and had got their initiation on 7th October, 1955 at Y.S.S. Ranchi. Paul E. Lucey, field representative public relations service division G.E.C. Schenectady N.Y. (America) got the primary techniques on 31st December, 1955 at Delhi Exhibition, in his own room. Number of people who took initiation from me grew steadily.

From time to time, I had to go to Y.S.S. Lakhanpur to give initiation to the boys of the school. On 8th January, 1954, 28 students took initiation into primary yoga techniques from me. On 5th January 1955, 32 more students got their lessons on the primary yoga techniques, and on 7th June, 1955, nine boys got the same. Sometimes, even more than fifty students took their initiation from me at a time. On the 20th July, 1961,

38 boys and three teachers of Y.S.S.K.V. Lakhanpur had their initiation from me.

At the request of Sri Mahendra Pratap, Principal Uday Pratap College, Banaras, I visited the College in January 1955 [14th to 17th] to give initiation. I delivered lectures there. 23 persons took initation from me including the Principal and his sister Shailo at the residence of the Principal. His other sister, nephew and niece had their initiaiton on 18th January 1955 at the residence of Sri K.C. Srivastava, Retired Custodian General of India, Delhi at 33, Kasturba Road, Allahabad. K.C.Srivastavji himself took his initiation on the next day at his residence. Mahendra Pratap was with me. We returned to U.P. College, Banaras, on the same day. On 20th and 21st January, 1955, I initiated number of students of the College at the residence of Sri Mahendra Pratap; on 21st January 1955 also.

I visited Dadri, Bulandshahar with Mahendra Pratap and initiated his mother and other family members on 27th and 29th December 1955. Sri Mahendra Pratap shifted from Banaras to L.S. College, Mazaffarpur as Principal. I visited Mazaffarpur at his request. I delivered two lectures, one on "Yoga in relation to the Theory of Relativity of Einstein" and the other "Self Realization through Yoga". The response was appreciable. Fifty students of the College including many students of the University had got their initiation at the residence of the Principal in January 1956 (between 13th and 23rd). I was invited to deliver lectures at Janta College, Turki, Muzaffarpur by the Principal of the Teachers' Training College. I delivered a lecture, on the26th January 1956 on "Yoga in relation to modern Science". The response was satisfactory. Forty two teacher trainees and members of the Teachings Staff including the Principal took initiation.

On invitation, I visited many Colleges in Mazaffarpur like Ram Dayalu College, D.D. Mahila College, where I delivered lectures. Many got the instruction in the art of Yoga there. Similarly, I was invited by the devotees to different parts of India, e.g. Shimla, Aligarh, Delhi. The reports of some of the lectures were published in the S.R.F. Magazines, U.S.A. (Western Headquarters) and also in our Yogoda Magazine (Eastern HQ). The response at Shimla was very satisfactory, where a centre of Y.S.S. was established with the initiated members. Another similar centre was established at Aligarh.

I received requests from several persons like G. Nulliah Naidoo, his wife, Mrs Jagathabal and G.K. Nalliah Naidoo from South Africa for initiation. Mrs. Sarojini Nulliah Naidoo and Mrs. Jagathabal got the

Kriya Yoga initiation from me at Y.S.S. Guru Mandir (vision room), Ranchi. Sri Sri Daya Mata and her party were present on the occasion. Sri Sri Daya Mata had approached me for permission to have stenographic notes at the time of initiation. I told her that it was the same rules and regulation which I got from Paramahansa Yoganandaji. I showed her the original typed copy. On looking at the copy, she told me, "I myself had typed the copy". However, Mataji on her behalf took the stenographic notes during the function on 20th January, 1959.

Mr. Constantine J. Tenukest, Incharge of the SRF, Sydney wrote to me in his letter dated the 15th October 1962, "Two devotees, both kriyabans are planning to visit Ranchi in March or April of the next year. One is your correspondent Jim Martini and the other one is John Goodwin of Rochhampton, Queensland. Both are devoted souls and both hope to find at Ranchi something they could not find here - the inner strength. May I request you most sincerely and humbly to look after them. Most probably they will be able to serve the Master's cause in Australia. I think that some most devoted souls fail to understand that Kriyabans can find their liberation in service to Master.

In a few years, I will be retiring. Who will look after His work? I know God will look after us. Master will look after us but something is left to our discrimination and to our sense of loyalty. You will see that essentially both men are very fine and full of devotion. Help them to channel this devotion" October 15, 1962. After a month, he again wrote to me:

"My dear Swamiji,

My previous letter was addressed to you at Ranchi. On the second day after this letter was sent, your letter from Dakshineswar was received. Did you receive it? It was dated October 15, 1962. In it, I have written about the work we are doing here for the Guru's cause. Also I have related to you that two Kriyabans Mr. J. Martini and Mr. John Goodwin intended to come to Ranchi - to receive some training and guidance under your direction. Mr. J. Martini intended to leave at the end of January and Mr. J. Goodwin at the end of February ..."

On 2nd December 1962, I received a letter from Mr. Goodwin: "Dear Swamiji, I am writing to you to enlist your aid, if possible, for my forthcoming trip to India. I have made formal application to S.R.F. in Los Angles to enter the YSS Ashram in Ranchi, and at the moment I am awaiting their reply. Mr. Tenukest advised me that you last wrote to him from Dakshineswar, so I am addressing this letter to him with the hope that it will find you.

"Both Mr. Tenukest and Mr. Martini have advised me that they have mentioned me to you recently. However, I wish to advise that my intention is to enter the Ashram as a renunciate disciple, and it is to this effect that I have made my application to Headquarters. My acceptance depends on the grace of God and Gurus, though I feel sure that they shall not fail me... if upon some reason or another, I was to be refused permission to enter the Ashram as a renunciate, would I have your permission to come as a paying student?"

Yours in Masters service John Goodwin

Mr. J. Goodwin wrote to me on 17th January 1963: "Our good friend, Jim Martini is now on his way to India and to Dakshineswar where I also wish to go".

Mr. C. J. Tenukest had written to me on 19th February 1963.

"I write to express my happiness that you are looking after one of our best devotees Jim Martini. This is your first hand opportunity to learn about our life here — about our blessings and about our trials. Jim was one of the two regular attendants of the Kiribill Meditation Group. With God's grace and through your love and attention, he may be a living support for Master's work in Sydney. I remember your willingness to help him and all of us, and I am thankful to Master for your being his instrument of wisdom and spiritual discipline."

I am in touch with Mr. John Goodwin. He intends to sail on March 27th but at present is having difficulties with the YSS Secretary in understanding that one should not present one's conditions before giving the views of renunciation. I have suggested to him to abandon very advanced plans and to proceed to Dakshineswar on the same conditions as Jim Martini. During six months of study and meditation under you, he will be able to resolve all his difficulties. Then, with your recommendation and approval, he may be fit to vow his unconditional surrender. 3rd April 1963."

"It is very comforting to know that you are pleased with the spiritual zeal of J. Martini and that John Goodwin will receive a similar support and attention."

I have quoted above only a few lines from thousands of such letters in order to express how the works of God and Gurus were progressing all over the world.

Chapter 5
With Sri Bhupendra Nath Sannyal Mahasaya

I first met Sri Bhupendra Nath Sannyal Mahasaya on Sunday the 8th August 1937 at about 9-30 a.m. along with some members of Y.S.S. at his temporary Calcutta residence close to our Calcutta Centre at 52A, Vivekananda Road. I asked him 'How long should one practise the Kriya exercises?' He said, "At least one hour a day. It is better if one can perform more". On my request, he advised, "Be always cautious to be away from the path of the senses." I have seen many devoted enthusiastic Kriyabans cool off as they enter into the world of activities. Be firm in trials and tribulations."

I came back home at 11-30 a.m. and revisited him at 3 pm again. We discussed the spiritual centres in the spine and their realization for nearly 75 minutes. He also told me, "Man does not know the importance of the Guru. If he has full faith in him, he will surely reach the Goal. If he does not even practise Kriya, he will get everything. But you should know the meaning of Faith. Sri Sri Lahiri Mahasaya used to say, Faith means "the cessation of breath". (Bi + Swas = Biswas. Bi means without; Swas is breath; Biswas means faith) which comes from breathless state.

On the 13th August, the college was closed at 12-10 p.m. I went to his residence at 2-50 p.m. I requested for some light on his Sadhana. He said "At the age of 15, I got the grace of Sri Sri Shyama Charan Lahiri Mahasaya. I used to meditate 14 to 15 hours a day, specially on new moon and full moon days. I used to take a little clarified butter along with 2 or 3 ripe bananas at about 4 a.m. in the morning and a little quantity of water. Then I used to sit for meditation. Without any break, I used to do my 'Sadhana' upto 8 p.m. My spiritual progress during the year was satisfactory and my Guru very kindly gave me permission to initiate other seekers."

I met him once again on 14th at his residence direct at 3 p.m. We had a long discussion on the different plexuses in the spine, 'Kutastha'

(3rd Eye) and Samadhi. Let me reproduce a few questions and answers:

"At the time of meditation generally a very dazzling point is seen - is it Lord Krishna?"

"Yes, but it is really His reflection. You will have to penetrate it and enter inside".

"Is it Kutastha"?

"Yes, You can see Kutastha every where".

"Do the 'Chakras' in the spine open one by one or simultaneously?"

"Nearly at a time. When the sensation starts in the spine, the Chakras from the base of the spine begin to blossom one after another quickly. But generally by the grace of the Guru, the centre at the medulla (3rd Eye) opens first".

"Are the descriptions of the Chakras in the Yogic books true?"

"Yes".

"Is it possible to realise the same?"

"Well, you should know the real meaning of the words of scriptures".

On 15th I revisited Sannyal Mahasay along with Bibhuti, Kalidas, Mohini and Krishna Chaityana. We entered into another session of questions and answers from Gita, Upanishadas and Vedas, Pratyahar, Dharana, Dhyana and Samadhi, 'Jivanmukta', Jagrata Samadhi and varieties of Samadhi. On our request Sannyal Mahasaya agreed to preside over our weekly evening meeting. Mohini Babu, asked. "How many steps are there in our Sadhana?".

"There are many. It is not necessary that we shall have to cross one by one. Some can cross three or four steps at a time, others may find their salvation at the 2nd or 3rd step itself".

Kalidas asked, "You have written in your book, that we can achieve the stage of Pratyahara with 12 Kriyas, Dharana with 144 Kriyas, and Samadhi with 1728 Kriyas. Is it possible to perform so many Kriyas at a time?"

-"Yes, but it takes a long time".

Mohini Babu enquired, "How to count such a long number?

- Why, how do they fix their numbers who count thousands at a time?"

- In that case, mind will be diverted towards the any counting".

Sannyal Mahasaya explained, "That does not matter. It is negligible.

If you can't count so much, and if the mind is absorbed within before that, well and good. Then there is no need of counting anymore".

I used to visit him from time to time. Once he came to Ranchi to give initiation to some persons. When he visited Y.S.S. Ashrama, I was teaching Yogasans. He was pleased with the Yogasana demonstration by the boys. He later sought approval of the authority of the Ranchi institution for my leave to serve the Veda Vidyalaya at Gurudham Mandir (P.O. Bounsi) Bhagalpur, Bihar as Yogasan teacher. I went there on this assignment. The place was charming due to its loneliness. The small temple dedicated to Lahiri Mahashaya overlooking Mandar hill was beautiful. There were 6 or 7 solitary caves at the base of the temple that served as beautiful meditation rooms. I got one for my personal meditation. I was getting various kinds of experiences in that meditation room.

I started teaching Yogasanas on 11th January, 1946. Some of the workers also joined. I went to Sannyal Mahasaya on 11th requesting him to observe my Kriyas. He carefully watched and commented, "You are doing the Kriyas well". He advised me to perform the revolving of the head slowly during the practice of 2nd and 3rd Kriyas. All the Kriyas, starting from the 3rd to the 5th are performed holding the breath in the lung. Hence, if the breath ceases automatically while performing 1st and 2nd Kriyas, then there is no need of performing the others". I came to know from him only that the 3rd Kriya mentioned in the pracepta was really the 2nd one. "The Kriyas are not the end but a means," he remarked, "Calmness and divine intoxication should be the aim. You will have to watch your mind, whether it is running hither and thither. If not, and it is fixed on any centre in the spine, and if you feel the electric flow there accompanied by divine intoxication, then it can be be taken for granted that you are performing Kriyas correctly".

He narrated one of his personal experiences on revolving the head during Kriya, "Once I was sitting with my master Lahiri Mahasaya. One of my spiritual brothers was performing the higher Kriya in the presence of our Guru. He was revolving the head with jerks. Gurudeva touched his head and told him to do the same slowly. I immediately learnt that it should not be done forcefully; "it should be done with deep attention so that with every revolving you will see the flash of lightning".

I requested him to help me see the flash of lightning; see the 'Chakras' in the spine. "That will be an artificial experience. It won't help you much. Go on with your Sadhana. You will yourself be able to realize the spiritual centres in the spine. Many devotees had meditated here for long years. Dive deep in meditation here. You will get their beneficial vibrations", he replied.

He reached Gurudham on the 7th Jan. 1946; I reached on the 8th. Sannyal Mahasaya used to explain the Bhagavad Gita based on the spiritual interpretation of Lahiri Mahasaya. While reading his own commentaries, he would occasionally cite examples from the life of his Guru. Once, while explaining the control of the body of a true Yogi, he mentioned, " Sri Chandra Mohan Dey, son of a spiritual brother got his medical degree. At the instance of his father, Chandra Mohan visited Lahiri Mahasaya. He was speaking about health and medicines. Gurudeva listened patiently. He, then asked, "Well, you have learnt well. What is the sign and symptoms of the existence of life?" Chandra Mohan explained like a professor in a medical college. Lahiri Mahasaya extended his hand towards the doctor and asked him to feel the pulse. There was no pulse beat. Gurudeva smilingly requested him to use his stethoscope to examine the heart. There was no heartbeat. Lahiri Mahasaya asked him whether he was alive. Chandra Mohan was clueless. Lahiri Mahasaya comforted him, "Well, you have learnt a lot, remember that there is lot to be learnt yet".

On another occasion, Sannyal Mahasaya cited another instance from the life of Lahiri Mahasya. "Once, a gentleman had come to test my Guru at 11 p.m. and told him, 'I have one question to ask; please tell me, what my grandfather is doing now'. Gurudeva replied 'He is copying something from scripture'. He also mentioned the place and name of the scripture. The gentleman laughed loudly and retorted, 'My grandfather is more than 90 years. He goes to sleep at 8 p.m. sharp daily'. Lahiri Mahasaya said, 'may be'. Later on, the gentleman enquired and realized the truth of Lahiri Mahasaya's statement.

On 16th, at the end of the Gita class, a devotee enquired, "why does the devotee who has dedicated his soul to God suffer most?" Sannyal Mahasaya explained, "It is his Prarabdha (result of the past deeds already in action)". I asked, 'Is it for this reason, we find in the scriptures, that the result of the pre-natal work must be worked out, etc.' Sannyal Mahasaya's voice rang with compassionate finality: "We shall have to work out the result of evil deeds of various past lives. Sometimes, it so happens that a devotee with tremendous good actions and meditation has to face supreme trials and sorrows, but he accepts them all gladly with a smiling face and waits for the final destruction of effects of the evil deeds, otherwise he won't be able to unite with his divine Beloved. Those who have once been touched by the divine Beloved, this power of endurance, patience becomes unparalleled. They do not falter from their spiritual path even amidst cyclonic storms of trials. You all know the life of Prahlada. How many times did his father try to kill him. Did he falter from the path of God? You also know the life of Haridas. From place to place and in different markets he was caned. When after being caned in two markets, his whole body was torn and bleeding profusely, he was asked to come back from the path of God, he responded, 'if my body be torn to pieces and my life goes out, I shall not forsake the name of God'. Can an ordinary person imagine such power of endurance and discarding life for God? Such is the extraordinary trial of the devotee of God and his power of endurance. If there be any rotten boil inside the skin, how would the disease be cured, it should rather be operated and removed; you must endure the pangs of operation".

On 18th January, at the end of his class one devotee enquired about the death of a Yogi. Sannyal Mahasaya replied, "The Yogis achieve the power of full control over life force. They can know the time of death before hand and accordingly they prepare their body and mind. Just at the time of death, they withdraw the life force from the body and send it to the thousand-rayed lotus in the head to unite with the Divine Father. Those who have not got such control on the life force, have to go to the astral world. There they have to work and meditate for final emancipation. Thus, they achieve the gradual salvation". He then explained the process of Gradual-liberation quoting Chandogya upanisada.

Another devotee asked, "How do the 'Jivanmukta' Yogis embrace their death?" Sannyal Mahasaya expressed, "They have no death. They have conquered it. To the human eye they seem to leave the body, but to them both life and death are equal. They are one with the Supreme. They have achieved omnipresence".

A devotee muttered, "I don't understand". He quoted many verses from the scriptures and cited the example of Lahiri Mahasaya, "My Gurudev came to know the time of leaving His body six months in advance and he intimated his wife, how his body should not be cremated. Just after six months he left his body. All his relatives were aggrieved. The mother of Taraknath Sannyal Mahasaya, wept bitterly and went to where Lahiri Mahasaya used to meditate. She bowed her head; when she raised her head, she was astonished to see Lahiri Mahasaya sitting on his cot as before smiling happily. She called all others saying, "Why are you all crying? He is sitting in his room. They all came and saw his flesh and blood body".

He related another story. "Once one gentleman came to my Guru with an oil painting portrait of Kabir in his hand and asked, "Is it all right? Gurudeva said, "Nearly all right". Then he amended the portrait with the pen and told him, 'Now it is all right?' The gentleman enquired, 'Have you ever seen Kabir?' 'I see him always', was the response. 'Where is he now?' Pointing to his own body Gurudeva declared, 'He is sitting before you'. Let me relate one incident from my own life. I can swear before my Guru, sitting in his temple, that what I say is true.

We all protested, "Why do you speak like that? Are we disbelieving your words?" He remarked, "Who knows what is there in whose mind?" He then added, "After the death of my Guru, I used to cry day and night. My relatives used to ask, 'Has he gone mad?' I myself did not know why I was crying. I was at Deoghar at that time. At about 2 a.m., my Gurudeva appeared before me in flesh and blood and asked me, 'Why are you crying?' I remonstrated, "You are no longer on this earth; next moment I laughed at my ridiculous statement. He is standing just in front of me. He too, laughed heartily and consoled me, 'I am always everywhere. Don't cry any more'. Then he patted me and waved his hand over my body. I never wept again."

One of the devotees asked, "If any one among us do not get salvation in this life, what happens to him in the next incarnation? Will he get this Kriya of ours?"

"Yes, he will get this Kriya. He is fearless. He need not be afraid any more. He starts from where he was forced to leave the body". In an imploring tone, the devotees voice rang: "Will you come to give us initiation again? In what way will we receive initiation?" He avoided a direct response and turned towards the mystery of Sadhana. "Encircling one great power a number of persons are working as initiators, all drawing their power from the original source. There are many such centres connected with one grand centre. You will not understand all these mysteries".

At the instruction of Paramahansa Yoganandaji, I went to Puri and met Sannyal Mahasaya on the 23rd May 1951 at his residence and handed over the photograph of Paramhamsa Yoganandaji. In return, Sannyal Mahasaya also gave me one of his photographs to be sent to Paramhamsaji at U.S.A.

He told an interesting incident.

"My Gurudev and our holy mother (wife of my Guru) were then living at Banaras. When she heard about insanity of her son (Dukari Lahiri), she approached her husband and pleaded, "Well, you are giving medicines to so many people, why are you not looking after your son in your house?" Gurudeva replied "Prarabdha is very powerful. The disease is difficult to be cured". The Mother was adamant, "You must do something for the son". Then he foretold, "he will be cured to some extent, so that he can work". Dukarida was locked in a room. Lahiri Mahasaya entered his room and asked, "Dukari, how are you?" Dukari bowed his head and touched His feet. Lahiri Mahasaya passed his hand over the head of Dukari. Instantly, he was cured."

I asked:

"Once you had initiation from the astral body of Lahiri Mahasaya, is that true?"

Reluctantly he replied, "Yes, but may be that was a hallucination or a dream. Hence, I don't like to divulge that fact."

"For how long did you have the privilege to have his company?"

He replied, "After initiation, I got his company only for two and a half years. I got 'darsan' twice or thrice, because He used to tell me not to visit. However, I have got His blessings in abundance and He had suffered much for me."

"When did you get the second higher initiation after the first one?"
"After three months."

"When did you get the third or fourth initiation?"

"Within one year I got up to the fourth initiation. So long I have not disclosed all these to any one. Please keep them in strict secrecy".

I agreed; I also mentioned that I shall note down in my diary and not make public now.

He compassionately said, "Maha Mudra, Pranayam i.e., 1st Kriya, and Jyoti Mudra, sometimes he used to impart instruction regarding the 'Nabhi-Kriya', or such other kriya considering the need of the devotee".

Once, I was suffering from malaria, on the verge of death. My elder sister wrote to Gurudeva. In response, he wrote, "Death will not visit him now, he will have much work to do". Now, I realise it is nothing but the work of preaching. Three to four thousand people have already got Kriya initiation".

"How many persons had got the power to give initiation from him?"

"At Bishnupur, there were four persons. There were many from other parts of the country.

On the 24th May 1951 at 3-30 p.m. I visited him again at his residence in Puri. I requested him to tell something about the life of Lahiri Mahasaya".

"In 1899 A.D., I first ventured to write on his life, and with that motive, I noted down some points. Later, I sent that short note to Tinkari Mahasaya. He promised to help me. I also approached others. Realising the vastness of his life and opposition from some, I dropped the idea. I attempted to express his teachings and counsels in poems. Many could not understand his words. For many years, I had pondered over his writings. The truths that I have realised and the meaning that I have understood from his writings, specially in Gita, have been expressed in my commentaries on the Holy Bhagavat Gita. I do not have, however, the audacity to claim that I have realised all his writings. Afterwards, I published his Kabir Gita and one or two other books".

During our discourses some of Sannyal Mahasaya's devotees were present. One from that gathering enquired about some miraculous story pertaining to the life of Lahiri Mahasya.

Sannyal Mahasaya reluctantly replied, "It is not judicious to narrate miracles even if it be an eye-witnessed fact. Incident gets exaggerated and deformed as it passes from one person to another. It becomes hard to get at the truth. Many persons do not investigate about the truth". Sannyal Mahasaya's youngest son was sitting by his side. Looking at him affectionately, he narrated one incident.

"Ramdas Maitra was a relative and a disciple of Lahiri Mahasaya. All his children had died just after their birth. Once Ramdas approached Lahiri Mahasaya for the protection of his children. Lahiri Mahasaya advised him to construct a delivery room, its front door, window, etc. "If you observe some blue light form a particular corner of the delivery room, rest assured the child will not die, it will survive this time".

"Just after the delivery, Ramdas's wife cried. Ramdas thought probably due to sudden death of the child made her cry. On enquiry, he learnt that she had seen an unnatural dazzling blue light from one corner of the room."

I requested Sannyal Mahasaya to narrate the story of that monk with long hairs like sticks. He said, "Once a monk approached our Gurudeva for initiation. Gurudeva was not responding. Then he entreated Lahiri Mahasaya and repeated his request. Lahiri Mahasaya said, 'You are willing to get initiation, but I do not want to give'. The monk asked, "Well, you are initiating people without any discrimination, then why do you decline a monk like me"?

Lahiri Mahasaya retorted, "Shall I divulge what sort of monk you are before this gathering"?

"Yes, you are at liberty to tell what you like".

"Lahiri Mahasaya asked, "Do you remember the rape you committed in the pulse field"?

"The monk fell at his feet, "If I can correct myself, I shall come back to you". The monk fled away.

The youngest son of Sannyal Mahasaya enquired, "Is there any definite proof of this act? From whom have you heard this story"?

"I have heard the story from my spiritual brothers who never spoke untruth".

On the 27th May 1951, during our usual conversation he talked about the life of Paresh Kaviraj Mahasaya. "Paresh Kaviraj Mahasaya was a vastly learned person. He was the student of Sri Gangadhar Kaviraj. One day, Gangadhar Kaviraj Mahasaya told Paresh Kaviraj, "I have explained Charak Samhita to you according to my ability but if you want to know the real inner meaning of it (Charak Samhita), you will have to take shelter under the feet of a true Yogi". After completing his education, he wrote a book explaining the meaning of the Charak Samhita which one day he presented to Lahiri Mahasaya for his comment. Lahiri Mahasaya after going through the book only commented, "fair". When he insisted on more precise comment, Lahiri Mahasaya said, "Everything is wrong". He was very upset. He spent the whole night in finding the mistake. All of a sudden the word of his teacher struck in his mind, that the true meaning was kept in secrecy with the Yogis. Lahiri Mahasaya was a yogi and hence, he must know the true meaning of the book.

"Next day, he went to Lahiri Mahasaya and sought forgiveness. Apologetically, he asked for the real meaning of the Charak Samhita. Lahiri Mahasaya explained it for hours together. At the end, he took initiation from Lahiri Mahasaya."

On my request, Sannyal Mahasaya hesitantly narrated another incident. "Once, there was some trouble in the Jamindar Estate of Mahantaji of Pausibir near Bishnupur. One of our spiritual brothers was also entangled in the case. A few persons were murdered. After the incidence, the Mahantaji was arrested by the police and an arrest warrant was issued against the spiritual brother. The spiritual brother was perturbed over the involvement in a murder case. He wanted to take shelter in the hut of his Gurudeva Lahiri Mahasay. The moment he entered the room of Lahiri Mahasaya, Gurudeva became furious, "You murderer, get out from my room". Our spiritual brother fled away. Then our spiritual brother thought, "Death is imminent. If I shall have to die, why to be hanged. Let me die in the sacred water of the Ganges". Thinking thus, he went to the bank of the Ganges and was waiting for the suitable time when another thought flashed in his mind. "Before death, I should meditate at the feet of my Guru. I could not see the feet at that time due to his anger. Let me have a glance of his feet from a distance". Slowly and stealthily, he went to the house of Lahiri Mahasaya. As the door opened he was looking at the feet of his Gurudeva from a distance. Lahiri Mahasaya shouted "Who is there?" and he was caught red handed. Gurudeva then remarked, "You, liar, thief, cheat, murderer you have committed all sorts of sins, now you are thinking of committing suicide. Take your seat in the corner of that room. Now meditate, if you leave your seat, I shall break your legs".

He was confined in that room for months together. He used to get leave at meal times. That case went upto high court, where he was released for want of proper evidence".

This reminded me of one verse in the Guru Gita where Lord Siva says, "O Parvati, the Guru can protect a person if he is sweared by the Munis (saints), demi-gods and the gods and also from the fear of death."

During our free discourses, Sannyal Mahasaya related: "Many people from the furthest corner of India heard His name. One day I met a monk of the temple of Mahakal in Ujjaini. When he came to know that I had come from Banaras, he enquired about Lahiri Mahasaya, whether he was still living. I expressed my sorrow he is no more in his mortal body on this earth. I (Sannyal Mahasaya) asked him, what is your notion about him?" The monk replied: 'He had reached the highest goal".

Sannyal Mahasaya mentioned that Lahiri Mahasaya was very calm and quiet, and so reserved that no one could understand the depth of his Sadhana. He controlled all his senses. Once, on the street, a person abused him. At the end, Lahiri Mahasaya commented: "Are you now satisfied?"

I asked, "How many disciples of Lahiri Mahasaya are there?"

"Most probably, three to four thousand. He got his initiation between the age 32 to 34 years. He used to give initiation while he was in service. He retired in 1880 A.D. and left the physical body in 1895 A.D. Hence he had got full 15 years after his retirement for giving initiation though I don't know exactly how many years he devoted himself to the spread of Kriya Yoga. Generally he used to give initiation from his own room at Banaras. The wooden cot on which he used to sit and the shoes made of cloth that he used to wear are still preserved in his room".

In another occasion, I requested Sanyal Mahasaya to tell me about the life of Lahiri Mahasaya and his devotees. He narrated: 'Sri Kailash Banerjee and his wife, both were initiated by our Guru. Once Kailash Banerjee Mahasaya was seriously ill at Bishnupur. I, too, was then at that place. The father of my spiritual brother Hrishikesh Kaviraj was a very good physician. He could foretell the death of a patient by feeling the pulse only. He used to visit Kailash babu besides many other eminent doctors and physicians. All had given up hope of Kailash Babu's life. All in the family were morose and sullen. But the wife of Kailash Babu was performing her household duties in a natural way. I used to address her as sister. I enquired, "Didi, (we call the elder sister as Didi) what's your opinion regarding the condition of Dada (elder brother is addressed as Dada)"? She commented; "Gurudeva has intimated me that my husband will not die this time, and that is why I am not worrying about him".

"After sometime, Kailash Babu came around but after the lapse of seven or eight months 'Didi' left her physical body. She had come to know the time of her death, having heard it from her Guru, and accordingly she intimated everyone the time of her final day of departure from the world. From mouth to mouth the news of her death got circulated throughout the town. The people of the town used to criticise her, pretending Bhishmadeva on her bed of arrows, and waiting for the auspicious moment. Her family members were apprehensive because of her stout and strong physique without any sign of imminent death. But she left her mortal coil just at the time she predicted."

As Lahiri Mahasaya, having expired earlier, she must have got her message during meditation. Some of the devotees had got the vision of Lahiri Mahasaya at the very place, where afterwards, Gurudham was established.

"Dr. Radhakumud Babu was a very devoted soul. He once came to my ashram and shared one of his experiences regarding this place. He got the vision of Lord Gourangadeva and his devotees who were singing devotional songs ("Harinam sankirtan)". Sannyal Mahasaya quoted one verse from the scripture: "Where mind naturally becomes absorbed in God and becomes calm and delighted, that is, the feet of Lord Bishnu".

I enquired: "How were the footprints of Lord Gouranga printed on the stone?"

"Everything can melt at the touch of that supreme spirit. The solid matter has no power to resist His power and that is why the solid rock melts at His touch. But human beings have the privilege to accept or reject Him and hence, He cannot cause to melt the heart of man easily'.

Once, while discussing about Lord Buddha, Sannyal Mahasaya spoke at length regarding the power of non-violence. He quoted the words of Patanjali to explain the subject. He cited many examples from the lives of many devotees. "Lastly I shall tell you one incident of my own life. Once I had gone to Sahebganj with some of my fellowmen for a walk. All of a sudden a mad he-buffalo was running towards us, nodding his horns. People shouted: 'that is a mad buffalo' flee, flee". If we tried to run away we would fall from the hill and if we did not leave the place we would die of the attack of that mad creature. However, finding no other alternative, I instructed my fellowmen to sit down there, thinking the buffalo not to be an enemy, but a friend. They, too, finding no other way, tried to follow my advice. For the time being, I realised the animal as part and parcel of my soul, a friend. The buffalo, with nodding horns, came to me and placed his head on my shoulder. I patted his mouth, passed my hand on his shoulder and neck without feeling any fear. After a few minutes I told him, 'we are afraid of you.' Then he went away. According to my horoscope predictions, that day was the day of my death'.

On 28th May, 1951, after dinner, Sannyal Mahasaya sat on his easy chair in the outside verandah of his residence. We took our seats on mats around him. He quoted a verse: "If there be any pre-natal karma to be worked out, it remains as it is for eternity".

Forthwith, in a protesting tone, I said: "What if there be a tremendous effort to overcome it?"

Sannyal Mahasaya: "Such a tremendous effort is not generally applicable. The life of Vishwamitra is the only instance where we find such an effort. According to our pre-natal works, we have got this physical body, the particular parents, and the present joys and sorrows. It is true, we can alter the resultant force of our pre-natal works by the application of tremendous effort in this life. But we should not misuse our efforts for comforts/welfare of our physical body. Lahiri Mahasaya used to instruct us. Every one gets some food for the upkeep of the body only, clothings to cover it and a shelter for rest, may be like the king or like the beggar. Hence, our efforts should be applied for the spiritual progress only".

On the 29th May 1951, he himself narrated one miraculous incident from the life of Lahiri Mahasaya. "Once one of my spiritual brothers had gone to the market at Banaras and saw that our Gurudeva was also marketing. He then came to the house of Lahiri Mahasaya and found him sitting on his cot. The spiritual brother thought that he had committed a mistake. In order to clear his doubt he again went to the market. To his astonishment he observed that Lahiri Mahasaya was still busy with his work in the market. He again returned to Gurueswar noticed Lahiri Mahasaya was meditating on his own cot. His mind was perplexed. He hastened again to the market to see Lahiri Mahasaya was still there. Again went to the meditation room for solution. Lahiri Mahasaya then laughed and he got the answer."

"Lahiri Mahasaya instructed Sri Ma (his wife), just six months before his death not to cremate his body but to preserve it. He also foretold her the exact time and date of his death. Within that six months he had a carbuncle on his back near the spine. I don't remember exactly who operated that malignant boil but I know definitely no anesthesia was used during that serious operation. When all the work was over, He enquired from the surgeon: 'Have you finished your work?' as if He had no connection with the operation. The wound was healed up and he was cured of all ailments. In due course, he left his physical body.

"We did not know the wish of Lahiri Mahasaya as Sri Ma did not inform us of Lahiri Mahasaya's last wishes. Hence, according to the Hindu custom, his body was cremated. Only afterwards when other members of his family and our spiritual brothers came to know of the last instruction of Lahiri Mahasaya, all of them were sad that they could not preserve his body."

Sannyal Mahasaya continued, "Brahmachari Sri Krishna Ramji had served Lahiri Mahasaya day and night. A few days before his demise

Lahiri Mahasaya very affectionately addressed Krishna Ramji, 'Krishna Ram, you have served me whole-heartedly. I am satisfied with you. I shall give you whatever you ask from me to-day'.

Sri Krishna Ramji prayed 'Gurudeva, you have given me all. Due to your blessings I have got everything. If you are willing to confer anything on me, I pray, please bless me so that my mind does not deflect from your feet for a moment and my deep devotion (Bhakti) does never flicker'. From that day, Brahmachari Sri Krishna Ramji became silent for the rest of his life. We never heard him speaking to anyone".

Sri Sannyal Mahasaya enthusiastically narrated another story: "Once one of my spiritual brothers was going with his family members to visit our Gurudeva in a cab. As they were at a distance of two or three miles from the residence of Lahiri Mahasaya, the wheel of the cab broke down. They saw a man approaching towards the cab; the man enquired, 'What's the matter?' The spiritual brother explained the problem. The man helped him to fit the wheel. Soon they reached the residence of Lahiri Mahasaya and narrated the incident. Lahiri Mahasaya nodded his head and expressed that he was aware of the fact.

"The spiritual brother asked: 'You have not seen the accident, then how do you know the fact?'

"Lahiri Mahasaya commented: 'Then, who had fitted the wheel'? The brother then realising the depth of his compassion felt ashamed over his interrogation and expressed regret and his deep gratitude as well".

On Saturday 23rd June 1951, at Ranchi, I received a letter from Paramahansa Yoganandaji to go to Puri and collect the life history of Lahiri Mahasaya and Sannyal Mahasaya. He wrote, "Don't delay, please carry out the instructions immediately. Act immediately ...."

I intimated Girinda, then incharge of Y.S.S. Ranchi. He said: "Without the order of the General Secretary, Prokasda, I cannot send you to Puri. Intimate him and I shall obey." I realized that order must come through proper channel. Hence, I hastened to the G.P.O. Ranchi and had sent a wire to the General Secretary, intimating the content of Gurudev's letter and requesting necessary instructions to Girinda. On receipt of the telegram, Prokasda ordered Girinda to release me for a few days. On 30th June, 1951, I started for Puri. In the mean time, I had typed the materials that I had already collected from Sannyal

Mahasaya for onward transmission to Paramhansa Yoganandaji. I reached Puri on the 4th July 1951. On the 6th I was fortunate enough to participate in the car festival of Jagannath Dev at Puri. On the 7th, I visited Sannyal Mahasaya with Gurudeva's letter to Sannyal Mahasaya, which he had sent along with my letter. I handed over that letter and all the typed materials, that I had collected from 23rd May to 29th May 1951, for correction to him.

Sannyal Mahasaya presented one of his duly autographed portraits to me to be sent to U.S.A. At the back of the picture, it was written: "Presented to Sreemad Swami Yaganandaji with my blessing, affection and love.

Bhupendra Nath Sannyal, dated Puri, Gurudham, Chattack Pahar, 7/7/51."

In the afternoon at 4-30 p.m. I revisited Sannyal Mahasya when he returned the two sets of typed copies corrected and duly signed, and the remaining one he kept with him. I observed that he had omitted the names of one or two persons from the typed copies and remarked: "I should not publish the name of anyone who is still living. Further, what will his relatives think of me?"

During our conversation, he narrated one story: "Once Sri Keshab Dutta Mahasaya had gone to Lahiri Mahasaya to know the spiritual interpretation of Srimad Bhagvad Gita from him. Keshab Babu reached when Lahiri Mahasaya was taking the Gita class. Keshab babu requested him to explain the 24th verse from the Chapter 8. On hearing the commentary, many devtees felt happy that their doubts were cleared, but observing that Keshab Dutta Mahasaya had not asked any question, one devotee enquired: 'Well Dutta Mahasaya, have you nothing to ask?' To that, Lahiri Mahasaya himself remarked: 'Dutta Mahasaya has already got the reply to his querry.'

Sri Sannyal Mahasaya related another story about Keshab Dutta Mahasaya: "Due to the fervent request of Sri Sri Ma (wife of Lahiri Mahasaya) and Joyrama, Lahiri Mahasaya had to go to Bisnupur to cure the insanity of Dukarida. On his return journey, he was passing by the side of the house of Keshab Dutta Mahasaya as the route was by the side of Dutta Mahasaya's house. Many devotees had come to visit Lahiri Mahasaya. They were accompanying him. There was a river on the way. On the other side was the residence of Keshab Dutta Mahasaya. As they were crossing the river, Keshab Dutta Mahasaya was thinking of inviting Lahiri Mahasaya to his house but at heart he was hesitant.

"After crossing the river, Lahiri Mahasaya requested Dutta Mahasaya to offer him some drink. Dutta Mahasaya was so moved by his unconditional Kripa that tears rolled down his cheek."

On the 8th July, Sri Sri Sannyal Mahasaya complied with my request. He went on, "Lahiri Mahasaya had ordered me to give initiation to the public, but I used to take permission before initiation. Once I wrote a letter to him asking permission to initiate three persons. In reply, he had returned my letter, putting his remark by the side of each name. The remarks were as follows:

1. Initiate at once.
2. Initiate after three years
3. Tell him to approach after seven years

To my astonishment, I observed that the third person had gone astray within those seven years.

Sri Sannyal Mahasaya continued: "Once a devotee was waiting patiently for the Divine command at Baidyanath Dham. He received the Divine command: 'Go to Banaras, your desire will be fulfilled.' After receiving the Divine order, he went for initiation to many Swamis, Saints at Benaras but no one accepted him as a 'Chela'. When he visited Swami Trailanga, he commented: "I am not your Guru but your Guru is living here in Banaras". Then he went to Lahiri Mahasaya. He accepted him and fixed the date for initiation. When he, with the thought of clearing his doubt, said: 'Divine one, I have one doubt'. To it, Lahiri Mahasya responded: 'Do you mean the incident of Baidyanath Dham?' The spiritual brother was surprised.'

I requested Sannyal Mahasaya to clarify one of the most vital point for which Gurudeva had sent me to him: Sannyal Mahasaya agreed to clarify, I then enquired: "How many times, have you got the 'Darsan' of Lahiri Mahasaya?"

Sri Sannyal Mahasaya replied:

'Publicly I had seen him (Physical body) thrice, twice at Banaras, and once at Bishnupur. Besides, I have seen him once or twice with his physical body but that was not publicly. Many times I had got his vision. To speak the truth, I had got my initiation from his Astral body. Afterwards, when I approached him for initiation, he said: 'You have got your initiation'.

'Once I had got the vision of Mandar (Mandar hill) — The vision was as follows: Many saints, swamis; monks, munis, and rishies were meditating on that hill. Among them were Lord Jesus Chirst, Mohammad, Lord Buddha, Acharya Shankar and such others and many holy saints. I was about to burst into tears for not seeing my Guru.

Indian synonim of Disciple.

Lahiri Mahasaya addressed me from the top of the hill and said, 'I am here'. Afterwards, when I had gone to the hill of Mandar, I could recognise the place.

'On another occasion, I had his vision at Bishnupur, just one month before his demise. In the vision, I observed that he had come to Bishnupur. A large number of people were rushing to have his company. I was feeling hesitant to push through that huge gathering. He himself appeared before me and told, 'I am now leaving'."

On the 9th July 1951, as usual I had gone to Gurudham in the afternoon. The health of Sannyal Mahasaya was not good and hence, I could not collect any new material on that day. On the 10th July 1951, after dinner, I managed to type all the new materials collected in the month of July 1951.

In the afternoon, as usual I visited Sanyal Mahasaya and produced before him all the typed materials including the corrected retyped materials. He, after going through all the pages, passed his remark at the end: "permitted to print in the Autobiography of a Yogi by Paramahansa Yogananda".

Duly signed, he handed over to me two sets of materials and one set he kept aside for him. Then, I returned to my residence and left for Ranchi via Calcutta.

Chapter 6
At Ejmalichak

On the 5th August 1940, Sri Janardan of YSS Brahmacharya Vidyalaya officially introduced me to the students and asked them to be attentive to my religious instructions. I was to address them every Monday for ten minutes during the regular prayer meeting.

On the previous day, Sripati Babu, Assistant Headmaster approached me with his son who was then in class VII, "Brahmachariji, my son is dull; please do something so that his memory may become sharp. I hand over my son to you. Kindly admit him in your regular yoga class". I accepted the boy. Another student of class X had requested me to explain the benefits of Kriya Yoga. I designed and delivered my first lecture accommodating response to both of them.

"My dear young brothers, I am really moved with your devotion and simplicity. I am truly thankful to you, as you have given me opportunity to serve you all. I shall tell you something regarding the development of memory.

I have noticed that your mind does not concentrate on your lessons; rather it wanders around. Hence, you can't commit the lessons to your memory or learn them by heart, even after reading for a long time. Many of you think that your memory is not sharp. That is not the fact. Those who complain that they can not remember anything, can narrate accurately a long interesting tale or a ghost-story or can describe the scenes from a movie. If they are dull headed, wherefrom comes this? The fact is: they don't find any interest in that particular lesson. If any way we can create interest in the lesson, this problem will not be there. The duty of the teachers is to create that interest.

But you can scientifically develop your memory through kriya yoga. Those who have got our kriya initiation will understand and realise the truth. You have read in your science class that if the electric current passes through a coil around an iron bar, it becomes a magnet. If the iron bar is soft, magnetization lasts so long as there is the current; but if the bar be a steel, it will be a strong magnet. Our spine can be compared with the electromagnet. With the help of kriya exercises, if you can send the life force, your spine will be a magnet, it will draw or attract all the energies in the spine. You know the function of a lens. The scattered sun's rays can be utilised for the ignition of paper, cloth or such inflammable substances. Similarly, if the scattered waves or rays of the mind when concentrated through meditation can do immense work. Your mind will be so powerful that you can do marvellous works. You can concentrate on any subject. But that is not meditation. When mind is concentrated on God or on divine only then it is termed as meditation. You know the life history of Swami Vivekananda. How in a very short time he could read so much and also could memorise them. It was due to his concentration of the mind.

Those who have not got kriya initiation, I shall suggest another simple way. When you sit to study, sit for a while silently and try to recollect the words of the teachers in your classes. You will realise that you have forgotten many of their words. You can take the help of your books for remembering the words. Repeat this exercise for 2, 3 or at most 4 days. When you are sure that you need not memorise any more, drop that from your regular thinking. Practical experience will tell you the truth of my words. You can argue, 'how can I memorise so many words of so many teachers? I tell you, mind can travel very fast, faster than sound or light. In conclusion, I request you all to find the truth in my words through experiment, Om Shanti."

On the 16th August, 1940, I received a letter from Swami Satyananda Giri, the then in-charge of Y.S.S. Ranchi. He wrote: ".....you have not been sent there as an ordinary teacher. I have no doubt in my mind that you will be a good teacher there, but you should also bear in mind that you have been sent there to serve the Y.S.S. institution. Accordingly you should preach, not only through your speech but also through your thoughts and actions. This way, you will be able to deliver good lectures; but be cautious not to be light and cheap while preaching. Acquire new experience from those students that will be beneficial to you. You will have to do a lot of work, the direction of which you will get from within. Don't be proud. Be a humble servant of the Lord..

What's the news about Dhiren Shree and others? Silently, steadily and firmly try to draw their devotion. However, you should not take the initiative. Last Tuesday we felt your absence. Your devotion and faith in God and Goddesses will uplift you and thereby we will be benefited too"..

Inspired by this letter, subject matter of my next speech for the staff and students was "Aims and ideal of Y.S.S.".

"My dear colleagues and young brothers, to-day I shall try to throw some light on the aims and ideals of our Society. Have you ever looked into your life, the way you are leading. Do you know, what is your longevity? According to the official report of the Government, the average longevity of an Indian is 24 years only. Do you know in what way your days are passing by? Eight years during your infancy were spent in ignorance and darkness. If you sleep for eight hours a day, then 1/3 of your life will be wasted in sleep. Now you have only 1/3 of your life, or 8 years at your disposal to know and learn. Now calculate yourself how many hours you spend in the school, and how many hours are essential for attending to the daily chores. You will find that there is very short time for higher persuits, and for God. This valuable time is spent in reading novels, playing cards and chatting! When do you think about our Divine Father, who has given you this beautiful earth? Should we not devote one percent of our time within this 24th hours, for him? Can we not preserve a few minutes for Hari who has give us affectionate parents, friends and all sorts of articles for our enjoyment" Have you ever thought, who are you? Why have you come to this earth? And where will you go after your death? I can tell you for certain that if you think even for a moment about these, your life will be noble and an ideal one.

"It is my request to the Kriyabans to spend at least a few minutes for kriya exercises. If you can devote a few minutes daily for God and His thought, in course of time you will be a great man in this world. In the Gita, Sri Bhagavan said, "Of thousands of men some rare soul strives to realize me; of those striving yogis, only some rare one (devoting himself exclusively to me) knows me really". Hence, if any one among you follow my words or at least try to follow, my efforts and speech will be fruitful. Om Shanti."

On the 17th, I had a discussion with the authorities of the school regarding starting a Gita Class which they gladly agreed. I requested the Assistant Headmaster to issue a notice calling for a religions meeting after the school at 2-15 p.m. I persuaded Sripati Babu to preside over the meeting. Sripati Babu introduced me, "Brahmachari Animanandaji will speak on religious matters every Saturday. Those who are willing to attend the class may join, those who are unwilling may leave the place". No one left. All took their seats silently. I began my speech.

"My dear friends and young boys, last year I spoke regularly on many Saturdays. This year too, I shall try to throw some light on Gita and such other subject on every Saturday. Before entering into my subject let me tell you about our aims and ideals. Many people think that our aim is to create Brahmacharis and Swamis. That's a wrong impression. Our aim is to impart such instructions so that you can guide your life. Like a hero, you should fight your own battle and win. Whatever vocation you choose, you must be an ideal one, so that others may emulate.

Now let me explain what Gita is. In the introduction of Gita, there is direction for study of the scriptures. You are instructed to worship Gita and to meditate on the thoughts. Gita is a garland of mantras. Lord Sri Krishna is the supreme spirit. He said, 'You grieve over those who should not be grieved for, and yet speak like the learned one. Surrendering all duties to me, seek refuge in me alone. I shall absolve you of all sins, grieve not, which will protect you in all the stages of your life.'

Gita should be read with a pure heart sitting in seclusion. If the mind is disturbed with impure thoughts you can not grasp the real meaning of the scriptures. If you do not have interest in a subject, you cannot understand it. Hence, you must have deep devotion while studying Gita and such other scriptures.

Why should one worship the book, Gita? In the words of lord Krishna, "Gita is my heart and the best part of my body. It is my imperishable knowledge. Gita is my best abode and the supreme place. It is the supreme saint and it is my Guru. I rule the whole world abiding by the knowledge of Gita. There is no doubt that Gita is the supreme knowledge".

We have been instructed to recognise Gita as a Garland of mantras. Mantra means a 'word', realization of which can lead to salvation. There are some mantras in Gita that are so powerful that even if we can realise a part of it (say half or one fourth) we can achieve liberation. Take for example verse 18, Chapter 2.

• First one fourth is: "All these bodies are perishable". The 2nd 1/4 part is: "The soul residing in it is everlasting, i.e., indestructible.

• The first 1/4 of the verse 20, of the same Chapter is: 'The soul is never born, nor it dies" Another 1/4th is: it is unborn, eternal, everlasting and primeval'.

If you can realize any 1/4th part of the verses quoted above, you will reach your goal — the eternal abode in the highest Heaven. This is known as Self Realization for which we have taken this garb and the vow of Brahamacharya.

Sri Bhagavan Vedavyasa had seen these mantras, who had realised then at heart through the power of his yoga; and had composed them for us in 'Anusthup' rhythm. But why in 'Anusthup' rhythm?

In every particular rhythm, there is a peculiar vibration, the wave length of which differ from one another to a great extent, some of which are beneficial to us, in one way, others may not be so. The vibration of Anusthup rhythm is highly beneficial for our spiritual upliftment.

Even in ordinary words, you can mark the difference. Suppose someone addresses you, politely, "Hello brother, will you kindly accept my invitation"; and another in a rough tone, 'You rogue, I shall kill you". Now mark the difference. One person has created a very peaceful and happy vibration in your mind, and the other has upset your peace of mind, and you become very furious.

Poet Valmiki also composed the Ramayana in Anusthup rhythm. Many of our scriptures had been composed in this rhythm. Chandi is one of them. All the mantras are meant for the revelation of some divine. In Gita, our aim is Self realization i.e., revelation of our own soul. Lord Krishna is the God for the purpose. In the introduction of Gita, it is stated that He is not a man or a King or an ordinary hero of a novel, but the supreme Spirit.

What is the 'Bijamantra' of our Gita? 'Bija' means seed. You have seen the seed of a banyan tree. It is very small, but within it lies, the potentiality of the huge tree. Drawing the analogy, I quoted earlier, 'You are grieving over those you should not, and yet you are speaking like a learned person'. This world is not ever lasting, even your body will be destroyed one day. The riches, the family, the friends — all will be left behind at the time of final parting from the world. Moderate temperature, air, light, water and earth are required for the germination of seed. When a seed gets all these, it rises from its slumber and spreads its limbs that were dormant so long and gradually becomes a very big tree. Such is the case with us. If the above words of renunciation, (the seed of Gita) get the water of devotion, moderate temperature of regular meditation, air of good company and the light from the scriptures, it will germinate into a large tree, under the shade of which the people of the world will seek refuge one day.

As the seed gets nourishment and strength from the earth, the seed of Gita derives nourishment and strength from: 'Surrendering all duties to me, seek refuge in me alone'. The supreme soul resides in our body. We shall have to meditate to realize our own Supreme soul. We have the privilege to be good or bad. Don't misuse this free choice and free power and merge into the darkness of hell. If you rightly use this freedom, you can get Self-realization.

Right at the beginning of Gita, Dhritarastra asked Sanjaya what his and Pandu's children did in the battle field?" But why start this battle? Also, Krishna who is the supreme spirit was the charioteer of the fighter Arjuna. What is the meaning of chariot? In the Upanishad, it is stated that human bodies are the chariots and the soul residing in them are the passengers. Lord Krishna explained to Arjuna in the first sloka of the thirteen Chapter of the Gita:

"O Offspring of Kunti (Arjuna), by the knowers of truth, this body is called kshetra ("the field" where good and evil karma is sown and reaped); likewise, that which cognizes the field they call kshetrajna (the soul)."

Then comes the question who is 'Dhritarastra' and 'Sanjaya'?

In the Mahabharata, 'Dhritarastra' was blind. Mind cannot see; it was the mind that had been allegorically described as Dhritarastra. The derivative meaning of the word is 'That which upholds the Kingdom is Dhitrarastra'.

'Sanjaya' is the introspection. Who are fighters about whom Gita described in details? Mind is searching, through introspection, result of the internal battle of the individual soul, between the evil propensities and the good qualities resisting them. This internal battle is always going on in every human being. The names that had been mentioned in the Gita are lust greed, anger, avarice, pride, ignorance, sleep, drowsiness, affection, jealousy, and such other evil propensities of the mind fighting from one side, and on the other side, are the resisting forces such as consciences, judgment, controlling power both physical and mental, to be unaffected in hot and cold, devotion, love for God, prayer, meditation, desire for Salvation, Samadhi, renunciation and such other divine qualities. These are the allegorical names.

Let us examine a few such names. In verses 4 to 6 in Chapter I of the Gita, we get following names.

1. Bhima, Arjuna, Satyaki, Virata, Drupada, Dhristaketu, Chekitana

Kasiraj, Purujit, Kuntibhoja, Saibya, Yudhamanju, Uttamanja, Abhimanyu, the son of Subhadra and the five son of Draupadi.

- Virat — Samadhi, (Vi=unconscious + rat = Kingdom, world)
- Drupada — (Dru means quick, pada means to go) hence electrical flow or current in the spinal centers.
- Dhristaketu — controlling power.
- Chakitana — remember and or part memory. It also means the very first sound that the Yogis can hear at the initial stage of Sadhana.
- Kasiraj — Knowledge, illumination.
- Purujit — pratyahara is the 5th stage in the eight fold yoga. It also means rest.
- Kuntibhoja - Asana
- Saibya - Niyama, the 2nd stage in the eight fold yoga. It also means the power to do good.
- Yudhamanyu — Pranayama is the 4th stage of the eight fold yoga. Sitamanya - Internal strength.

In the verses 8 and 9 we get the following names.

Bhisma, Karna, Kripa, Aswatthama, Vikarna, Somadatta.

- Bhisma - ego, or pride due to ignorance
- Karna — attachment
- Kripa - imagination or ignorance
- Aswathama — result of the prenatal works
- Vikarna - illegal works
- Somadatta - wordly works.

Gita is a 'Kalpavriksha in which the yogis get their yogic meaning, the scientists get their scientific searches, the renunciates get the laws of renunciation and so on. You have read in science that when the disease germs enter into the body, great fight ensues among the white blood corpuscles and bacteria. Some say Gita is the history of the bacteriological fight in our body.

Subject matter of my next speech was Aims and Ideals

"Dear friend and young brothers, as promised during our last meeting, today let me explain what should be our aims and ideals.

Have you ever thought of the way, you come to school daily? Are you coming here willingly or your parents forcing you to come? What are your aims? Sometimes we set question: “write an essay on the aim of your life” to know your inclination or aim of your life. If we analyze the human life, we can surmise that whatever he does he is doing for the peace, joy and happiness in life following either a right or a wrong path. You must search happiness in the proper way. You cannot get it through a wrong path.

It is stated in the holy Bhagavad Gita, “The joy that is derived through senses, appear like nectar in the beginning (at the time of enjoyment), but tastes like poison in the end. Such a joy is Rajasic. The joy which deadens the soul, both in the beginning and in the end, and which is derived from sleep, indolence and carelessness is Tamasic”. Hence, according to the words of Gita these are not the right causes. The enjoyment that you get through sense like pleasure in smoking or such other intoxication may prove to be nectar at the time of smoking, but be sure it is really poison, destroying silently both body and mind.

But real joy is very difficult to get. For it, you will have to labour hard, under the feet of a Guru, who has already attained the state of true happiness in God through meditation. We can only get true happiness in Sattvic joy. Sri Bhagavan said: “That in which one finds enjoyment only through practice of Bhajana, meditation and Kriya exercises, whereby one reaches beyond all sorrows. That which may appear like poison during the practice, but tastes as nectar in the end, is said to be Sattvic”

I spent, thus, some happy days with the boys of the Y.S.S. Brahmacharya Vidyalaya at Ejmalichak, Midnapur.

Chapter 7
Samadhi

I was invited by Y.S.S.K. Vidyapith, Lakhanpur, Purulia to preside over the Birthday Celebration of Paramhansa Yoganandaji in January, 1953. The function started early morning with a special puja of the Gurus, devotional songs, recitations, reading from the book of Paramhansa Yoganandaji and so on. In the afternoon, there was a special meeting for the occasion. I had to conduct the function as its President.

There were several speakers to deliver lectures on the life of Paramahansa Yoganandaji. But every one spoke very short in order to hear the life history of my Gurudeva directly from me. Hence, I had to speak at length on the subject, on the spiritual side, how he achieved the highest stages of realization and became the saviour of mankind. It took me one hour and forty-five minutes to explain the same.

In the evening, I had got special blessings from my Guru. My mind was partly withdrawn inside. Though it was very difficult to fulfill the outward duties, I could manage. As the mind was gradually going inside, I was afraid to be conscious fully. After the supper was over, I hastened into my room and closed the door. On my bed, I was fully withdrawn. Gurudeva, intimated me that he was so long working out the 'karmas' of the devotees who had got kriya initiations from me. He also intimated me many secrets regarding the 'karmic' laws. In the conclusion, he said, 'As I have left my physical body, you will have to work out some of the karmas of the initiated members which have to be worked out in a flesh and blood body. You will also fully realize at heart what things you are offering at the fire ceremony at my feet at the time of kriya initiation. Don't be afraid, I shall give you the power of endurance. Further, I shall be with you in spirit. Thus, you will get some new knowledge in the field of initiation, which will help and guide you for future selection of worthy persons for initiation. You will also come to understand how great is the responsibility of a true Guru. It is the sacred duty of a Guru to relieve some of the karmic burdens of the disciples and consider himself fortunate in being able to render such aid and I hope you will also willingly accept this responsibility. In order to set an example for the disciples and also to alleviate their sorrows, I want to put these mental and physical sufferings on you. You know how our gurus, Lahiri Mahasaya, Sri Yukteswarji and many other Self- realized souls have suffered to redeem the mankind from sins to make them fit for salvation. While I was on the earth, I had to work out the karma of the devotees from time to time. If you yourself will try to work out the said karmas you will die. Hence, I shall be with you not only in spirit but also in mind and heart. It will take several days to work out the same. My beloved son, do you understand now? Are you willing to help me in this noble cause?" I responded: "Yes, revered father, most willingly I shall help you to work out the karmic debts of the devotees"

Then came the sufferings. The pangs of the sufferings are beyond description. Sometimes my body became so much heated that it seemed to me that it would be burnt to ashes, but that condition would not last for a long time. After suffering for a few seconds, the nature of the horrible pain would change. Sometimes I was entering into a very dark deep region of hell. The horror of the place, induced in me so much fear that I would die of heart failure. But, as the Divine Father was with me, that condition could not last long. Within a few seconds, I was pushed to a different region, a region of all happiness, joy and light. Sometimes, I would shiver from intense cold. The intensity of the shivering was so stormy that all the warm clothings of my room would not be enough. However, within a very short time, that would change. I was pulled to the blessed heaven, the coveted paradise of men. Once I was entering into the horrible hell and in the next moment into the heaven as if I was swinging like a pendulum, though the period of oscillation was not the same always. I spent the whole night like that. Early in the morning, I regained my consciousness partly to manage my worldly duties of instructing the new boys in the preliminary Yoga techniques.

On the 9th morning, Gurudeva intimated me, 'The acute sufferings of the initiated persons are now over. Today, you will be blessed with a new light of knowledge. However, there is a great purpose behind your suffering. I want to intimate or rather help you realize, what you are offering at my feet at the ceremony of karma-burning during initiation of the public. You will have to give initiation to thousands of people, hence, realize what you are offering and what I am taking"

As I was very anxiously waiting for the new knowledge. Sri Abanindra Lahiri, the Asst. headmaster of Y.S.S.K. Vidyapith came to my room and intimated me, 'The sun is just rising.' On hearing his words, I approached the door, wherefrom the sun was visible. I kneeled down at the door of my room and began to worship the sun by chanting some scriptural and Vedic hymns, the meanings of which are as follows:

"Oh Sun, you are the only eye of this world. You are the creator, preserver and destroyer of the world. You are the embodiment of the three Gunas (dispositions) and hence, you are Brahma, Vishnu and Mahesh incarnate. On whose rising the whole world is awake and is engaged in works and who is the giver of success to all works; whom Brahma, Indra and Narayana worship, he imparts us blessings.

I bow down my head to millions and trillions rayed sun who has divided himself into thousand different rays and who appears to the yogis in thousand different manners, I worship that sun devotionally. Thousand Yugas or Ages are moving in cyclic ways around him. Oh Supreme Lord, your face is covered with intense light. I am very anxious to have the vision of your real nature, please remove the curtain over your face".

Instantly, the cover was removed. I perceived the real nature of the sun. During meditation, the yogis used to get the vision of Kutastha (the Spiritual Eye), it was similar to that Kutastha but much larger and more enticing. I was withdrawn by Lord God, residing within the sun and I became one with Him.

I realised how the Supreme Spirit plays with the souls in eternity. It was so sweet, so relishing that cannot be imagined or described. It has to be realized only at heart. I realized, I was one with Lord Krishna Himself.

Then one after another like motion pictures, the astral visions along with the accompaniment of thoughts and realizations were flashing before my mental eye. It lasted for a few hours. It was strange how I could mix with the people of the place and how I could attend to worldly matters though I was fully withdrawn. But I had a very faint recollection that I had spoken a word or two to the Headmaster.

At the end of the visions, Sri Gurudeva ordered me to go to Yogoda Math at Dakshineswar. I intimated my desire, to go to the Dakshineswar, to Hiralal Babu. It was 10th January 1953. Then came a new and most realizable state in me. I realise myself as spirit. He himself had become my body, mind and everything. I used to hear within myself, not I, I, but Thou, Thou.

The time for my departure came, but I was so much withdrawn that it was not possible for me to move even. I had a faint remembrance that the boys had dressed me up in the shirt and Abani Babu (most probably) put on the stockings on the feet. Due to my fixed inward state, which they too could guess, looking at my fixed eyes, Abani Babu sent one boy with me to help me to have the ticket at Purulia station and to get a seat in the train for Howrah. My Guru, Paramahansaji was guiding me from inside and eventually, I was able to reach Yogoda Math, Dakshineswar.

I had new experiences at Yogoda Math, Dakshineswar from 11th January 1953 morning onwards. I had lost my outward consciousness totally on reaching Yogoda Math. Always, everywhere I used to see and see my Gurudeva. I used to see the Divine Father in every body. Once, the servant of Yogoda Math, Raja Ram came before me. I saw Lord Krishna had come and I instantly prostrated at his feet in due reverence. Raja Ram was taken aback and he caught hold of me and guided me to my bed room. At Raja Ram's touch, the vision vanished and I saw Raja Ram instead of Lord Krishna. He deluded me in many ways, because everywhere I used to see and perceive Him. But the moment, I would try to catch Him, He would vanish. The mental agonies for not getting Lord Krishna in the way I wanted Him was beyond description. I don't know exactly how long or for how many days that play lasted. Generally, Lord Krishna would play with me in that way during day time, but at night I used to enjoy the Divine Realization.

At night, I used to experience myself as the Supreme Spirit of Lord Narayana. Then I became many, the trees, the insects, and all. Paramhansa Yoganandaji appeared before me, and I requested him to withdraw the perception of diversity. And then, he withdrew his power and I became Brahmachari Animananda again. The moment, I regained my consciousness as Animananda, I became an atom and was moving freely like air in the world.

Then came one danger. I saw myself as a man in one of my former lives, and was suffering and crying. I was crying and praying at the feet of my Guru, "rather, please tell me, who am I? Am I living or dead?" Due to my intense prayer, the vision changed, and I saw myself in another way. I found myself as a person made of light, and all the people, animals and insects of the world were my counterparts as different images.

Then came another trouble. I saw myself as Narayana but simultaneously another thought flashed whether I am the doer or an instrument? Gurudeva intimated me, 'You are the Jagannath of Puri". (Jagat + nath =Jagannath. Jagat means the great cosmos and Nath means the Lord, hence Jagannath means the Lord of the Universe). I instantly realized, 'I am not the doer'. (In the image of Jagannath at Puri, there are no hands and feet - symbolic of the instrument). Then came another trouble. At heart, I realized myself as Narayana, the Creator, Preserver and Destroyer in One; but Gurudeva intimated me as Jagannath, the instrument and not the doer. I was crying to know exactly "Who am I?" The vision changed.

One night, I experienced myself as one Being made of strong light. I was soaring higher and higher. The velocity of which was so great that I could pass worlds after worlds within a fraction of a second. All the worlds that I had passed are round. At the end of the journey, I reached the highest Heaven. When the motion stopped, I found myself seated on a throne made of multi-coloured light, I am that Narayana again. There I saw that arrangements had been made for my marriage. But to my utter astonishment, I realized that there was no bride for my marriage; I was wondering how the ceremony would be performed. The most attractive astral music for the marriage ceremony was going on. However, at the end, I was fortunate enough to find my Divine Beloved, residing within me. I regained my outward consciousness for the time being. It was 9 a.m., the next morning.

Let me revert back to my arrival at Yogoda Math, Dakshineswar on the 11th morning. At the entrance of the Chapel (Guru Mandir), there was 6 ft. tall portrait in oil of Paramhansa Yoganandaji. It was the life-size portrait painted by His brother Sri Sananda Lal Ghosh. I was so moved to see the portrait that I instantly lost my consciousness as I sat down at his feet. Many of the future incidents of Y.S.S. at Dakshineswar flashed in my mental eye like quick motion pictures. I was there most probably upto 11 a.m. Then I was led to the Guru Mandir to participate in the Birthday Celebration of Paramahansaji. Though His birthday was 5th January, the celebration was arranged on Sunday, 11th January since 5th January was Monday, a working day so that all the participants would have their weekly off day and would be able to join the function.

Brahmachari Sri Prakash was performing the Guru Puja. After the puja we all assembled in front of the Guru Mandir on the bank of the Ganges. The portrait was shifted and placed there. Instead of sitting on mats or carpets I sat on the grass in Vajrasana; I kneeled down in front of the portrait of my Gurudeva in the sun. So long the meeting lasted, I was in that posture, looking at the picture of Paramhansa Yoganandaji. Tears were flowing from both the eyes, all the time, at the thought that we had lost his physical body forever.

One after another, speakers were delivering speeches, but to my utter amazement, I perceived that I had taken the other form and was instructing my other forms in the audience. After a while, I was puzzled, and afraid when the vision changed and I realized that the speakers and the audience were different forms of Gurudeva. He was scolding me through the speakers.

At about 4-30 p.m. the function (meeting) was over. I regained partly my outward consciousness. I could recognize the spiritual brothers, who had come to me. Swami Benoyananda Giri, Swami Dayananda Giri, Sri Girinda (now known as Swami Bidyananda Giri) came to me. I told them: "We all shall have to walk hand in hand".

On 11th, when the function was over in the evening, I was again withdrawn fully. I perceived that the whole world was crying for the light of knowledge. All were suffering in every way; I, alone, was trying to cross the ocean in order to reach the other world, the highest heaven where everyone of the world were my own self. For days together, I was in that state. I could perceive the thoughts of people who came to me, both good and bad, and at the same time I could feel that the Supreme Spirit was playing in disguise. Hence, I became indifferent.

The inmates in Yogoda Math and some of my spiritual brothers thought that I had gone mad. The information of my madness reached the ears of my relatives in due course. They selected my old friend, Jagabandhu Kabiraj, (who once cured me from the after-effect of over-medication) for my treatment. After a few days, Jagabandhu Kabiraj visited me at Yogoda Math, Dakshineswar for my treatment. Brahmachari Sri Prakash escorted the physician to my room.

He realized my state of mind looking at my fixed eyes, turned upwards. He asked me, "Brother, do you recognize me?"

I replied, "Yes, you are Jagabandhu Kaviraj. Your chamber is at Sri Guru Ausadhalaya at 46/B, Amherst Street, Calcutta-9".

Then he enquired, “Well, brother what has happened with you?”

I replied, “Missing the links. I don’t find where is the link of the worlds. By the worlds — I mean dream world, meditation world and this physical world. I am, hence, deluded and puzzled. I could not recognize anything, all were one to me”. He then very affectionately pulled me out of my bed, and we went out hand in hand. He said: “Let us go out for a walk”. He directed me towards the bank of the Ganges pointing at the setting sun. He enquired, “Is it due to this sun? Have you gone through the sun and have got this state of mind?”

“Yes”, I replied. He was glad and remarked, “I too, had once gone through the sun and had realized this state of mind”. Then we went out of Yogoda Math for a stroll. I very anxiously enquired “Then how have you solved the problem of this missing link?” He went on quoting verses after verses from the Holy Bhagavad Gita in order to solve the problem. The words of Lord Krishna, however, helped me to a great extent to solve the problem. At night, during usual meditation, I tried to pull the life force downwards from the head. After a long struggle, I succeeded and send the life force to the coccyx.

Sri Jagadbandhu Kabiraj visited me thrice. He helped me to come down from that state of mind and to be a normal person again. He prescribed some medicines for the outward remembrance. These were “Bishnu oil” for massaging the head, to drink the extract of the Brahmi-leaves in the morning and also one glass full of cold drink made of sugar candy. When my mother heard that I had gone mad, she visited me with a bottle full of cold drink made of sugar and some fruits. She was weeping looking at my fixed eyes, thinking that I had really gone mad. I was shocked to see her weeping.

At night, I laboured hard to pull down the life force from my medullar region and to send it to the coccyx; I succeeded at last. Next morning, I thought I must not get over drunk with ecstasy. I must now visit my friend Jagabandhu and along with him I should pay a return visit to my mother and report my return to normalcy.

Jagadbandhu came in when I was about to start for his chamber. After a few minutes, we started for Calcutta for my sister’s house where my mother was then residing. All the relatives including my mother were very happy to see us. My friend-physician explained to them, “Brahmachari’s state of mind is a common yogic state, which I myself have experienced. My Guruji had to pass through this state of mind. Our Mohanto Maharaj, Mandaleswar Mahadevanandaji became more mad than Brahmachariji. He was in that state for more than a month. If you look into the mental condition of Sri Ramkrishna, you will find similarities with the state of mind of Brahmachariji". On hearing this elucidation, all of them were pleased and free from anxiety.

Now, let me explain the Divine Motion pictures that were responsible for the missing links. From 23rd December to 23rd January, I was in the region of another world with occasional little breaks in the show of motion pictures. These breaks were in the beginning from 23rd December to the 5th January. But from 5th to 23rd January, though there were few breaks, my mind was always inwardly fixed, sometimes fully and sometimes partly. Many of the future incidents of my life and also of the world had been shown for several days. Sometimes, the motion pictures were passing slowly and sometimes quickly and sometimes they became fixed for sometime. Most of the pictures were soundless, but at times there were talkies, like the cinema shows now.

In cinema, incidents are cut short sometimes, and rearranged through editing for entertainment. In the Divine Motion Pictures, to serve the same purpose instead of omitting any portion, it was passed over very swiftly. It served two purposes, one, to impart an idea of the incident, the other, omission of the details through too quick a movement. For example, when I was entertained with film (Divine) show of my own life from birth, it passed very quickly upto the age of 4 years. From the 5th year it was moving slowly, that is, normally.

I was in my native place playing, meditating, walking and so on. It took approximately 8 to 10 minutes to display the incidents of one year. Once at the age of 12 years and again at the age of 21 years, the film became fixed for sometime in order to make me realize that I shall have to struggle hard to get the Divine Knowledge fully. Then from the age of 21 years to the age of 38 years, the motion pictures passed very quickly. I had been "entertained" with my future life till retirement from this world. As regards the play of the world, the passing of the different yugas had been shown to me, sometimes without sound, sometimes with it. These parts of the divine film moved very quickly.

On my physical body, my whole tree of life i.e., the spine from the coccyx to the medulla was alive. Tremendous electrical flow was passing through the whole length and breadth of the spine. The whole body was paralyzed, but sometimes I could feel (when my mind was drawn towards the body) the electrical flow throughout the whole body. As a result, I could not realize where I was, and in which yuga — Kali or

Dwapar. I was perplexed which made me mad to some extent.

There may be a question, whether all this was hallucination or a mental chloroform or real madness. The great Masters of India, in order to mould the lives of the world in right direction, authored Stellar Science. Though the Stellar Science i.e., Astrology, is too vast, both mathematically and philosophically, for outwitting the evil influences of the stars, the Masters discussed the natal chart elaborately. They stipulated many rules and regulations for right interpretation of the horoscope, so that we can get some way out to escape the universal thralldom. They invented through research and, above all, through intuition a lawful channel for the outward operation of cause-effect equilibriums that the individual had set into motion in the past. The horoscope, hence, is a challenging portrait, revealing the unalterable past and also the probable future results. Astrological books had been written in order to judge the character of a native.

They had written the following laws by which we can judge nature of a mad person:

1. Moon, Mars, Jupiter and Saturn are in one house.
2. Sun, Moon, Mercury, Jupiter and Saturn in one house.
3. Jupiter in the ascendant and Mars in the 7th house.
4. Saturn in the ascendant and Mars in any one of the 5th, 7th or 9th houses.
5. Weak Moon and Saturn in the 12th house
6. Day of birth should be Tuesday or Saturday, and Moon and Mercury should be in any one of the ascendant, 4th or 7th or 10th houses, but they must not be under any good influence.
7. Sun and Moon should be in any one of the ascendant 5th and 9th along with Saturn and Jupiter in any of the ascendant 4th, 7th or 10th.
8. Saturn in the ascendant, Sun in the 12th house and either Moon or Mars in the 5th or 9th house.
9. Sun, Moon, Mercury, Jupiter, Venus and Saturn in one house.

My horoscope is as follows:

Jupiter in the ascendant and in Pisces. Hence, Pisces is my 1st house. In the 2nd house i.e., in Aries is Mars. In the 3rd house i.e. in

Taurus resides Venus. In the 4th house (Gemini) are Sun, Mercury and Saturn. In the 5th house, there is one Ketu, and obviously, in the 11th house is Rahu. On the 6th house, there resides the Moon. This reference to my horoscope reveals that there is none of the signs of madness.

The Rishis had also discussed many rules and regulations to find out the good fortune of a man and also for high spiritual development. (Yotish Prabhakar). It is stated that if any planet becomes the owner of the 1st and 10th house, he himself can confer the kingdom to a native. Looking into my horoscope, I find Jupiter i.e., Guru is the owner of my 1st and 10th house, and hence he himself will bestow the kingdom of the world.

Also, if owners of 9th and 10th houses reside in their own houses, they will make the native a world famous man. He will be the most fortunate man. The Rishis had explained that the native will get the kingdom if he is born of a King's family; otherwise he/she will get wealth, unparalleled name and fame, both in the field of spirituality and worldly matters. The planets can only bestow wealth, fame and powers to the individual during their 'Dasha periods'. In my horoscope, the owner of the 9th house is Mars, and the 10th house is Jupiter and they are residing in their own houses. In January 1953, the Dasha period of Mars, the ruler of the 9th house was in full motion. The ruler of the 9th house governs religion, dreams, visions and fame in the field of religion. Jupiter is the ruling planet of my horoscope. He was also entangled with the Antar Dasha periods. This gave me such high spiritual experience and visions through the Cosmic Motion Picture. My Guru, conferred on me the title of 'Dharmacharya' (spiritual director of all religions) on the 30th January 1952. It occurred also during the Dasha period of Mars.

Chapter 8

Some More Visions, Some More Motion Pictures

Quite often, I had to visit the different Y.S.S. centres and work there for different spells. But formally, I was placed at Y.S.S. Ranchi. I had to spend many days at Puri, Bhagalpur, Lakhanpur, Midnapore (Ejmalichak), Dakshineswar and such other places, and got various kinds of spiritual experiences. In this Chapter, I shall take out a few leafs from my old diary to reveal the nature of these experiences.

On 14th September, 1941 (Sunday), during morning meditation, first, I had the vision of Goddess of Learning, Saraswati, for a long time at the Christ Centre. After Her departure, Goddess Durga Mata appeared with all Her splendour. She had ten hands with Her usual arms or weapons, She blessed me only for a few seconds.

On the 7th March 1945, I had the vision of two goddesses along with Lord Krishna. On 21st May 1945, at night, with the advent of golden light I was about to lose myself and I prayed to Paramhansa Yoganandaji not to dissolve me since my parents were not yet initiated into kriya. "I don't want to taste the nectar as a devotee" was my concluding prayer, when gradually, I regained outward consciousness. On the 20th September 1945, I had the vision of the Divine Mother and requested Her to appear before me in the form of my Guru. On my request she disappeared and in Her place appeared 'Kutastha'. She intimated me, "Kutastha is the Guru".

On the 12th October 1945, I had the vision of Lahiri Mahasaya at about 4-15 a.m. He appeared to be old, bald headed, not all the hair were grey. He told me, "After five minutes your cousin brother will die of an accident".

I told him, "I had written about that brother (he was a stammerer) to Gurudeva. He had written, 'I am sorry about your cousin. I am praying'. On it, Lahiri Mahasaya commented: "What else can he write"? Afterwards I came to know that my cousin died at that time in a railway accident. Lahiri Mahasaya consoled me, "He will not suffer much. Have faith and devotion, you will get everything".

On the 26th September, 1946 at about 3 a.m., Gurudeva came and helped me out of the physical body. Then he held me by the left hand and we both swept over the lands, hills, rivers and then reached before a gathering where I was nominated as President of the function.

On the 2nd December, 1947, at night, the life force at the coccyx during its ascent turned round twice or so and then within a few seconds rushed to the brain. I felt I was out of the body and was flying upwards. Instantly I mentally bowed my head with devotion at the feet of the Gurus, when the astral body's velocity became very high; for nearly 15 minutes (it was not possible to know exactly the time taken during that flight) I was in the air. At the time of coming back to the body, I felt a tremendous sensation at the medulla. Gradually I descended at the heart centre. As I was meditating, on 'OM' (chanting mentally), the life force again rushed towards the brain and the astral body came out of the physical casket as before. Roaming in the astral body for several minutes, I descended in the physical body and regained the outward consciousness.

On 7th May 1950, early in the morning during meditation, I had the vision of Paramhansa Yoganandaji at the Christ centre. On the 21st September 1950, during meditation (between 6 a.m. to 6-30 a.m.), I had the vision of many gods and goddesses of the astral world. Among which the vision of the Divine Couple (Lord Krishna and Sri Radha) was the most attractive one. Generally during such visions, I became so much absorbed that I used to forget to pay due homage and respect to them. My mind was fully engrossed on the objects of visions. After their departure, I used to bow down my head and regret that I had forgotten to pay due respect to them.

On the 4th May, 1951 (Friday), during meditation at about 4 a.m., I had the vision— the map of India made of dazzling light appeared at the Christ centre. It appeared and disappeared for several times. Then it became stationary, though restless (i.e., trembling) at first, then it became fixed at the Kutastha. The map was not the old India. But a changed one. In the middle of it, appeared the Divine couple, Lord Krishna and Sri Radha. My mind was overwhelmed with joy to see our parents in the middle of my motherland.

On 13th June 1951, at 2 a.m., I sat for meditation. Generally, I used to pray and remember the Gurus of our line. That day instead of remembering and praying to the Gurus in the customary way, I prayed to the invisible saints and Divine Angels present there to help me in my meditation. Within a few seconds, I was withdrawn inside. I lost the outward consciousness completely. The vision started. At the outset, the vision of a temple appeared, in the middle of which there were many gods and goddesses. The vision directed me to enter the temple with reverence, bowing down at the feet of the (deities). In the temple, I saw the different forms of Divine Mother (Durga, Kali, Lakshmi and others). After paying due homage, I entered into the adjacent room of the temple.

That room was meant for the 'Vaahanas' - the carrier-creatures or bearer-animals like owl, the conveyance of the Goddess Lakshmi; lion that carries Mother Durga and such other Divine creatures, all made of light. I was afraid to see the lioness along with her cubs at a distance of 6 to 7 feet, and hence I left that room and entered into another adjacent room.

In that room, there was a divine guide. As I entered that room, the guide pressed a button on the wall and it flew like rocket, soaring higher and higher, with the velocity of lightening. Through the windows, from both the sides, I could see various scenes, the beauty of which was beyond description. After a few minutes the divine lift came to a halt at the main gate to a new land. The guide then guided me to visit that astral town. There I found human beings like us. After a walk for a few minutes, we reached the gate of the underground town, like the metro in France. We entered into the underground town. After a very short time, the guide led me to a small room (like the roadside telephone booths in modern towns). As I entered the room, the guide turned the handle and closed the door. To my astonishment another lift, like a lightening flash, came and joined with the room (in front of our room). There was another guide in the new lift who enquired from my previous guide. The new guide requested me to sit quietly, and pressed the button (The button was like the button of a calling bell). On pressing the key both the rooms, like the electric train, were running with tremendous speed. After three minutes we reached the destination. On reaching the destination, the new lift along with its guide vanished. The guide, pointing at the entrance gate of a palace, advised me to enter it. He told me that he would wait for me at the exit door.

After visiting the palace, I came out through the exit door. The guide directed me to another small room at the exit. As I entered that room, the guide pressed a key attached to the closed door of the new room. Instantly the room turned its direction and the door automatically opened to a spacious road. Many people were walking on the road. After a few minutes, we came at the junction of the two roads controlled by a policeman. Here, we could get running roads on payment of money like the taxies in the town. My guide paid the necessary money and reserved a seat on the road. As we occupied our seats, the collapsible gate on our backside closed. Other persons, who were coming, like us, would have to wait there for a few minutes. When we would reach the destination, the collapsible gate would open automatically. The road (like the escalators in modern towns) ran like the trains and reached the destination. The stage manager switched off the energy of the operating room, and the show came to an end. The motion, rather the momentum of the machine parts was still in action which I could perceive due to the tremendous sensations that were going on throughout the centres in the spine. I regained the outward consciousness. The vibrations or the sensations in the spine became slower and slower, and ultimately stopped.

I thanked heartily the Rishis that entertained me with that Divine show; I looked at my wristwatch, it was 4 a.m. then.

Chapter 9
Dharmacharya

As mentioned earlier Paramahansji had conferred on me the title 'Dharmacharya' on 30th January, 1952. 'Dharma' means religion and 'Acharya' means one who practices. The end of all religions is the realisation of God in the soul. Ideas and methods may differ but the realisation of Supreme Spirit at heart is the main point. It does not consist of dogmas or doctrines. One may commit to memory all the religious books and may believe in all the churches in the world, he may take initiation from all the Gurus, still may have no perception of God; he is equal to an ordinary person or may become an atheist. Paramahansaji has given to the world various methods of yoga, that have to be practised. Only purchasing and collecting the S.R.F. lessons on Kriya Yoga will not suffice. It is Being and Becoming. Hence, we should always remember Religion is realization. It is not hearing and acknowledging the theories or talks. One can listen to hundreds of speeches or doctrines, but without practice of the Kriya Yoga, our body and mind will not be changed at all.

The Vedas called, "Hear, children of the Imperishable Soul, I have realised Him as the Sun and His kingdom as beyond darkness". Our Gurus also proclaimed similarly, but the Truth is hidden in the cave of the spiritual eye. We shall have to practise Kriya Yoga faithfully and daily with full love for God; then only we shall be able to enter into that cave and be able to realise the Truth.

In gratitude for the title of "Dharmacharya", I wrote an article "You have made me the king". Paramahansaji had also sent me the copy of the letter which he had given to Sri Girindra Kumar Dey (now known as Swami Bidyananda Giri) along with the letter of 30th January 1952. In that letter, Gurudeva wrote, 'I am giving Brahmachari Sri Prokas and Brahmachari Animananda the title of 'Dharmacharya'. Brahmachari Animananda has been very faithfully following my spiritual instructions.'

The copies of the letter were also forwarded to Swami Premanda Giri, International Secretary of S.R.F. and Y.S.S., Br. Sri Prokas, General Secretary, Y.S.S., India, and Sri Prabhas Chandra Ghose, VicePresident, Y.S.S., India. Paramhansa Yoganandaji made me the "king" on the day he authorised me to initiate and ordered me, "Try to convert thousands to the path of Kriya". But on 30th January 1952, he made me the "king of kings" publicly.

Haridasi Mata had taken her initiation (preliminary techniques) from me on the 7th January, 1952. The next morning, she invited me to take my breakfast in her house. Seeing her small room I had remarked, 'This is like the Himalayan cave, pure and solitary". Though she disagreed with my statement and had passed some adverse remarks about that room, still she worshipped with flowers and had garlanded me with a very small garland. She regretted the thin and small garland. I commented, "Don't worry. It was like the necklace'. In the afternoon, Sri Ramakrishna Paramhansa Deva appeared before her and blessed her. She requested Paramahansa Sri Ramakrishna to give some tangible thing as a token of his visit. Paramahansa Sri Ramakrishna gave her a few rare Himalayan flowers and a big garland made of various Himalayan flowers and Tulsi leaves not found in the plains. In the evening she came to my residence and offered the garland and flowers to me.

I was astonished as the garland with such rare Himalayan Tulsi leaves and flowers could not have been purchased from the Calcutta market. I had seen these sort of flowers and leaves in the Himalayas at Kailash hill; local people call it 'Pawali". On enquiry I came to know of the divine origin of the garland and the flowers. The flowers were distributed among the devotees present for the group meditation as a token of blessing.

On the 10th January 1952, the Divine Mother (Goddess Kali of Kalighat, Calcutta) appeared before mother Haridashi Devi and handed over her one garland made of tuberose (Rajanigandha) and two garlands made of marigold and ordered her to garland the pictures on the altar. On the altar in the room were the pictures of Goddess Kali of Kalighat, Goddess Lakshmi and my photograph from a Studio. All the garlands were as fresh as ever even after seven days.

On the 4th & 5th February, I had several visions during my daily meditations in the evening which imparted me the future guidance as regards preaching work.

The Gurus first appeared before me in all their glories, and one by one all of them merged in the body of my Guru Paramahansa Yoganandaji. As I was puzzled to see when Babaji Maharaj, Shyamacharan Lahiri Mahasaya and Swami Sri Yukteshwarji melted in the body (the body of Paramahansaji also was made of light like the figures of all other Gurus) of Paramahansaji, the vision changed.

There was the ocean of light in the middle of which the glorious body of Gurudeva was visible. I was approaching hurriedly towards the feet of my Guru. While running I looked behind for a moment and saw thousands were following me. I jumped into the ocean and reached the feet of my Guru. As I prostrated at his feet, he embraced me and I was drawn within Him.

The Divine Love, that I have received from my Guru is beyond description, and would like to cherish the same in my heart forever. However, I am quoting a few lines from the Autobiography of my Gurudeva, Ch. 34, to express the nature of that Divine Love.

"At his magnetic touch, (a wondrous current swept through my brain, releasing the sweet seed-memories of my previous life)".

'I remember, my voice was half-choked with joyous sobs. You are my Guru Babaji, who has belonged to me always. Scenes of the past arose vividly in my mind; here in this cave I spent many years of my last incarnation. An ineffable recollection overwhelmed me. I tearfully embraced my master's feet'.

'For more than three decades, I have waited for you to return to me'. Babaji's voice rang with celestial love:

'You slipped away and disappeared into the tumultuous waves of the life beyond death. The magic wand of your karma touched you, and you were gone. Though you lost sight of me, never did I lose sight of you. I pursued you over the luminescent astral sea where the glorious angels sail. Through gloom, storm, upheaval, and light, I followed you, like a mother bird guarding her young. As you lived out your human term of womb-life, and emerged a babe, my eyes were ever on you. When you covered your tiny form in the lotus posture under the Nadia sands in your childhood, I was invisibly present. Patiently, month after month, year after year, I have watched over you, waiting for this perfect day. Now you are with me. Here is your cave, loved of you; I have kept it ever clean and ready for you. Here is your hallowed asana-blanket, where daily you sat to fill your expanding heart with God. Here is your bowl, from which you often drank the nectar prepared by me. See how I have kept the brass cup brightly polished, that some day you might drink again there from it. My own, do you now understand?"

'My Guru, what can I say?' I murmured brokenly. Where has one ever heard of such deathless love? I gazed long and ecstatically on my eternal treasure, my Guru, in life and death'."

This is the real state of an 'Acharya' or 'Dharmacharya'. 'Acharya' also means demonstrator. In the Vedas, the Rishis said, "Recognise me as an 'Acharya' or demonstrator. The real Guru is the Divine Father, or the Lord of the Universe. The founder of our Renunciate Order with all its branches was Acharya Shankar, the incarnation of Lord Siva. He too, never used to call himself as Lord Siva but the humble servant of Lord God. Shyamacharan Lahiri Mahasaya, Swami Sri Yukteshwarji and Paramahansa Yoganandaji never called themselves God, but the humble servants of the Divine Father.

Though Acharya Shankar was the founder of Monism i.e. One God or spirit pervading the Universe, still he had accepted the world of ours as 'Vyavaharik Jagat' or the practical world. Likewise, though the 'Acharyas' denied themselves as Guru or God, they could not deny themselves a 'Acharya-Guru's.

All the Acharya-Gurus have the dual personalities, one as the ordinary persons — sleeping, eating, moving or acting like the ordinary persons, and the other, the inner side, where they are equal to God. Paramhansa Yogananandaji, in his Autobiography, has given innumerable instances regarding the Acharya-Guru's attainment of spiritual power.

The Materialization of a palace by Babiji, the grandeur of which is beyond the imagination of the public, is an instance of creation like God.

How seven drops of lamp oil had foiled the power of Death is another instance of Lahiri Mahasaya's power to infuse life in a dead body. Rama died at noon and Lahiri Mahasaya brought back his life at dawn the next day.

Swami Sri Yukteswrarji also demonstrated many miracles. He cured Sasi who was on the verge of death from his tuberculosis instantaneously. He, while working at Calcutta, appeared before Paramahansaji with an extra body at Serampore. By touching the chest of Paramahansaji Sri Yukteswarji had transmitted the cosmic consciousness to him.

In the same way Paramahansa Yoganandaji had transmitted to me the cosmic consciousness sitting at a distance of thousands of miles. He was then at U.S.A, and I was at Y.S.S., Ranchi.

While describing my state of cosmic consciousness, I narrated that all the Gurus merged in the body of Guru Paramhansa Yoganandaji. At first I could not understand the meaning of it as I used to think that Swami Sri Yukteshwarji was superior to my Guru and in the same way Lahiri Mahasaya was superior to Sri Yukteshwarji and so on. Through series of visions, Paramahansaji made me realise scriptural truth, "Mad Guru Jagat Guru" "Mad Atma Sarva Bhutatma" i.e., "My Guru is the Guru of the Universe" and','My Soul is the Soul of all".

The scriptures had explained that if you always think of the chain of Gurus, Param Gurus, Partapar Gurus and Paramesthi Gurus, then you won't get any fixed state of rest. Scriptural Truth cannot be perceived through intellectual means. By intellectual acumen we can come to a conclusion today but might change the same next day; but when it is realised at heart through perception that can never change. It becomes part and parcel of the soul. This is known as Being and Becoming.

Let us see some more instances. On the 18th February 1952, I had a vision of Sri Sri Lahiri Mahasaya at Y.S.S., Ranchi, at 5-25 a.m. Those days, I used to look after the young boys of Y.S.S., Ranchi, helping them attending the general prayer in the Guru Mandir. I used to request the Gurus to pull me out from my meditation so that I can join the general prayer timely and help the boys. On that day, I was roused from my daily meditation at 5.25 a.m. As I had a few minutes at my disposal, I again closed my eyes and requested the Gurus to help me so that I might not be late. The moment I closed the eyes, Lahiri Mahasay, appeared in the Kutastha' (Christ Centre) in shimmering blaze. Shining flood of light gave me a thrill from head to feet with joy. Tremendous electric sensation passed through all the cells of my body. My mind was absorbed to see his glorious form for five minutes only.

On the 17th March 1952, I had a vision of the Divine Mother during my morning meditation at Y.S.S., Ranchi. At the Chirst Eye the dancing figure of the Divine Mother appeared in a blaze of very dazzling light. At Her every playful step, the waves of the flooded light rushed in all directions. My whole body was electrified with that unending light. She had put on a 'Banarasi Sari', decorated with beautiful flowers. From every flower, flood of white light was flowing. On the feet there were tinkling anklets from which there was the jingling sound. I was so much intoxicated with that vision that it persisted for hours together.

These are only two incidents that explain the difference between intellectual assimilation and realization. On the 25th January 1951, Paramahansaji wrote, 'You must, for all times, as a religious preceptor teach Ongsan, Pranabasan (our technique, listening the Oum Sound) and Kriya and a precept as compulsory to all students." Though Paramahansaji had written several times in the same way, I could not realise the depth of such words. When Paramahansaji through various visions and ecstasies communicated his last wish, 'I came to realise the true meaning of a religions Preceptor'. It is the role of an 'Acharya Guru'.

I perceived through visions which Gurudeva very kindly imparted to me that my role in this life was that of an Acharya Guru, which he tried to confirm by the words for all times. On that day, when I got the vision of Guru, I realised that all the Gurus are 'One'. When all the Gurus entered into the Body of my Guru and I too was drawn into His Being, then I realised that I am He', which was confirmed when I saw that all the devotees, who had taken initiation from me and the people who would take initiation afterwards, had merged into my One Being.

Paramahansaji once wrote to me: "You are my hands and feet." I thought then that he would work through me, but when any body being melted became One with Him, then I became He.

Chapter 10

The Divine Guidance

The Supreme Spirit guides His children in many ways. Generally, the devotees get His direction through their Gurus, either through direct verbal counsels or though letter, if the Gurus are at a distance. Now comes the question, if the Guru had left his, mortal coil, how would the devotees get the Divine guidance through the Guru.

The Gurus like Paramahansa Yogananda, Sri Yukteswarji, Lahiri Mahasaya, Babaji Maharaj, Sri Ramakrishna Paramahansa, Swami Vivekananda, Lord Buddha, Acharya Shankara and such other souls who are one with the Divine Father help their devotees in many ways.

The devotees who are highly spiritually advanced can contact their Gurus in meditation and receive direct guidance. There are other highly advanced souls who receive Divine Guidance at any time and at any place, only by closing their physical eyes; they enter into the realms of the Divine Souls. Such advanced souls are, of course, rare. They are self-realised souls, and are free from the mirage of the world.

The devotees, who are not so much developed or advanced, may get the guidance in dreams where and when meeting the Gurus is possible. Such dreams generally are accompanied by blaze of light.

During the day, when the devotees are engaged in worldly duties, the Gurus may appear before them either in flesh and blood or in the Astral costume. When they come with their astral bodies, they generally appear or descend with a blinding flash of light.

On many occasions, when they want to impart some instructions to differently advanced souls in a group meditation, they may send their words like radio-waves audible to physical ears of all the devotees present in the group. Such voice may be heard, as if coming from the roof or from any corner of the room or from any divine image. If among the group, there is any advanced soul present, who can enter into the divine realm or can dive deep into meditation, the Gurus may use the vocal instrument of that devotee and speak like the human being. The devotee, whose voice is heard, can see the divine Guru or Gurus like Astral television and also hear the divine voice while absorbed in meditation. Other devotees not capable of diving deep into the sea of meditation can only hear the communicating words of the Gurus.

The Divine Guru or Lord of the Universe can send His help or His guidance through various kinds of signals, to the ordinary public, either devoted to the spiritual path or devoid of any spiritual pursuit. These signals can be interpreted only through Astrological ways:

a) through the sounds of lizards,
b) through the different sounds of the crows, sitting in different ways, etc. and
c) various other kinds of signals
i) Good or auspicious signs: At the time of starting, if the man or woman sees the following — fish, cow with her young one (calf), Jar-full of water or empty jar on the way to be filled, lady with her child, horse, and such other signs mentioned in Astrology, he/she will have success for the purpose he/she is going out.
ii) Evil or inauspicious signs: Opposite to the previous signs: such as empty jars, visit of person or persons not blessed with any child, etc. Regarding the various auspicious and inauspicious signs, there are many stories and incidents narrated in the scriptures such as Ramayana, Mahabharata, etc.

In this Chapter I shall try to narrate or explain the various different ways, by which I got the Divine guidance through my Guru Paramahansa Yoganandaji directly by words or letters during his life time and after his demise. I have mentioned elsewhere in this book direct guidance received through meditation and ecstasy. The second way is through dreams. Sometimes the gurus or the gods and goddesses come and guide the children. Sometimes, the guidance comes through kinds of dreams and a dream on such an incident which would have the greatest impact on a devotee when and where the vision of God and Gurus might not be present. Let me cite an example.

The incident occurred at Y.S.S. Lakhanpur on 25 th October, 1946 at about 3 a.m. in the night. 'I am in a dilapidated boat trying to cross the river with a strong current. One of my spiritual brothers is also with me on the boat. When we reached the middle of the river, the boat was about to sink. The spiritual brother was helping me to drain out the water from the boat with the help of buckets and I crossed the river'.

What is the significance of this dream? The river is the world which I shall have to cross to reach the abode of my Father, the highest heaven. Boat is the physical body, which is in a dilapidated condition due to the visit of diseases. (It is the law of the Universe that no one is absolutely free from any disease in life). The trials and tribulations are allegorically mentioned in all the scriptures as the current of the river of the civilised world. The spiritual brother who helps me signifies those who will practise the kriya yoga can cross the river with me and also can help me not only in the spiritual world but also in the physical world. Gurudeva used to describe the value of group meditation. It helps the devotees to a great extent. At the time of weakness, the cross-currents of other spiritual brothers help the weak brother.

Another incident took place at Jagatdal Police Station, (at the residence of my younger brother who was an officer of the Police Station) on the 11th January 1947. In the early morning, I clearly got the vision of Paramahansa Nigamananda of Saraswat Math. The vision was so vivid that he appeared to be in a flesh and blood body. I bowed at his feet. He very affectionately infused spiritual current in my body. I instantly remembered the Gurus of my life and death, when the spiritual eye appeared with all the glory. I enjoyed the blessings for some time. In my early life, I used to recognise Paramhansa Nigamanandaji as my Guru and that is why he came to satisfy my soul.

Similar incident took place at Y.S.S, Ranchi, on the 6th March 1952 (at dead of night). During the last week of March 1952, I was deeply absorbed at the thought of my lost memory of the previous lives. My mind was very heavy from the evening of 6th March' 52. At night, my mind was so heavy that I was arrogant not to perform any Kriya exercise; why have I lost the ever-blessed-bliss of my soul? Though the inner soul asked me to do the Kriya exercises, my vanity forbade me to do the same. However, due to habit, unconsciously, I had performed a few Kriya mentally and remembered the name of God and Gurus at the time of sleep. Like 'Yoga-sleep' ("yoganidra"), the vision of the Astral world appeared. I believed that I was floating in the astral sky. In that beautiful bright sky, there appeared one or two astral trees, which vanished instantly at my touch. I realised at heart that I was floating on the astral sky without any support and my body also was very fine, befitting for the soul's expansion. In that state, I realised my soul's glory for the whole night.

Physical body is a dream body, soul is not the physical or astral body. It is above all like ether or a very fine elastic substance that can be expanded and can cover the whole cosmos.

Another way is the way of Astral television for the advanced kriya yogis or astral radio for the public at large especially the devotees of God following some sort of spiritual discipline. My whole life is practically guided by this way. The Gurus and Divine Angels used to impart instructions off and on by this way. Here are a few examples.

The incident took place on the 27th December 1960 at 6-30 a.m. at Dakshineswar. Paramahansa Yoganandaji appeared before me and communicated the following (The gist of which is given):

"I used to love you from my heart, that's why what I had given you something which no one had ever got it, not even any monk. But you could not preserve the same. If you could preserve the Yoga-power, which I had given you then I had not to labour so much for your 'Gadi (Gadi means seat of power i.e., a king, minister, president, etc). You have misused the yoga-power; without discrimination you have scattered the power and have given the same to the undeserving ones. Without due consideration, you have taken the sins and diseases of many persons. Had I not taken the poisons (sins and diseases), your body would have been attacked with unbearable diseases...

Haridashi (Paramahansa Haridashi Mata) is praying much for the good of the Ashram. The world is benefited by her thought of Brahma. Afterwards you will be able to understand how far she had worked for your Ashram. She is doing good for the millions and millions of the people of the world through her constant thought of Brahma and deep prayer She had the power to enter, into the highest heaven. She had gone to the inner chamber of the Divine Mother and had played with Her "Many storms will come over Your Ashram. Due to her prayer, all the storms will fly away. No one could recognise her... "

A similar incident took place on 1st January 1961 at Dakshineswar at dead of night. Paramahansa Yoganandaji appeared and told me: "I had gone to Babaji Maharaj on the 27th December 1960 at Kailash (to discuss about you), from where I had come back on the 28th December 1960. On my arrival, he came to understand everything". He himself commented, 'you have come to discuss the matter of Animananda. Well, he should not go to Australia now..' Paramhansa Yoganandaji then explained to me the reason, why I should not go to Australia now.

"If you go to Australia now, Haridashi would leave her mortal coil. She is now trying to leave this world and to fly to the highest Heaven for good. She has one desire to die at Banaras. Hence, don't allow her to go to Banaras. If anyhow can she go to Banaras, she will never come back and will die there on the day of her arrival. Secondly, if she does not get permission to go to Banaras from you, she is contemplating to go to Kamakshya. She has got one companion, who will bear all her expenses including the train fare, etc. If she could get the chance to go to Kamakshya, she will discard her physical body there and would be one with Divine Mother in the temple."

I have given the details of my Gurudev's instruction on this event in the Chapter, 'we do not visit Australia'.

I have mentioned another incidence that took place on the 17th January, 1961 at 8 a.m. Babaji Maharaj appeared before me with this message. "Yesterday, we had a meeting regarding Haridashi. We don't find any way to bind her in this world as she has no desire. She has dedicated everything at the feet of 'Narayana' (One aspect of the Divine Father). If you can bind her with the help of your love, the world will benefit. Please tell her not to go anywhere. Please always keep your eyes on her so that she may not abstain from her meal. She was the playmate of the Divine Mother. Due to the curse of Sage-Durvasha, she had to come to this world.

"The words that Paramahansa Yogananda said to you are all true. He decided to do many works, but could not finish them. You will have to work out the same. He will have to be born again. Daya had binded him through her love. Paramahansa, too, got her at the tender age and it was he who could bloom the flower of love in her... "

While Babaji Maharaj was speaking, Paramahansa Yoganandaji appeared. Turning his face towards Paramahansaji, Babaji Maharaj commented: 'Paramahansa, I am very pleased to see the work of your son. Paramahansaji said 'That's your grace'. Babaji continued: "But he has misused much power, as you have given him permission to give initiation at so early age".

I mentally begged pardon and requested him to tell me the way to atone for the misuse of power. He responded to my prayer: 'Well, you are blessed to have Paramahansaji as your Guru. He has laboured hard for you. If you could preserve the power, what he had bestowed upon you, you could safely sit on the Gadi. However, now work hard and absorb your self in the work of the Ashram. Labour four times the labour you are now doing; only then you will be able to conquer the world. I don't think it is advisable to go to Australia now. Go to Ranchi, work hard there. After 14 or 15 days come back to Dakshineswar and perform the work whole heartedly. You will get success. Now I am going to Kailash".

On the 8th February, 1961 at Dakshineswar, Param Guru Sri Yukteswar Giriji appeared and said: "Oh Nara-Narayana Satchidananda, just now Paramahansa Yogananda fervently implored me at Kailash in front of Babaji Maharaj for you. He is very anxious to hand over the charge of the Sansar (the world) to you. Now I ask you, in what way have you spent the power that Paramahansaji had bestowed on you?" I prayed mentally to excuse me for my misdeed and requested him to mention the remedy for it. Sri Yukteswarji also ordered me as Gurudeva and Batbaji Maharaj had done.

There are mysterious other ways by which God can impart instructions to His children for their guidance. This incidence took place at Kakdwip Gouria Math on 1st May 1955 at about 8 a.m. in the temple of Radha-Krishna. My younger brother was then an officer of the Kakdwip Police Station. I went there to spend the holidays.

I had gone to visit the temple. As there was no one in the temple and as the then in-charge of the temple allowed me to worship the Divine Ones, I entered the temple and touched the feet of the Divine Father- Mother. The moment I touched the white marble stone image of the Divine Mother, tremendous electric current passed through the fingers of my hand, charging the whole body.

Divine Guidance: I realised that the spirit is all pervading i.e., Omnipresence.

This incident took place at Ranchi in the afternoon. I was reading a holy book. While I was deeply absorbed in my study, unconsciously my toes of one of my legs touched the adjacent plant. An electric shock passed through the leg, imparting a thrilling sensation in the body. I realised why the rishis proclaimed that the Divine Father is residing in fire, in water, in the plant and trees. He Himself has entered into every atom of the universe.

Through prayer, hundreds of times I got the Divine response and guidance. Through holy books, scriptures, Vedas, Upanishads and the sayings of the Masters, according to the calibre of consciousness of the individual devotee, such guidance and instructions are perceived.

Through floating words, they say, that Lala Babu, one of the very rich persons, while walking, in the afternoon, heard a young girl calling: "Father, the sun is setting, time is passing, awake, arise from the sleep". He instantly realised in his soul that the days of his life were passing and forthwith renounced the world and became a renunciate.

Such are the mysterious ways of the Divine.

Chapter 11
Paramahansa Haridashi Mata

From her very childhood she used to get the vision of the Divine Father Lord Krishna in the form of the Giridhari Gopal, her family deity. They had a temple, where the golden statue of Giridhari Gopal decorated with various kinds of jewels was worshipped by the family members, specially by her grand mother, Sarnamoni Devi. He used to appear before her every now and then as a playmate and used to play with her. She was then five years old. At that time, the Divine Mother too, used to appear before her as a little girl who used to help her in various ways.

As per Her instruction, Haridashi Mata had learnt cooking at the age of 5/6 years. From the age of 7/8 years she used to cook some of the items of feasts on special social functions. The Divine Mother always would appear at the critical moment and most of the time She Herself used to cook on her behalf. Due to the Divine Mother's guidance, she became a renowned cook among her relatives and kinsmen. Indeed, they were surprised with her extraordinary skill of cooking at that early age.

The Divine Mother, as she used to see, as her playmate, appeared to be same as she was at 5/6 years herself. She used to wear red bordered sari like the married girls or the mothers in India. She had three eyes, two like the human being but a bit longer than the average girls, and the third one was visible on the forehead vertically glowing like a dazzling sun.

While speaking about the 'Rathayatra' of Lord Jagannath (the ruler of the Cosmos) of Puri, she narrated one amazing incident of her early life. At the age of eight, once Haridashi Mata, along with some 25 to 30 villagers including some of her relatives, was going on a boat to visit the 'Rathayatra' festival at Kalna. While they were passing through a marshy pool, they saw that a larger boat carrying jackfruits was slowly rowing ahead by the side of the bank of the pool.

Haridashi Mata requested the boatmen to overtake the jackfruit boat. On her request, the boatmen accelerated the speed of the boat and was passing through the middle of the pool. It was the rainy season, the whole place was flooded with water. While they were passing through the middle of the pool, the people of the bigger boat requested them not to pass through the middle since that was a dangerous place. The occupants of the pilgrimage-boat could not understand them. Moreover, the boatmen did not apprehend any danger. Disregarding their warning, as they were about to cross the danger zone, all of a sudden the motion of the boat was arrested by magic. The man in the bigger boat could understand what had happened. They brought their boat by the side and helped them to leave the boat and board the other boat by placing, a ladder across.

On enquiry, the pilgrims came to know the reason of the miraculous arrest of the motion of the boat. The businessmen going to sell the jackfruits at Kalna fare told them that there was a very big snake in that spot who had devoured many people. It had arrested the boat by its teeth from the bottom. They were very much frightened on hearing this. Then the businessmen told the pilgrims that they had with them a revolver to save their lives from the attack of the robbers. If any one could use the revolver when the snake would come out of water then they could search it with the help of fishing devices. Haridashi Mata suggested firing at the snake, and the villagers and relatives supported her proposal. The snake raised its head from the water as soon as the fish catching device was thrown into the water. Haridashi Mata immediately fired at and killed it with just two bullets. The businessmen then dragged the snake out of water with thick rope and put it on the bank by the side of which the pilgrims for Rathayatra festival were going on foot.

As the distance from the village Kurmira (the birth place of Haridashi Mata from where they started) to Kalna was about four miles only and the incident took place midway between them, the news of the death of the man eater snake had spread from mouth to mouth. As a result, people from different places visited the dead snake. The businessmen then invented a new way of income. Tickets were being sold for seeing the snake. The policemen, too, had to arrive there in order to control the rush of the public. Afterwards, in the presence of the police officers, the stomach of the snake was exposed and various kinds of' gold ornaments were found. The digestive fluid of the said snake could not digest the ornaments of the ladies that it had eaten or devoured.

I enquired from Haridashi Mata: "Where did you learnt the art of using the revolver at the age of eight?" In reply she said: "At that early age, I had all the recollections of my previous births. I was Brahmacharini in all my prenatal existences. I could use the yogic power that I had acquired in my previous lives. That's why I could use the gun, or rifle or revolver or could do any work that I would like to do. What to speak of early age, even I could remember all when I was a baby. My grandmother was a God-realized soul. She could understand me and all my achievements through her yogic power. She used to tell my father not to get me married." I requested her to narrate the details of her previous lives. She declined on the ground that it was not necessary to know all the details".

While speaking about the use of gun, she narrated one incident of her early life when she had to use the gun. She said: "There were a few persons in my village, who were robbers by occupation. Usmita was their leader. We had a fruit orchard. The large garden was on the back of our house. Once, Usmita, along with his eight to ten fellow men, entered our orchard to discuss about their future place of robbery, while I was eating Kow fruits along with my friends there. As we were all very tiny girls, aged between 8 to 10 years, they overlooked our presence and began to converse among themselves. Though we were chatting while eating fruits, I was very attentive to them, and I could hear their discussion. The leader Usmita said, 'I am not afraid of any one. Only I am afraid of a cat on land and a 'Bowal' fish in water'. One of his fellow men enquired: 'Why are you afraid of a cat and a fish, the most insignificant creatures in the earth? Usmita replied, "I know a very secret technique by virtue of which I can take the form of a rat, and can cross the river throwing dust to the eyes of men. So, I can enter in any room and can open the doors at dead of night. Then assuming my former body I can rob the house".

Then he said, 'Well friends, let me tell you the important reason for which I have called you here. Tonight we shall go to the house of Anukul Ghosh, the jaminder of Korati. Be ready with our band party, day-light and guns'. Saying thus, the party left".

"Sri Anukul Ghosh of Korati was my uncle. He married the sister of my father. Hence, I was very anxious to save the life and property of my uncle. As my aunt was not blessed with any issue, she used to love me dearly. Their house was at a distance of half a mile from our house. With the permission of my parents, I started, in the afternoon, for the house of my uncle which was protected with compound walls. After taking our meals as we went upstairs, we heard the sound of the band party with day-lights and occasional firing approaching our uncle's house. It appeared to us as if a marriage party was going to celebrate the marriage ceremony.

The party came to the main gate of the house of the uncle. By that time, I was ready with the my uncle's gun. My uncle was puzzled to see the party. I could see the people through the holes in the wall. I had already closed all the doors and windows as they were approaching. A few of them entered into the compound. Usmita had entered first assuming as a rat through the drain and had opened the bar of the main gate. I could recognise them as many of them were present in our garden. Without delay, I fired killing three of them. Rest fled".

I enquired: "What happened afterwards?" She replied, "Next morning after breakfast, my uncle and aunt both came to my father with me. My uncle requested my father not to chide or rebuke me. "She had saved our lives last night". Then my uncle narrated the whole incidence.

I further enquired: "Do you remember, what happened with the dead bodies of the robber?" She said, "They could not carry the corpses with them. I don't remember, who informed the case to the police and what happened with dead bodies."

I asked, "Did the leader Usmita die?".

"No, he fled that day, but died a year after". I enquired: "How and where?" Haridashi Mata continued: "A year after, Usmita went to my uncle's house to take revenge of the death of his fellowmen at dead of night. I intuitively knew that Usmita would go to kill my uncle. Initially, he did not know where my uncle slept, how to reach there. But during that year, he managed to get the right information. Through intuition I perceived the time and date of his misdeed; a few hours before that time, I reached my uncle's house and expressed my wish to stay there".

"My uncle, as asked for by my aunt purchased various kinds of sweets for me. Though the walls of the main, building was made of bricks and cement, the grain store was not so strong. There was a spiral stair that connected the main room where my uncle used to reside at night. I knew from my inner heart that Usmita would enter first the grain store. I had learnt many yogic techniques. As I was thinking of my grand mother, Usmita was entering into the room through a hole assuming the form of a rat. I saw a huge cat came out from my own self and stood before the body. It instantly had cut the throat of the rat with its teeth. Usmita died on the spot. Profuse quantity of blood oozed from the cut throat and drenched my clothing. The miracle was that the body of Usmita was still the body of a rat and the head took form of Usmita. The body was outside the wall, and the head was inside it.

"Then I spoke to my uncle to inform the case to the police station of Korati. When he tried to contact the office through the phone in the ground floor, he realized that the cable was cut into pieces. He went upstairs and informed the Officer-in-charge of the police station from his personal phone. Aswani Babu, then Officer-in-charge of Korati. Police Station came within a short time. I told him that a cat had killed the rat. He was astonished to see the dead body, the head being the form of a man and the body was that of a rat. He could recognize Usmita."

Haridashi Mata continued: "After the death of Usmita, Lodha, one of the fellow robbers once came to our house to steal. It was the month of December or January. That night, due to a sudden rainfall, the earth became muddy. I was with my mother-in-law residing in a house, the wall of which was made up of tins. My mother, who came to visit me the day before, was also there. Lodha could see us from outside through small holes in the wall. To satisfy his evil desire, he pushed an iron rod through one of the holes just on the back of our wooden seats. The rod passed under the wooden seat of my mother. I at once caught hold of the rod and snatched it away from his hand. My mother-in-law remarked, "due to the disturbances of the thieves, it is difficult to live in such a village". Lodha counter-remarked in the most vulgar language. It angered me and I threatened him, 'Wait a bit, I shall teach you a good lesson'. Lodha ran away. In order to teach him a lesson, I came out of the room under the pretext of nature's call. I ran to the police station of Korati and reported the matter.

Aswini Babu, the officer-in-charge of police station replied, "If you can give me any definite proof, I shall go, otherwise not." "Yes, I have definite proof with me." Then Aswini Babu ordered some of the constables to follow him in the police-van and he started on his motor cycle. On arrival, Aswini Babu enquired from mother-in-law what the matter was. My mother-in-law, pointing to me, said: "Haridasi will tell you what has happened". I then narrated the incident. "Look at this iron rod, you will find the name of Lodha engraved". He examined the rod and was satisfied to see the name of Lodha. Then asked: 'How did you get this rod? I replied: 'I snatched it away from him, when he had pushed it in our room through the tin wall'.

"Aswini Babu, in an astonishing tone, remarked: 'How was it possible? You are a little girl, how could you snatch the rod from a strong robber?" I commented: "You know, the robbers besmear oil on their body, and as all of a sudden, I with a jerk I pulled the rod, it slipped out of his hand. Then I requested him to call Lodha in order to examine the footprint on the mud. Aswini Babu, then sent a constable and the village watchman to his house for arresting him. He was brought. "The police men extracted the truth from him. He was then sent to the police station for further enquiry".

Haridashi Mata narrated another incident of her fight with the robbers to preserve her chastity. "In our village Kurmira, my uncle Haren Kaka once sold sixty maunds of jute (about 22.38 quintals). Haren Kaka had to go to deposit the money (Rs.1200) in the Savings Bank at Munshiganj. His other two brothers went with him. As all the male members were absent, I was invited by my aunts to sleep with them at that night.

Those jute traders were actually robbers. The business or the trade was their facade, and rather a side business. At that night, they came to rob the money that they had paid. The three aunts were sleeping in different rooms attached to one another. I was sleeping in the room of Haren Kaka. At dead of night, I was awakened by the sound of digging earth. I observed that a thief had already made a big hole in the earthen wall of the room a few feet away from my bed. The moon's rays had flooded the room passing through that cavity. I realised that within a few minutes the thief would be able to enter into the room. If the thief entered the room, he would not get the money, but molest us. Hence, to save our chastity, I decided to kill the robber. In that moon light, I could see a heavy scythe in front of me. I took that scythe with my both hands and knelt down by the side of the cavity waiting for the entrance of the robber. As the head of the robber was visible inside the wall, I took the name of Kali ("Jai Ma Kali ") (Kali is name of the Divine Mother) and struck on his head with all my might by the back side of the scythe. Instantly, the skull was broken into pieces. My garments were drenched with blood. My body became immobile, the clench of my hands became fixed- the scythe still being under my grip, I went into trance which lasted for hours together. During that ecstatic state I could see the Divine play of Goddess Kali, who was chopping the heads of the demons.

"My aunt was observing what I was doing. She shouted as I killed the robber. All the other robbers fled away as one of them was killed. All the kinsmen and other relatives living nearby rushed on hearing the shrill cry of my aunt. They instantly informed the case to the police station of Korati. Aswini Babu along with other assistant officers came there to investigate the case and saw me in that state. The next morning as the uncles arrived from Munshiganj, Aswini Babu, with the help of my relatives, snatched away the scythe from my hands from behind. I instantly fell down on the ground. After a few minutes I regained my outward consciousness.

I had to go to the Munshiganj court along with Aswini Babu and other relatives. The magistrate asked me: "Why have you killed a man?" In reply, I commented: "Your honour, he was not a man but a beast in the shape of a man. He had entered into our room in the night to rob my chastity; I had killed the beast." The magistrate was satisfied and offered me rupees five hundred as a prize for bravery."

I enquired: "How did you utilize the money?"

"I did not use that money for my personal gain. I had given that money to Aswini Babu for taking sweetmeats. He gladly accepted that money and spent it for the purpose I gave him."

"How did you know that your money was spent for the purpose you gave to Aswini babu?"

"On a particular day, the whole of my family members, along with the staff of that police station, were invited to satisfy my wish and that was how I could know the fact".

I enquired, "Did you ever see any ghost or spirit in your life?"

"Yes, but what is the use? It would not benefit the public. We should discuss about spiritual matters. However, since you have asked me, I shall narrate one incident about the visible spirit of a dead person with whom I had to fight in my early life". She continued, "I had learnt from my grandmother, the art of fighting with the wizard and witches, and especially with the visible spirit of a dead person. Accordingly, I had subdued many ghosts of evil nature. A few years after my marriage, when I was 14, I had to attend a marriage ceremony of one of my relatives in the village. Nearly 250 ladies and girls were dining in an open place on the occasion. Since I was a strict vegetarian from early childhood, I did not join those guests. I was sitting alone on the veranda, witnessing the feast. One disembodied spirit took the form of a female ghost and had taken a seat among the guests. No one would guess that an evil spirit would take a visible form and enjoy the royal dishes in that marriage ceremony. All of a sudden my attention was drawn to the crippled like peculiar form of the legs of that (apparition) lady, whose face was covered by the veil of her sari.

When the feast was over and the ladies were ready to leave the seats, the ghost in a very peculiar voice requested the girl who was serving the dishes to serve her more quantity of the sauce that she had served at the end. Hearing that peculiar voice, the ladies could make out that she was an apparition, and fearing for their life everyone fled. Instantly, I applied a special mantra and arrested her. She could not move an inch from that place. Then, I had to fight for sometime in the presence of all. The fight was really a mantric battle. I ordered her to leave the village and as a sign of her departure for good, she should break a huge branch of a tree in front of us. She could not object or disobey due to the pressure of the mantric power. She followed my order, and went away breaking a branch of a tree.

The next day my husband arrived at our house, and came to know from the relatives all about the fight with the ghost. He became very angry; his life would be in danger since he used to tease the spirits. The disembodied spirits may kill him at an unguarded moment. He was so angry that he was ready to divorce me.

My parents pacified him. He told my parents: "I can accept her on one condition. She shall have to pass a test. She shall have to jump in the middle of river 'Padma' and come back safely. Further, she should not fight with any spirit in future. I gladly accepted the test and the proposal. I, along with my husband, parents, uncles, and several others boarded a boat. When the boat reached the middle of the river Padma, I, remembered the Divine Mother and jumped into the tremendous current and waves. As I jumped into that dangerous waves, I was received by my Heavenly Mother and I became unconscious outwardly.

She embraced me and I saw in a vision, a very beautiful palace, where she entertained me. I was in that ecstatic state for more than an hour.

All my relatives were crying as they could not see me and thought that the crocodile had taken me for good. When I came back to my normal sense, I floated and saw our boat in front of me. As I raised my hands, my husband pulled me on to the boat by his hands. From that day, I never used any mantra to fight with any spirit during the life time of my husband."

Chapter 12
Srimati Saraswati Das

Srimati Saraswati Das, born on the 19th August 1948 in Calcutta, is the youngest daughter of Late Charu Chandra Sarker and Paramahansa Haridashi Mata. At the instance of her mother, I initiated her on the 21st July 1955. On that day, she received only the preliminary yoga technique. On 3rd February 1963, I initiated her into full kriya yoga along with her elder brother Paresh Chandra Sarkar and James Martini of Australia. Her mother was also present on the occasion. At the time of her initiation, she got the vision of Lord Sri Krishna in the blaze of light.

Babaji Maharaj told me on the 3rd March 1963 at 7.42 p.m., "Don't scold this little girl. She is the incarnate of Lakshmi (Goddess of riches). Whatever she demands, please supply and keep her pleased. In future, she will take the place of Mother". On the 6th November, 1970, Babaji Maharaj said, "Saraswati is the most fortunate girl; a worthy daughter of a worthy mother". On the 30th January, 1971, Babaji Maharaj intimated me, "Brahmamayee Ma Tara is born in the womb of Haridashi Mata. She is free from all desires. She will lead the life of a renunciate (Sannyasin) after the birth of a child. Tens of thousands of people will rush to visit her. Can you tell me among the yogis who has ever been able to extract the footprint of the Divine Mother? But Mother Saraswati extracted the footprints of the Divine Mother at Lakhanpur".

Babaji Maharaj thus created in me the desire to know the details regarding extraction of the Divine Mother's footprints at Lakhanpur. I visited Saraswati at her house at Calcutta. On enquiry she told me, "I was at that time reading at Yogoda Satsanga Girls School (Basic) at Lakhanpur, Purulia. I used to get the vision of the Divine Mother Kali. At first, I became very afraid to see the sword in her hand, but afterwards I came to realise that she was my affectionate Divine Mother. I was forced to remain in trance for days together as the

Divine Mother was always with me. When I regained my normal consciousness, I wrote all the incidents in my notebook, but sorry to inform you that the notebook was missing".

However, I collected the addresses of the two teachers of the Girls' school who were present at that time. I dropped two postcards to the respective addresses requesting them to write to me about the incidents. One of the cards came back. The reply of the second letter was received on the 16th April 1971, the free translation of which is as follows:

"Aum Ma, Sri Charanesu",

Revered Swamiji, I have received your letter a few days ago, but I am very sorry that I could not reply to the same earlier, hope you will very kindly excuse me for this delay.

Now I am working in a village Higher Secondary School. But I received your letter at my house at Ranchi as I was on leave at that time. What you had heard about the incident of Lakhanpur was true. I was working there as a teacher. It seems to me that to witness the Divine play, the Divine Mother dragged me there as I had not even heard the name of Lakhanpur. I could not understand what happened; all of a sudden, Swami Bidyananda Giri came to me and appointed myself and a friend of mine as teachers of the Y. S. S. Basic Girls' School at Lakhanpur. After a few days, I could realise the presence of the Divine Mother.

Here is the account of what I experienced, heard and witnessed at that time. On my arrival there, two temples, one for the Divine Mother and the other for the Divine Father were created. Being invited, the Swami of Puri came and established the same. Though Swamiji established the temple of the Divine Mother, the local jaminder Choudhury Babu took full charge of the temple on the ground that they had a temple on the very spot where it was created. Hence, the school was deprived of the worship of the Divine Mother but the temple of the Divine Father was under our control. The schoolgirls, Headmistress and one lady of Ranchi who was known as the 'Didimoni' (elder sister) used to worship the Divine Mother twice daily devotionally. But the priest engaged by the jaminder Babu used to worship the Divine Mother half-heartedly. He would not even clean the stale flowers and 'Bel' leaves which would rot at one side of the room. As the priest would not worship the Divine Mother devotionally, we had no interest to witness the same. The adjoining areas of the temple too, were very unclean.

We, the teachers and girls did not pay much attention. At dead of night, the girls used to hear the sound of crying.

The Goddess of the temple was alive. She appeared before Saraswati Sarker of Class V and ordered us through her not only to clean the temple as well as the surroundings of it but also to maintain the sanctity of it. Before this incident, many, among us, used to hear the lamentations of a neglected girl. Though this was beyond our imagination, supernatural and surprising, yet it was a fact.

For a few days, Saraswati felt unwell. During daytime she was free from any trouble, but as the evening set in she used to get breathing trouble. We could not help her. Nearly a week had passed. The older girls used to stay with her for the whole night and used to prepare themselves for the examination. The grown-up girls used to live in the hostel adjacent to the temple. The teacher-in-charge of that hostel also resided in that hostel with her youngest child. One day, at dead of night, one girl of that hostel heard the intense crying sound near the window. She woke up some of her roommates and requested them to hear the crying. They thought that the child of their teacher-incharge was crying. They approached their teacher-in-charge and saw the child was in deep sleep. They could not trace the source of that crying sound. Somehow, they spent the night. In the morning, the girls came to me and disclosed their experience. I told them, 'most probably it was the crying of a cat'. They protested, saying, "It was not the incident of one night, many of the hostel inmates used to hear the sound as they went out of their rooms". I could not make out what the matter was. At that time a number of dogs would chase as if they had seen an unknown person. I, too, became afraid but could not think otherwise. I could not even imagine that there may be any real reason behind it.

The day was Saturday. Early in the morning, a batch of girls, who used to reside in the room of Saraswati Sarker, rushed to me and disclosed that Saraswati had got a vision of the Divine Mother Kali. In that vision, she became very afraid to see the Divine Mother with the sacrificial sword in her hand. On enquiry they came to know the reason of the fear of Saraswati. She intimated them that the Divine Mother had commented, "You are all worshipping your Divine Father with show, if you don't worship Me, I shall destroy your Ashram". On hearing this, Saraswati cried in that vision, "Don't beat Mother, don't beat, I shall tell them to worship you". The girls, on hearing these words, pushed her to bring her back to outward consciousness. Saraswati then narrated her vision to them. I intimated the fact to our Headmistress. She confessed: "Yes, it is true we worship our Divine Father with pomp, but really we neglect our Divine Mother. However, to-day in the evening I myself shall clean the Mother's temple".

The priest-in-charge of the temple told us that he, too, had got the similar dream. If he did not worship Her properly, She would destroy his family. In the evening of that Saturday, as usual Saraswati was feeling uneasy. The Headmistress had gone to clean the temple of the Divine Mother. Before starting the cleaning work she instructed me and another colleague of mine to look after Saraswati.

That evening I myself had gone to attend the Puja ceremony of the Divine Mother in the temple. After the 'Arati' (Puja ceremony) was over, I returned to the room of Saraswati as if drawn by a magnet. On my return, the girls informed me that Saraswati was speaking in a trance state. We, too, noticed that Saraswati was free from the breathing trouble. She was lying down on the ground with closed eyes, on her back, and was moving on all sides pushing the earth with her legs while at the same time conversing with the Divine Mother. "Ma, don't beat. I shall tell them to worship you. They will clean your house daily". Saraswati did not know when Headmistress had gone to clean the temple. We could realise from their conversation that Saraswati was blessed with the vision of the different temples of India; how they had kept clean all the temples and how devotionally they were worshiping the Divine Mother.

The Divine Mother led her to the house of an old lady and showed her how the old lady had kept her very small cottage neat and clean and how devotionally she used to worship the Divine Mother. The main purpose of visiting those temples and the cottage of the old lady was that we, too, should worship the Divine Mother devotionally and should keep the temple neat and clean. Though I could not see the Divine Mother, still from the words of Saraswati, I could understand what the Divine Mother was saying. Saraswati was speaking with the Divine Mother constantly. It appeared that she was not our student but a goddess. On hearing her conversation with Divine Mother, we became puzzled and perturbed and mutely stared at her. In order to dispel all doubts in the matter, let me quote a few words of her conversation with the Divine Mother.

"Mother you used to weep daily as your temples were very dirty, the surroundings too were filthy. The putrefied leaves of flowers were emitting such an obnoxious smell that you cold not stay in the room. That's why you would roam over the compound wall, lamenting. Were you not crying that night, by the side of the window taking the form of a little child? What? If any one would try to see you opening the door, you would lead her to the other world with you"?

"Mother, beholding you would the dogs bark and would chase you?"

When I reached the village, I had seen a devastated mound on the very place where the temple was erected. I had come to know from the villagers that the Divine Mother used to live in that mound. Once, a relative of a villager had come from a town to visit his relatives. One day, they went to that place. The villagers told him that their Divine Mother lived in that heap. That gentleman from the town not only ridiculed the belief of his relatives, but also to prove his words stood over the mound with shoes on. The gentleman died on the spot vomiting blood.

Saraswati enquired, "Mother, ridiculing you, he put his legs on your temple due to which he died on the spot vomiting blood, is that so?" Saraswati went on, "tomorrow girls would clean the environment of the temple, and would sprinkle the cow dung water".

The girls, very gladly, waited for the morning. At 12 o'clock midnight, I and a friend of mine returned to our rooms. I used to live alone in a room but that night due to fear I could not sleep alone. I went to the room of my friend.

Early next morning, I saw the girls cleaning the Ashram temple with tremendous enthusiasm and energy as if some one was supplying them energy. After tea, we went to the room of Saraswati and noticed her lying down in the same condition. We saw her face beaming with joy and satisfaction all the while conversing with the Divine Mother.

We were all surprised to realise her supernatural power as we attentively heard the said conversation. She was lying down on the ground unconsciously in her room, but she could understand what was going on in the Ashram and temple; most probably the Divine Mother would intimate her all the facts. Saraswati asked, "Are you now pleased with the girls as they have cleaned and have sprinkled all the places with cow dung water. That's why you will visit all the rooms. On hearing that the Divine Mother is pleased and would visit our rooms, I became afraid and said, "We don't observe spiritual laws regarding cleaning, let us go to our rooms and sprinkle some Ganges water in the rooms." We hastened to our rooms. I was surprised to see the condition of my bed.

The cover of the quilt was half-opened, the cover of the pillow was removed and the bed itself was in a topsy-turvy condition. I had a suspicion that someone had entered my room for money, I used to keep under the bed. But I saw the distinct footprints on the quilt as if the Divine Mother had just walked over the quilt, first putting her feet on the cow-dung.

It was not possible for me to describe my mental condition. I touched the footprints with reverence and then disclosed the matter to my friend. She could not believe. I brought the matter to the eyes of many a one. Inmates of my adjacent quarter said, "so long as the foot-prints do not appear in my room, I won't believe".

By that time the staff and students had gone to the school but I went to the room of Saraswati as I had no class in the 1st period. As I entered her room, I heard her words, "Mother, the lady believed in whose room you had gone, but the others could not. Mother, please don't take offence, kindly enter into her and create faith in her mind". I could understand then that the Divine Mother, being pleased had promised to go to the rooms and gone and as a token of Her appearance had left footprints in the room of the lady. I was not within myself with joy as She had entered into mine. Being over-drunk with joy I hastened to my friend and said, "Mother had not taken ill. Saraswati had already begged pardon on your behalf and prayed for different types of footprints on everybody's bed.

All of a sudden, Saraswati in a pleading tone said, "Mother, she does not know, please excuse her who is scattering dust over your footprint." On enquiry, I came to know that a girl, Tulsi, was throwing dust over the dusty footprint of the Divine Mother in order to make it more prominent.

Suddenly, Saraswati laughed and said again, "Mother, that little girl had spread her cloth on her bed and was crying for your footprints for a long time. Please, bless her with your footprints. Within five minutes of the pleading of Sarawati, the little girl crushingly informed me with tears in her eyes and face beaming with joy that she was crying for the footprints for a long time, and in the long run her desire had been fulfilled. In that way, everyone was blessed with the divine footprints. Saraswati once exclaimed by way of talking, "Mother, today you are pleased and hence, you will visit the room of everybody tonight dancing with your play mates."

We all became very happy with the hope of witnessing a new thing.

Among diverse conversation between Saraswati and the Divine Mother, the day passed. Saraswati had not taken anything, not even a drop of water for nearly two days. She was lying on the same posture with closed eyes. We all were anxious to find ways and means to feed her. In vain, we discovered many plans for feeding the girl who could not even bear the touch of the garment of anyone and who had no outward consciousness. Being helpless, at last, a teacher boiled a quantity of milk in a pure and holy way (changed her dress and had put on washed and cleaned ones, had put a tulsi leaf on the boiled milk) and kept it on the table, so that she (the teacher) could supply if Saraswati expressed her desire to drink. Then the teacher locked the door of her own room and went to the temple to attend the evening puja-arati. After the "arati" was over, she returned to her room and I hastened to the room of 'Saraswati. The moment I entered her room, I heard her words; "Mother, let me see what you have brought in a glass. Oh! You have brought milk. There is a tulsi leaf in it. Mother, like a thief, you have stolen it. What will they take? They will drink the remnant mixing with water".

Till then we were quite ignorant that milk for Saraswati was kept aside by teacher, hence became astonished on hearing the words of Saraswati.

After five minutes, when the teacher entered the room of Saraswati, she was informed of the incident of the milk. She informed us that she really had kept aside a quantity of boiled milk with a tulsi leaf in it for Saraswati but as she opened the lid on the vessel in order to 'Fetch it for Saraswati, she was astonished to find no trace of milk in the pot. If it was the work of the cat, it should have removed the lid, but who replaced lid? She could not make out what the matter was. On hearing from us, she realised that it was the work of Divine Mother. She Herself had brought the milk kept aside for Saraswati and had fed her. It was a matter of anxiety if the child won't take food and drink.

Another teacher had spread a cloth on her bed. She did not believe so long that the footprints of the Divine Mother would appear on it, at the same time she was feeling the sensation of fear, and she asked a girl to sleep in her room. The girl spread her bed on the ground. The teacher, at about 10-30 p.m. advised the girl to sleep and told her that she was going to Saraswati and would send some other girl who would also sleep with her. The teacher, on meeting Saraswati, got busy in assimilating the words of Saraswati and forgot about her promise to the little girl. On return to her room, she was asked to fetch the key from the teacher, but the teacher never sent any one! Further surprise awaited the teacher. As she lit the light, she noticed innumerable impressions of small but prominent footprints on the cloth spread over the bed as if someone had danced on her bed. With unspeakable joy she hastened to intimate the news to us. As she reached the door of Saraswati, she (Saraswati) remarked, "I think this time you have got faith". We all were dumbfounded. She silently returned to her room.

After sometime, Saraswati remarked, "Mother, to-night you would dance in the rooms of all along with your mates whereas one had kept her leg on your body." The girls rushed to the room of Headmistress who was sleeping. They intimated her. She came to the room of Saraswati and told, "I was not aware of it. That's why I had gone to bed; I was feeling very uneasy". Saraswati repeated the remark about someone being absent. It was found out that everybody except one teacher was present. Again the girls rushed to the room of the teacher concerned; she was pouring water on her head and face. She, too, after receiving the information said, "I too, was feeling very uneasy as I had gone to bed".

We all assembled in the room of Saraswati vacating our rooms for the Divine Mother to dance with Her mates. Both the Divine Mother and we became very happy. We said, "Let the Divine Mother dance in our rooms".

While speaking with the Divine Mother, Saraswati lifted her hand upwards and said, "As you are willing to give, give, give"; she collected something in her hand and handed it over to one, instructing her to show the same to the believers. Since we believe in the Divine Mother completely, she showed that to us. It was a long hair of the Divine Mother.

Suddenly, another girl spread her hand and began to cry. After sometime, we noticed a beautiful 'Bel' leaf by her side. Saraswati instantly said, "It is not her due, the former girl receive it".

The whole night rolled out. In the morning, Saraswati told us that she would go to the temple after bath. The girls made all arrangements for her bath. After bath, wrapping her body in a Sari, she proceeded towards the temple. A portion of her Sari (anchal) was wallowing on the ground while she was approaching the temple with closed eyes.

Her divine appearance was beyond description. She paid her homage to the Divine Mother as she reached the temple and returned to her room.

The divine intoxication continued for few more days. She regained her normal condition; at times the Divine Mother used to appear in her body, when anyone would violate the general spiritual rites. She had to work out all the consequence of the violation of the spiritual law. We had noticed at that time the pangs of her sufferings for the atonement of the sins of the girl or lady. When she could not bear the pangs of the suffering, she would fall down on the ground and would converse with the Divine Mother. From her conversation, we could know the nature of the sin, and the name of the person who had committed the same.

By the grace of the Divine Mother, I had seen and realised a lot. I have tried to express the same to you as far as possible. I hope, you will surely be happy to read it. Please don't forget to intimate me on receipt of this letter whether I could furnish you something worth having. Permit me to conclude this letter here.

Please accept my devotional pranam to you.

Yours,

(P. S. I could not furnish the address of the other teacher, as I don't have her present address.)

On receipt of the above letter I revisited Saraswati at her Calcutta residence to collect more information on her spiritual progress. I asked her, "Well Saraswati, have you ever seen any other God or Goddess besides the Divine Mother Kali?"

"Yes, once while I was at Tollygunj, Calcutta, I had got the vision of Lord Narayana in the blaze of light. In that vision or rather super-conscious dream, I was walking on the road in Tollygunj area with my relatives. As I was then a very young girl, I was very afraid. In the dream, I was uttering, "Jai Guru, Jai Guru" and also "Aum", "Aum". Instantly Lord Narayana appeared in a blaze of light. He had four hands. In each, He had different things. In one hand a very beautiful lotus, in other a 'Gada' or club, in the third a conch-shell, and in the fourth on the index finger a ring-like substance (similar to our playing discus chakra), emitting tremendous light.

He said, "Don't be afraid, I am with you, whenever you be afraid, remember Me, I shall come to you".

When I was at Dakshineswar, I got the vision of a Goddess. She had four hands. She was sitting on a peculiar type of animal, the face of which was nearly similar to a crocodile but the tail was like a very large fish. The middle portion was more or less like a big fish. The creature was swimming along the middle of the Ganges swiftly carrying the Divine Being with a roaring sound of the sea. The mouth of the creature was wide open. Thirdly, from time to time I get the vision of Lord Krishna-Radha".

"Have you written your experiences in any note book".

"Yes, but only a few incidents", came the reply. I brought that note book with me.

On my return to Midnapore, I came to know from her mother Paramahansa Haridshi Mata that recently Saraswati had the vision of "Ma Lakshmi". Ma had instructed her to worship Her during the coming "Lakshmi Puja" in a customary way with the help of a priest. Paramahansa Haridashi Mata Said, "Ma Lakshmi, instructed Saraswati to bring her earthly mother on that occasion by her side. That's why my daughter fervently implored me to go to her house during the Lakshmi Puja. Hence, I shall have to visit her at that time."

Saraswati and her husband both had gone through the letter, which I had received. I sought a few clarifications: "Well, Saraswati who was that old lady, about whom the Divine Mother pointed out to you regarding the sanctity, purity and cleanliness of her small cottage?"

"She was my earthly mother".

"From the letter, I came to know that you had the vision of different temples, will you kindly describe the same?"

"It was true, the Divine Mother showed me innumerable temples, including the Kali temples of Dakshineswar, Kalighat (Calcutta) and such other places. But I could not recognise them as I have never visited them in my earthly form. In some of the temples, I noticed that the Divine Mother was in a sitting posture; in most of the temples, the Divine Mother was visible in a standing posture".

In order to unfold the spiritual development of Srimati Saraswati Das, let me quote a few incidents or rather visionary super-conscious dreams from her own note book.

Case -1 (undated): On all sides, there was light and various sounds, tremendous light, and nothing else. The light was so strong that my eyes were throbbing with pain. Afraid, I sat down in a place and began to cry putting my face in between the knees. I do not know when I fell asleep crying. Suddenly, I was awakened with a push and beheld in front of me a very beautiful young man. He was of 22/23 years. He was calling me. Seeing a person after so long, I cried again loudly.

The boy enquired: "Why are you crying? What has happened to you? With whom have you come here? Have you lost the way?" He sat down by my side and said: "Tell me, I shall take you to your place".

Now, there was no such intensity of light. The environment was very beautiful as on all sides there were trees and plants of various kinds of fruits and flowers. I was thinking about the locality of his residence.

After a long time, I replied: "I can't recollect anything. I have not come with anyone. Well, I don't see any house in this locality. Where do you live? Are you one of such travelers like me and lost the way?" The boy laughed aloud and remarked: "Do you think everyone to be a wanderer as you have lost your way? It is not so. Well, there is no one here. You may cry in vain as you see there is no one within hearing range except myself". My blood dried up. Though internally I was about to be paralysed, I collected strength and enquired, "Why should you take me?"

He said, "I can do anything as I please. Even I can kill you" and looked at me angrily. I replied: "Do whatever you like, but please do not kill me. I am afraid of dying".

The boy said; "Well, I shall see that afterwards. Do you like to go to my house? You can see my residence." I replied: "How far is your residence? I can't walk long distance as I am very hungry". The boy said, "Well, let us go".

We were walking towards his residence. Suddenly, darkness was enveloping me; being afraid, I came nearer him. He understood my condition. He then pressed my hands within his own, and said, "Don't be afraid, let us go". Then total darkness encircled me. Out of fear, I could not walk. Holding his hands firmly I halted there with closed eyes. He enquired, "What's the matter? Why are you standing? Let us proceed". Out of fear, I could not utter a single word. Drawing me to his side, he remarked: "Silly girl, why are you so afraid? Being a girl of this land, why are you so afraid"? Affectionately passing his hand over my body and head he asked me again: "Are you still afraid?" Instantly, I understood and recognised him. He led me to our Divine Mother.

On arrival at the house, I embraced our Divine Mother. She (Divine

Mother) enquired, "Why do your eyes and face look so dry?" casting Her glance at our Divine Father. The Divine Father innocently replied, "How can I know?" I became very angry and disclosed to Her all that happened. Mother was also angry which she expressed through Her eyes. By that time, Mother had served me all palatable dishes. While eating I was looking at my Father angrily. Father, too, expressed His resentment through His eyes.

Case-2: "Multicoloured ocean of light. I was drinking it with my whole being. At times the waves of multicoloured light were lashing me. Like a little girl, as I was trying to hold them in my little hands they vanished like the will-o-the-wisp. As many times I tried to grasp them, they receded back to a distance. On all my sides there was only light, many coloured, dazzling light and nothing else".

"I became tired running after them and at last sat down, at a place. I had lost all the desires to catch the light. Sitting idle, I fell asleep. Suddenly by a push, I woke up and saw a couple of old beings lying down by my side touching my body. As I tried to sit down, the old man caught hold of me and forced me to lie down again. But when I sat forcibly, the Divine Parents too, came up and sat by my sides".

Chapter 13
Mahasamadhi

Mahasamadhi means the Samadhi or ecstasy that never breaks. It is always used in the sense of final exit of the life force from the body at the time of death. Mahasamadhi of my Guru Paramhansa Yoganandaji took place at Los Angeles, California, U.S.A. on March 7, 1952, after concluding his speech at a banquet held in honour of H.E. Binay R. Sen, the then Ambassador of India.

His body appeared to be the body of a living person even after twenty days after his Mahasamadhi, but he never came back to the same body that was later interred at the Los Angeles Mortuary at Forest Lawn Memorial Park.

According to Indian social customs, I had to perform special Puja and fire ceremony on the 18th March '52. On the 17th March '52, I personally went out to invite the Swamis, Brahmacharis, Saints of other institutions as well as the devotees of Y.S.S., Ranchi, to participate in the special fire ceremony on the occasion of the Mahasamadhi of my Gurudeva. As a general custom, the sons should, with folded hands, invite the relatives to participate in the Shradh ceremony of their parents. On the 18th, the ceremony went on from 5-30 a.m. to 9 p.m. which included prayers, kirtan and devotional songs.

As a sacred duty of the son, I had to perform the Guru Puja and the fire ceremony at 9 a.m. that was completed at 11-30 a.m. Narenda recited the Holy Srimad Bhagavad Gita and also conducted the devotional songs.

'Prasad' was distributed among the invitees. The 'prasad' distribution on the occasion of the Mahasamadhi of a saint is known as "Bhandara". Bhandara of Paramhansa Yoganandaji started at 12-30 p.m. and finished at 2 p.m. In the afternoon, the guests of Ranchi went away and I entered my own room for rest. The thought of Gurudeva overpowered me and tear-drops rolled down my cheeks. At that moment, a few devotees of Y.S.S., Ranchi, came to my room. One of them enquired: "Well Swamiji why are you weeping? I replied: "The thought of my Gurudeva overwhelmed me and that's why tears are coming out from my eyes."

In the evening, after the special Puja of the occasion and the general prayer, I sat for meditation. Gradually my mind was withdrawn and I perceived the difference between the ego and soul. My dwarf vision was enlarged and I could feel the three states simultaneously, first, the world outside; secondly, the inner feeling and thirdly, the consciousness of the Infinite.

After a few minutes, the outside feeling was lost, and my feeling was centred with the perception of the Infinite only. At 1 a.m. I regained my normal state of outward consciousness. After a short while, I again sat for meditation. Instantly, my mind was absorbed with tremendous electrical sensation in the spine. The life force from the coccyx ascended to the brain (medulla) with such a tremendous force that it took a fraction of a second to cross the spinal centres.

At different times I used to feel the upward journey of the life force differently. Sometimes, I used to feel the flow of the life current as the journey of an ant. At times, I could feel the same as the movement of a frog, jumping from one centre to the other. Again on other occasions, it was like the jumping of a monkey i.e., by two or three quick jumps the life force would cross the spinal centres. But, like a bird without stopping anywhere, it was the third time my life force had crossed the whole spinal centres within a fraction of a second.

As the life force had reached the medulla, I became Infinite as my Gurudeva appeared before me with all his glory. His body was made up of countless tissues of light, which became one with my astral body. The combined light of our bodies became reddish blue. Like the ocean of light, our combined body light covered the whole infinite Astral sky. The oceanic joy that embraced me is beyond description. Early next morning, for a few minutes, I regained outward consciousness. As I performed a few Kriyas, again I lost all outward consciousness and merged in the Infinite state of consciousness. At about 7 a.m., I regained the outward conscious state of mind.

When in the evening, I cried for a long time like an orphan child for the Divine Love and affection, and when the very existence of life became unbearable to me; Oh! Divine Father! You came silently from the infinite sky decorated with trillions of glittering stars; wiped away my tears carefully with your hand; looked at me with affectionate eyes filling my heart with solace. But in an unguarded moment, you went away silently again.

The above astral vision, though it gave me solace, my mind was not fully satisfied. I was craving for the physical touch of his flesh and blood body.

Sri Yukteswar Giriji left his mortal coil at 7 a.m. on March 9, 1936 at Puri Y.S.S. Ashram. Paramhansa Yoganandaji got the touch of the physical body of Sri Yukteswarji at 3.0" clock in the afternoon of June 19, 1936 in a Bombay hotel. The detailed description of the meeting has been narrated by Paramahansaji in his Autobiography (Autobiography of a Yogi, Chapter 43).

We know that the real yogis, even after their ascent to the Infinite, have the power to reappear on the earth, wearing the flesh-garb like Sri Yukteswar Giriji Maharaj. Innumerable instances can be cited from the lives of the yogis of India who reappeared to their disciples after their demise. That's why my heart and soul was hankering for the touch of the physical body of my Guru. In vain, I sought for the physical body of my Guru for years together. The mental agony that was tormenting me for years.

I felt: 'Alone, I am roaming in the world. You have gone to the other world and I am left alone to fight the battle of my life. The strings of my heart, though tuned by you, are out of tune now. I could not play the role of my life the way you wanted me to play. Would you come again to retune them? I would try to remain awake the whole night (in meditation) to get your physical touch. Would you come? Oh! My Guru, would you come?

Chapter 14
The Quickest Way to Contact God

From my early childhood, I had the notion that the noisy world was the greatest obstacle for the perception of God or Self-Realization. I was, hence, always attracted towards the Himalayas; and I was silently preparing myself for the flight.

When I joined the Ranchi Y.S.S. as a member and a worker, to avoid the noisy school hostel, I selected first Gita Kunja as my residence and the place of solitary Sadhana; and after a few months, the cottage near the Siva temple. I believed then that worldly duties/chores would disturb my mind and would cause restlessness. Hence, I always used to avoid crowd and the association of people. Since it was not possible to avoid the duties of the Ashram and the school, I used to do them unwillingly.

Once, I wrote to Paramahansaji (most probably in 1938-39) about my duties at Ranchi in order to apprise him of the pressure of work entrusted to me. I thought that he would surely suggest some way out so that I might get some relief from some of the duties. But in reply, he expressed his satisfaction over my packed daily engagements.

From time to time I used to communicate to him my spiritual progress and the progress of the institution. I could not then understand how he used to mould my life through written suggestions and orders. It took years to understand the way he moulded my life. In order to explain the same, let me quote some of the words from his letters.

'Self-less work for the Yogoda Satsanga and regular Sadhana should be the motto of every Yogoda worker. Try to recruit young educated men to work in the Yogoda Satsanga, as we need many men'. (February 5, 1940).

On receipt of the letter, I meditated on the above words for days together to understand the meaning and purpose. Nevertheless, due to the written words of Gurudeva, I could not avoid the association of men. In order to recruit young educated men for the society I had to be in the educated circle. I thought that as Gurudeva had ordered me to recruit young educated men, he would save me from the evil effects of mixing with the worldly people. Secondly, I thought self-less work was not in any way bad or the cause of bondage.

After a few days he wrote to me another letter: "you must meditate deeply every day and faithfully carry out your daily duties so that you can become a true Sannyasi in every way. My blessings are ever with you. Do your utmost to serve the cause in whatever way you are asked'. (February 24, 1940)

At that time, I was inclined to renounce everything for the sake of God and Gurus. But I was sorry to learn that the way I understood 'renunciation', was not the reality. By renunciation, I thought it included the renunciation of the worldly duties too. The above words changed my idea of renunciation. I used to do the duties willingly and faithfully. These words of Gurudeva taught me the value of the dignity of labour.

"Meditate regularly every day, perform your daily duties with perfection, knowing that in all works you are serving God and the Masters'. (July 16, 1940)

On receipt of this letter, my idea regarding 'Karma' (works) changed totally. Previously, I thought that one work would create another work, and thus, work would be the mother of bondage. Sri Gurudeva tried to draw my attention to the Truth that by serving the society, I was serving God and the Gurus. Previously, I used to think that the society was in no way better than the ordinary Sansar' (family). I now realized the difference between the ordinary family and the family of God and Gurus. The ordinary family members seek the pleasure and happiness for themselves only, whereas the society seeks the happiness for all in the world. Hence, I was attracted towards the work of the society so much that on many occasions I curtailed the time for my Sadhana.

Sri Gurudeva intuitively perceived my thoughts and wrote: "Please remember that sadhana and work must walk side by side. Work must not, under any circumstance, eclipse the sadhana which is the summum bonum of the Yogodans". (November 22, 1940)

I had, to some extent, deviated towards the work of the society as I thought that by serving it I was serving God and Gurus. The balanced rhythm of our life depends upon the combination of work and sadhana. While attending to different duties, we generally forget the Divine Father. In order to draw my attention towards the constant thought of God, Paramahansaji, a few days later, wrote another letter: 'Meditate much and be constantly merged in the thought of God that you may better serve Him and the Masters' (December 18, 1940). This is how Sri Gurudev used to guide me.

The most important thing in the spiritual life, particularly for those who want to contact God quickly, is the balanced life; work and meditation must walk side by side, and while working one should be constantly merged in the thought of God.

Many devotees have taken Kriya but they, most of the time, perform the Kriya exercises without devotion and love of God, as a machine in a factory. That's why they don't get appreciable results. If the Kriyas are performed mechanically, despondency, depression, giddiness will over-shadow the mind. Kriya is also a sort of work, a type of spiritual duty. We should not forget the purpose for which we are performing the Kriya yoga. Our aim should be not the acquisition of yogic power but self-realization. Month after month, year after year, Gurudeva used to impart the same instruction in different words.

Let me quote a few more words from his letters to this end:

"...Meditate more and give yourself whole-heartedly into God's service. Through unselfish and untiring service, you will receive many blessings from God and the Gurus. (Oct. 2, 1947).

'Meditate and balance your life by performing all your actions for the love of God to please Him and Gurus. Then you will be all right...' (March 1, 1950)

"Spiritual duties and meditation should never be neglected any time. For, then the outer environment tends to draw one away from the inner self'. (March 7, 1950)

Through me, Paramahansaji imparted the same instructions to all the devotees spread over the world who also are striving for God contact.

'I know you are doing utmost to aid others on the spiritual path and you must continue to do so whole-heartedly. Encourage all who have received Kriya to practice it daily without fail. Only by establishing the habit through repetition is one able to dive deep into His ocean of cosmic bliss. I am with you in spirit, in whatever duties you undertake. Believe that He is working through your body, mind and soul in all that you do and it shall be so." (March 7, 1950)

From 1935—36, what I had heard from his mouth had been written by Him year after year even till the end of His life and the same instructions were given by Him to all the devotees in the world.

Hence, obvious conclusion is that the quickest way to contact God is "Sadhana (meditation) and work must walk side by side; work must not, under any circumstance, eclipse the sadhana which is the summum bonum of the Yogodans."

In the Vedas and Upanishads, we find the echo of the same Truth. In the Isha Upanishada we find: "He, who is worshipping the Avidya (work) is merging into darkness, but he, who is worshipping the Vidya (meditation, Kriya yoga etc.) is merging into still more darkness". The meaning of this is as the aeroplane or bird cannot move in the sky with wing on one side only, neither work nor meditation alone can propel the soul of man into the Infinite sky of Bliss. Again the Isha Upanishad declared: 'Those who learn Vidya and Avidya simultaneously, through Avidya they can conquer death and through Vidya they can acquire the everlasting Bliss and Peace."

Those who do the worldly duties only, due to want of spiritual knowledge suffer a lot in the astral world after death. But those who perform only Kriya exercises without attending to other duties will fall down into deeper darkness during worldly trials. Due to want of experience in hard tests of life and the dearth of knowledge to outwit them, they succumb.

It is true, that the young yogis in the beginning stumble or fall down when hard trials or tests come. They sometimes commit such mistakes that cannot be pardoned by the veteran yogis. But such is the way of development. A baby cannot run. A child falls many times before learning the art of walking. What to speak of running, the same child can carry huge load when he or she grows up as a young man or woman.

The (unripe) green mango is sour. When the rays (heat) of the sun fall on it, it gradually becomes sweet. The soul of young yogi is like the green mango. When the heat of trials and tribulation fall on him, his transformation begins, and ultimately he becomes a ripe mango. In the march of life of the devotee, when cruel trials assail upon him and he cannot see the light of God, he becomes puzzled as to what to do and what not to do. The devotee sometimes becomes atheist. During one of such trials, I wrote to Paramahansaji. He instantly wrote to me:

"God hides Himself deliberately to test us, many times, and the devotee must learn to place full faith and trust in His imminent presence in spite of what seems to be the total removal of His beloved self from our inner ken..." (July 22, 1949)

This is the way of purifying the soul. The trial burns the dross of a man that covers the soul and obstructs the bright rays of the inner self to emit. Grace of God is the main factor for God contact, which depends upon the obedience of the Guru and the individual soul's sadhana. If the devotees labour according to the guidance of their Guru, they must get the blessings of God.

When a devotee, through regular practice of Kriya exercises, enlarges his calibre of consciousness to such a point, that he can hold the universal consciousness within himself, the grace of God is bound to shower on him; and he becomes one with the Divine Father. At that time, devotee feels that he is omnipresent and omniscient and that the Divine Father is working through his body, mind and soul in all that he does.

In order to achieve God contact, the first essential condition is self-control, specially sex propensities, greed and anger. The doors of the senses act like leakages in a jar which do not allow the waters of realization to collect in the hearts of men. The second condition that should be fulfilled is the unconditional surrender to God, deep devotion (Bhakti) and love for Him.

Chapter 15

At Yogoda Brahmacharya Vidyalaya, Ranchi

On 20th May 1938, for the first time, I had been to Yogoda Bramhacharya Vidyalaya, Ranchi (YBVR). On 1st November, 1938, I joined Yogoda Ashram Calcutta as a permanent worker of the Society and from there I joined the Yogoda Ashram, Ranchi, Eastern Headquarter of Y.S.S. India, on the 21st January, 1939, as a permanent worker. On 8th June, 1938 I got an opportunity to visit the Jonha Falls with some of the members of the staff of the YBVR. On my many subsequent visits to the falls also I was accompanied by both staff and students.

On the 29th June 1938, on the occasion of the Rathayatra of the Lord Jagannathdeva I had the privilege to visit the Jagannath temple on the top of the Jagannath hill with the staff and the students of Yogoda Brahmacharya Vidyalaya. Brother Sashilal was my assistant; he was always ready with the medicines to treat the injured persons. The whole day was spent with the first-aid service, since more than 2 lakh visited the Lord on the top of the hill. There was only one entrance and one exit. There were several beautiful caves. On four sides many camps were erected at the base of the hill.

I was entrusted by Swami Satyananda Giri, then in-charge of the Ranchi Institution with the duties of general welfare, conducting morning and evening general prayers, coaching the hostel boys, teach as a school teacher, helping the Librarian on Sundays or on off days of school. After a few days, I was also asked to look after the library. From the 14th February, I coached the boys of Class VIII in the library room. Due to the illness of the compounder of the Hospital, I had to attend to his duties from 9 a.m. to 10.45 a.m. temporarily. Kshitishda used to help me in the library.

The 22nd March, 1939 is a memorable day. For, 22 years ago, in 1917, on that day Paramahansa Yoganandaji founded the YBVR with seven children at Dihika, Bengal; a year later it was transferred to

Ranchi. On the previous day, it was announced that the YBVR would be closed on the 22nd and 23rd on account of the Foundation Day of the Vidyalaya. A detailed programme comprising devotional morning songs (Prabhat Kirtan) and round the clock was circulated.

I was asked to join the Astam Prahar Kirtan (round the clock devotional songs) with the boys of the 3rd Class from 10-30 a.m. to 1 p.m. I was, also, entrusted with the responsibility of reciting the entire Holy Srimad Bhagavad Gita. After Prabhat Kirtan, Kshitishda was requested to recite the whole Chandi and Sashida, the Upanishadas (only the selected Chapters from different Upanishadas). Kshitishda and I selected the Shiva temple for our recitation of the Holy Scriptures. Right at 4 a.m., we, the teachers, Brahmacharis and swamis, along with our students, assembled to join the Prabhat Kirtan. Our procession started happily from the Ashram with Khol and Kartal (drums and cymbals). According to the practice of such Sankirtan (Devotional songs with flute, Khol and Kartal praising the Lord & His blessed name) we all walked barefoot. We happily sang the Bengali and Sanskrit equivalence of

"How long would you sleep?
Awake. arise, sleep no more,
Behold, dispelling darkness,
The morning light is visible.
Oh Brother! The flood of light
Is rising in the sky.
Let us go to Him
Taking the name of Guru Brahma,
Shake all the deep slumber."

We went around the Ashram. Enthusiastic student and staff sang the sweet, melody with the rhythmic sounds of drums and cymbals. The long tour ended in front of our Guru Mandir at about 6 a.m. From 6 a.m, the Sankirtan accompanied by harmonium, khol (hand beaten special Indian drums commonly used in temples), and cymbals started from the Guru Mandir. According to the previous announcement, the teacher-incharge along with his assistant teacher-in-charge joined the Sankirtan accompanied by their students. According to the arrangement, there will be relay where one batch of students (class by class) would be present for two hours only. Sankirtan was on at Guru Mandir since

6'O clock in the morning and at Shiv Mandir, at the same time. Kshitishada and I lit the incense and special lamps, and started reciting holy scriptures as per the prescheduled programme. Reciting of scriptures continued till 10-00 a.m.; and, then I joined Sankirtan at 10-30 a.m. I remained with Sankirtan till noon. After lunch and a short rest, I rejoined the Sankirtan party. I remained with Sankirtan till the end which was a privilege.

According to the Tithi, (thirtieth part of the whole Lunar month) Thursday, the 23rd March was the Foundation day of the Vidyalaya. As usual, I conducted the morning prayer. After prayer, the prize distribution of the school was held. Anandada (grandson of Sri Sri Shyamacharan Lahiri Mahasaya) and Sashida (Headmaster) delivered the most inspiring lectures on the aims and ideals of the Vidyalaya and the institution as a whole. At 3 p.m. I conducted a batch of about 20 students to the Ranchi Hill at the initiative of the students themselves. On reaching the hill we enjoyed the views for a time; then I guided them into meditation for some time. We visited the Shiva Temple on the top of the hill. There I conducted the evening prayer. The sweet melody of our chorus hymn echoed and re-echoed throughout the hill, and spread all over the place. The visitors on the hill were pleased to see the Young boys trained in such a way.

On the 29th, the whole of Ranchi Town happily celebrated the Ramnavami festival marking the appearance of Sri Ramchandra. We too celebrated the occasion. I led the boys of the Yogoda Brahmacharya Vidyalaya in the early morning Prabhat Kirtan beginning at 4-30 a.m. in a barefoot procession along the encircling street of the Ashram till we reached the temple at about 5-30 a.m. I chanted from holy scriptures, selected Chapters from Srimad Bhagavad Gita and Upanishadas. We visited Tapoban in the afternoon where a Ramnavami fair was held.

On the 6th April, it was decided that all the students and staff would visit Jonha and Hundru falls on the 7th on foot. My right foot was seriously injured during a football game on 1st April. Hence, it would not be possible for me to join the pleasure trip. I felt sorry at the thought of my inability to participate in the excursion. The, distance from Vidyalaya to Jonha is 21 miles and from Jonha to Hundru is 11 miles. If I could go to Jonha by train still I would have to walk several miles. However, after supper, I sat for meditation which continued upto 1 a.m. Then I went to bed. When I woke up at 4-10 a.m., I was very thankful to God and Guru as I was completely fit. All the boys and staff had started on foot at 4 a.m.; and seven on bicycles. Several very young boys who could not walk for such a long tour were waiting for the train with a teacher to lead them. I joined the last batch. The distance from Jonha station to Jonha falls is nearly two and half miles. There is a marble temple near the falls. In the evening after prayer, we sat for meditation. We spent the night in that Buddha temple. From 1 a.m. to 5 a.m. I was absorbed in meditation.

On Saturdays, we used to have the weekly religious meetings in the Ashram. The 5th April being a Saturday, we held the weekly meeting and Kirtan here in the solitary jungle. The whole night, except a short break, was spent in meditation. On 9th, after breakfast, a batch of students and a few teachers started for a stroll on the opposite side of the temple crossing the falls. After a while, everybody came back except three of us. We planned to visit a hill that appeared to be 10 minutes walk. However, even after walking for an hour and half, the distance appeared to be the same; hence we returned. On 10th, we started for our Ranchi Ashram at 3.30 a.m. and reached in the evening.

A few days in the Buddha Temple within the Jonha Forest

The 12th March, 1941, was scheduled for visit to Johna falls. The students and teachers were excited at the prospect of visiting a jungle and a falls for the first time, free movement, picnicking and enjoyment. The school was over after two periods. All were busy in packing. The youngest ones would go to the falls by train. Sriman Banikantha, then in-charge of the Store room was most enthusiastic among the elderly ones, because he never had been to such excursion. It was decided that the Head teacher Kshitishda would be in-charge of the youngest batch and would go to the Railway Station where all others going on foot would take rest. In the afternoon, we all assembled in the gymnasium at 5-40 p.m. Kestoda, (Sri Krishnakali Banerjee), the physical Director arranged the boys according to their height. We were arranged in two rows. Brahmachari Sadanandaji became our leader. 'Quick March' came the order from our leader, and we proceeded towards the main gate towards the Ranchi Railway Station. As we reached the main gate, our leader raised the slogan, "Guruji Ki Jai"; we reciprocated with 'Jai'. Oh! What a thrilling sensation of joy pulsated through all the cells of our being!

By half past seven, we reached the Tatisilway Station, seven miles away from our Ashram. After our meals, we spread our beddings on the platform of the station. I meditated for two hours, from 1 a.m. to 3 a.m. On the 13th, at 3 a.m, we all started from the Tatisilway Railway Station and marched towards Jonha falls. It was the 14th day of the full moon, entire area was flooded with moonlight. We reached Jonha falls at 7 a.m. On reaching Jonha station, we noticed that the name of the Jonha station had been changed to Gautamdhara in memory of Prince Gautam, the premonastic name of Lord Buddha.

The temple of Lord Buddha accommodated us all. The whole day was spent in joy. As the boys got the freedom of movement, except that they were guided by a teacher, they were jumping, diving, swimming and playing in the water of the falls. At night, Sashida from our medical department showed various kinds of pictures of Lord Buddha collected from various countries with the help of a magic lantern. Mr. Basil Cramp had donated those pictures to the Society. Then Sashida explained to the local villagers from the adjoining villages who had joined us how malaria and pox could create havoc in the villages and how to prevent them with the help of the same magic lantern.

On the 14th, after the general prayer early in the morning, I started for the falls. As I was descending towards the place where the water fell from a height of 150ft. or so, there was a new marble statue of Lord Buddha. Instead of descending further, I wended my way to the feet of Lord Buddha; facing the statue, I performed some Kriya exercises and meditated for some time. After my meditation, with that calm and peaceful mind I turned towards the falls. I was thrilled to see the view in a new light. Above was the infinite blue sky; in front were the ever green trees standing tall at the feet of the Infinite — rows after rows on different steps of the Jonha hill trying to touch the Infinite sky. Below were the waves of the living hill arrested by the great Magician by His magic word 'Halt'. On the bosom of which the waters were playing and rushing to meet their beloved sea. As the waves were playing with their brother hill, foams and minute white particles of water like dust of diamond in the sun's rays were also flying to meet their beloved. As the Ganges, on the way to the earth from the matted hairs of Lord Siva moved away everything on her way, the Gautamdhara was moving away all the stones that mere falling from time to time from the hills on both the sides of the falls.

When I turned my gaze back to the statue of Lord Buddha, I was overwhelmed with his thought. His eyes was penetrating the earth and was beholding the Infinite. He was leaving the vast kingdom, beautiful wife and child. He was in search of the beloved of the universe. He must have got some of the infinite treasure for which he renounced all that he had. The worldly chain could not tie him in the earthly attachment. His vow to get the eternal knowledge was the ideal one for all the renunciates:

Spirit as soul be aim of us all:

Beneath this banyan tree, I take this solemn vow!

Let the flesh, skin and bone dissolve. Without learning the mystery of life I resolve, From beneath this tree, I shall never be free.

For the sake of praise and enjoyments, we had forgotten the Eternal spirit. Lord! Ignite in my heart the fire of renunciation that dragged you out from the jungle of civilization. My mind was searching the Infinite in the infinite sky. Totally filled with the thought of Lord Buddha, I slowly wended my way towards his temple above where we were residing temporarily.

Thereafter, we all got down on feet a few hundred steps. Gorada (Sananda Lal Ghosh, younger brother of our Gurudeva Paramhansa Yogananda) joined us. Following the course of the falls over the solid waves of the rocks, over a mile or so, there was a lake. At noon, we returned to the Buddha temple. At 3 p.m., Banikantha, Brahmachari Sadananda and I went to the opposite side of the falls and meditated for a long time in the lonely spot. At 6 p.m., we all returned to the temple. After the evening prayer, we sat for meditation. Sashida showed lantern slides to the villagers. Our return journey was fixed on the morning of 16th. A group of devotees promised to send a bus to fetch us. In the morning of the 15th, I went to the falls again to meditate at the feet of Lord Buddha. Banikantha and two senior students requested me to visit the hill on the other side of the temple. Through the villages, we walked about six miles towards the hill when Banikantha declined to proceed further. However, on request he agreed to walk for a few more minutes brining us to another falls in that jungle. There we discovered an embolic tree (Amloki). I was resting for a while and I noticed a villager was drinking something at a distance. When the villager went away, I reached the place and found out a very small spring out of a fissure in the rock. The clear water was collected in a ditch. The boys were very thirsty but were hesitating to drink the water. Though I had no thirst, to free their mind from any doubt, I drank a little water from the fountain. Then the boys drank water to their hearts' content. Then we returned to the temple.

On the 16th morning as the boys were busy repacking their bags and baggages, the bus came. The boys rushed to inform us of the arrival of the bus. At 7.45 a.m. the bus whistled on slowly carrying us all. Gradually, it gained speed as the road became free. Brahmachari Santanandaji and Br. Sadanandaji resumed the marching songs. Nearly the whole of our journey was spent singing the following song:

"Be hero at works. Don't be afraid and keep your head straight. Forgetting the differences proceed onward. God is with us, and success is sure. Oh, behold the unity among the different caste, colour and creed. The people of the world will be astonished to see the great united nation of India. We are thirty three crores, hence we are not weak. We may be poor but not weak in spirit. The fortune is coming in the sky of India again. Behold the sun is rising!"

The bus took only forty-five minutes to reach Ranchi.

I have already described how we used to celebrate The Foundation Day of the Vidyalaya. Hence, instead of describing the function for the year 1942, let me mention certain other things. Every year, we discussed various issues pertaining to the development of the Vidyalaya. Sports, yogasans, songs, drama, recitation and lecture were the main items of the function. In my lecture, I focussed on the history and the aim of the Vidyalaya.

About twenty five or twenty six years ago, out of realisation of the pitiable condition of the boys, due to wrong teaching, came the thought of establishment of an ideal school in the foot prints of the rishis for the harmonious development of body, mind and soul of the boys. At that time Paramhansa Yoganandaji had an opportunity to attend the religious conference held at Khardaha along with Swami Dhirananda Giri and Swami Satyananda Giri. He was charmed to see the simplest behaviour of Maharaja Manindra Chandra Nandi who was then looking after the management of the function.

Swami Dhirananda Giri had just passed the M.A. examination. Swami Satyananda Giri and Paramahansa Yoganandaji had already passed the B.A. examination. They chalked out a plan to establish an ideal school and started coaching a few boys in Calcutta. They used to meditate regularly and used to conduct religious meetings on Saturdays. According to their plan, they approached Maharaja Manindra Chandra and handed over their plan for the proposed ideal school to him. After going through the proposal, Maharaja said, "You are God sent. I too am thinking along similar lines. But for this noble work, we need selfless workers. Where shall we get such renunciates?" In reply Paramhansa Yoganandaji said, "We will take charge and will do the work ourselves". Maharaja promised to help them. Paramhansa Yoganandaji then invited Maharaja to their small cottage, the venue of their activities. On their request, Maharaja visited the place and was highly pleased to see their activities.

Under the patronage of the Maharaja, the school started at Dihika in 1917 initially as Brahma Vidyalaya. This created confusion with the existing 'Brahma' sect of people. To avoid the confusion, the name was changed to Brahmacharya Vidyalaya. At Dihika, the institution became famous, and Maharaja promised to build the required building. But his advisory board advised him to shift the institution to Kashimbazar in the District of Ranchi instead of spending thousands of rupees at Dihika.

During the World War I, the British Government received a large sum of money from Maharaja Manindra Chandra; in exchange, Maharaja got the Kashirnbazar jail. He was then known as Maharaja of Kashimbazar. According to the advice of the advisory board, Maharaja ordered the School Committee to shift the Vidyalaya to Kashimbazar. At that time, Kashimbazar was very unhealthy. The boys were suffering from malaria. Paramahansaji requested Maharaja to change the place. Maharaja shifted the Vidyalaya to "Jamai bari" near Kashimbazar. There was no relief to the suffering of the boys. Finally, at the request of Paramhansa Yoganandaji, Maharaja shifted the Vidyalaya to a bungalow near Ranchi Station temporarily in the middle of 1918. Maharaja then advised Paramahansaji to find out a suitable place for the Vidyalaya. There was a piece of land 40 bighas (more than 15 acres) at Madhukam for sale under Maharaja of Gumla. Maharaja Manindra Chanara Nandi purchased the same. A branch School of the Brahmacharya Vidyalaya was started there with the very young boys.

It was decided that when Maharaja would visit Ranchi, the bungalow should be vacated; but Maharaja never visited the place. Afterwards, Paramahansaji purchased the land from Maharaja Manindra Chandra's son, Maharaja Srish Chandra Nandi in 1935 and renamed the school as "Yogoda Satsanga Brahmacharya Vidyalaya".

The ideal of the Vidyalaya was harmonious development of body, mind and soul. The threefold suffering of men could not be mitigated through usual means. Paramahansaji discovered the yogic exercises for the physical development, yoga techniques of meditation for the improvement of mind and soul. By keeping the company of the renunciate teachers, the boys would get necessary instructions for the unfolding the real person within. For the harmonious development of body, mind and soul, it was not necessary that everyone should be a renunciate. Renunciation was a mental quality. Hence, the boys should see that the purpose for which their guardians had sent them to the Vidyalaya should be fulfilled. They should examine their heart, rather introspect within themselves and see their progress. The boys should be devoted to the ideals of the institution, love fellow brothers, and should follow the instructions of their teachers. It was the instruction of the scriptures to follow the ideal with dogged determination. They should be loyal to their teachers and the institution. Without loyalty, devotion, control of senses no one could achieve the goal of life. The boys should practice regularly the preliminary yoga techniques which they had got from the Acharya. The teachers, and elderly boys and workers who had got the Kriya Yoga exercises should perform them regularly according to the directions of their Acharya Gurus. They, too, should be devoted to God and Gurus, loyal to the cause and love the fellow brothers of the Institution as their nearest ones. Then and then only they would be able to fight the battle of life well. I urged all to have faith in the words of Gurus, to surrender themselves at the feet of their Divine Father. Then, I believe, you would get salvation. You all should not hanker after the fruits of your work, because that would divert your mind from the God, the goal of life.

On behalf of the Institution and the Vidyalaya, I pray to God and Gurus, for the all round success in life of us all. Aum Shanti!

Let me, now, share about the success of the boys of the Vidyalaya in physical development. From my early childhood, I used to practise Yogasana regularly. When I joined the Y.S.S. Eastern Headquarter at Ranchi, I used to practise the same regularly in my room. The interested teachers and students too, used to get Yogasana lessons from me. But after a few months, I was appointed as Yogasana teacher, in addition to my other duties mentioned previously. Hence from the very beginning of my joining the Ranchi Headquarters, I had to teach Yogasana to the staff and students of the Vidyalaya. The teachers used to come to my room for the lessons. I took regular Yogasana classes for the boys. From time to time, I used to take competitive examination among the boys and distributed prizes on merit. From time to time, the physical education department used to organise 'All Bihar Body Building and Muscle Posing Competition' at our premises. Various schools and colleges used to take part in that Competition. Boys of our Vidyalaya always used to get the first prize in Yogasana and occasionally in the other items of the physical show, such as weight lifting and muscle posing.

In the beginning, Sri Krishna Kali Banerjee, the then Physical Education Director (student of Sri Bishnu Charan Ghosh, well known body-builder, youngest brother of Paramahansaji Yoganandaji) used to organise the competition. Later when Sri K. Banerjee left the institution, Sri Sasi Bose Mullick, Assistant Physical Education Director became the Director and organised the competition for a few years. Though the boys used to get the first prize in Yogasana, once I allowed the boys to compete individually in order to see the results. On that occasion, I selected the first boys in Yogasana from each class. There were three judges who used to judge separately, and on the basis of the aggregate, the Chief Judge would declare the results. Our boys secured the highest marks. Not only they secured the highest marks but also each one of our Vidyalaya defeated all their competitors from other institutions. Hence after reconsideration it was decided that the first prize should be awarded to the Vidyalaya, and the other prizes should be given to other institutions in order of their merit. It was decided by the judges that instead of trophy, cash prize should be given to the Vidyalaya boys as first prize so that the amount could be divided by the teacher-in-charge among the boys.

On another occasion, our boys defeated all other competitors in weight lifting. A student of Ranchi College defeating all other competitors had established a record. Two boys of our Vidyalaya, Sri Benoy Banerjee (15 years) and his younger brother Sri Sisir Banerjee (14 years) appeared and stood before us. The elderly college students were surprised to see such young boys from a school as competitors. However, within five minutes, Benoy and Sisir defeated the Ranchi College student breaking his record.

I was the Yogasana teacher of our different Yogoda Centres. I used to invite boys of other Y.S.S. Centres to Ranchi for competition in Yogasana. Once there was a competition between Y.S.S. Ranchi and

Y.S.S.K. Lakhanpur on football. The boys of the Y.S.S.K. Vidyapith, Lakhanpur defeated the boys of Y.S.S. Ranchi by 4-1 goals. The boys in the Vidyalaya used to get training in Yogasana in the morning, every alternate day. On other days, they got training in physical exercises in the gymnasium under the Physical Education Director of our institution. In the afternoons, sports were a daily affair. Before teaching Yogasana, I used to impart lessons On 'Yogoda exercises' (free hand exercises) that I learned directly from Paramhansa Yoganandaji in 1935-36. Hence, during Asana-Class, the boys had to practise Yogoda exercises. Due to such special skills and qualities, when the boys enrolled themselves for higher studies they got various kinds of scholarships such as free boarding and lodging or free tuition or cash money. In the academics, too, the results of boys were good.

The secrets of success in Yogasana and other physical cultures were:

1. The boys used to practise the Yogic exercises regularly under trained Physical Education Directors and Masters of Yogasana.
2. Yogasana was one of the subjects of examination along with other arts and science subjects. I used to take regularly Gita class as a subject under religion. Yogasana was recognised as practical classes under religion. In order to secure good marks the boys used to take interest in Yogasana.
3. In order to create interest, I used to give prizes to three boys in each class in the order of merit.
4. In leisure time or Sundays, the boys used to practise difficult yogic poses. I used to help them.
5. I used to practise my yogic exercises along with them, so that they may understand correct postures, and also get inspiration from my practical demonstration.
6. I used to teach the boys Yogasana according to their adaptability and the nature and formation of their bodies. For example, Utthita Padmasana can be performed in four different ways. I used to demonstrate all the four ways. Some of the boys could perform the asana in one way, others in the second way and so on. Some of the boys could perform in more than one way.
7. Due to the prenatal tendencies towards the yogic exercises, some of the boys could adopt or learn the art more quickly than the others.

8. The judges or the persons entrusted to organise the inter-school and college competition on Yogasana used to select the most common yogic poses like, Mayurasan, Omkarasan, Baddhapadmasan, Paschimottanasan, Sirasasan and Vrischikasan so that the average student could perform the same. The students of our Vidyalaya could demonstrate all the Yogasanas correctly.
9. The boys generally used to come to our Vidyalaya at 6 to 8 years of age. From that tender age when all the muscles, tissues are flexible, the boys used to practise regularly the yogic exercises for years together. Hence, they could master all the yogic exercises during the five to eight years of their stay in our School.

On the Foundation Day function of the Vidyalaya, on the 22nd March, 1954, at 3-30 p.m. Acharya Brahmachari Rabinarayanji from Puri Y.S.S. Centre was requested to preside. The boys who finished the school career received Diplomas in the form of school leaving certificate. The best boy was awarded the special Diploma certificate. In the meeting, Girinda, Sri Abanindra Mohan Lahiri, Superintendent of Y.S.S.K. Vidyapith, Lakhanpur, Purulia delivered lectures on The Principles of Yogoda. I was asked to explain the aim of the meeting.

In my address on the Foundation Day of our Vidyalaya, I emphasized on the utility of celebrating the Foundation Day; and also on the results of ordinary instructions devoid of moral and spiritual values. Without appreciation of the moral values, no one can get real happiness and peace of mind. The right education for young boys was our aim and we should consider all round development of body, mind and soul. We should periodically examine whether we were lagging behind the ideal on which the Vidyalaya was founded; if so, what should be our duty to attain the target.

Should we consider these three points every year, on this particular day, we would know our duties for the future. Let us first consider whether we are at the right track as we began our journey? Secondly, let us examine whether we were going strong or lagging behind. Thirdly, if we were proceeding in right direction, what should we do for quicker development. The Vidyalaya was founded with one boy. The growth in the number of students indicates that we have progressed. Harmonious development of body, mind and soul was our ideal. We were following the same. Hence, we are not lagging behind, rather we are on the right path. Considering all these points, we may appreciate the utility of observing the Foundation Day.

After the evening prayer, we had one hour for group meditation. After the group meditation, Abani Babu (Sri Abanindra Mohan Lahiri) discussed with me regarding our Y.S.S. Vidyalaya. He asked me, "Which quality in man makes one the greatest person in the world?" I replied, "Love for the people of the world", in other words we can say, "Love for the Universe or universal love". The Universal love appears when the real man within fully develops. When we get the knowledge of the Supreme One, we are qualified to know everything. Hence, our first duty is to realise Him. Sadhana is necessary for the acquisition of His knowledge. As it was not possible to perform Sadhana for twenty-four hours in a day, selfless work was necessary. If a person works seeking fruits or results of his work, he would get hurt when failure would visit. If the person performs for self interest, he gets great shock when he finds that the fellow persons were trying to find faults, or playing mischief with the person for whom he was working. Hence, in order to please God, everybody should work selflessly.

Initially, one may not do selfless work. Every person would start his work seeking self-interest; after getting several shocks, one would learn to act selflessly without seeking the fruits of his work. Only then, he would get the glimpse of the love for the people of the Universe. When the devotees would advance on the spiritual path, they would get the power and desire for the performance of the selfless work. Without devotion and love for God, the Sadhana would be dry; and the devotee won't find pleasure in his work. When the devotee would pray and worship God with devotion and love for Him, He would shower blessings on him, and the power to work selflessly. Due to the blessings of God and Guru the devotee would get the power of endurance during hard tests in the field of work. Otherwise, it is impossible to perform selflessly; the love for all would remain at a great distance. He is the greatest person in the world who is a true lover of God, because he is full in every respect. And the followers of such devotees and lovers of God too, become full in every respect. The Omnipresence, Omnipotence and Omniscience power of God are transmitted in the true devotees of God. Lord Jesus Christ, Sri Ramakrishna Paramahansa Deva and such other persons were a few among the greatest persons of the world. Abani Babu said, "I may agree with you, but will everybody agree with you?"

I replied: "Yes, everybody will not agree with me. But the real worker will surely agree because he is advancing in the spiritual path. Those, who do not work or meditate, will not agree. We need not care for their views."

We celebrated the Bengali New Years Day in our Vidyalaya. It was 15th April, 1955. I conducted the morning prayer and the group meditation for 55 minutes with the boys; then Guru Puja in my own room followed by group meditation with the teachers and with the inmates of the Y.S.S. Ashram, Ranchi. After meditation, I explained a few passages from "The Master Said" by Paramahansa Yoganandaji. At 3 p.m. I presided over the general meeting with the boys and staff of the Vidyalaya and the inmates of the Ashram, Ranchi. In the meeting, the boys took the following solemn vow:

- We will meditate more attentively and devote more time this year than previous years.
- We will observe the rules and regulations of the institution more rigidly.
- We will not do such works which are against the ideal of the institution or create displeasure to all.
- We will study our lessons always mindfully and remain as brothers.

Recitation, songs, speeches were the main items in the meeting. I delivered the Presidential Speech in the meeting.

On the 1st October, 1950, Dr. N.N. Das, one of the Directors of Y.S.S. & S.R.F. in India came to Y.S.S. Ranchi. He took several group photographs of the staff and students; seven group photographs of Yogasan demonstrated by the boys; he also took photos of ten different most difficult poses of Yogasans by the boys. The photographs of Siva Temple, dispensary, football play by the boys and such other activities were also taken by him.

On the 2nd October 1950, we observed the birthday of Mahatma Gandhi. General prayer was held at 5:50 a.m. After the general prayer, we sang Mahatma Gandhi's favourite song 'Raghupati Raghaba Raja Ram ...' After Kirtan, the photographs of drill, physical shows, Yogasanas, etc. were taken. At 3 p.m. there was the general meeting in which Brahmachari Sri Prakas, the General Secretary, who had come that morning, Dr. N.N. Das, Sri Ramkishore Ray, the Directors of Y.S.S. & S.R.F. were also present in the meeting. I spoke on the life of Mahatma Gandhi.

During my long stay at Ranchi Institution, from 21st January, 1939 to 2nd November, 1959, there were many changes in the constitution of the Society, and also my duties and responsibilities. Around the activities of the Y.S.S. Vidyalaya, I had many realisations. Once Divine Mother mysteriously appeared before me and advised me to note down the words after reproducing them in my mother tongue, "I love and scold my God".

For a long time, Her words were resounding in my heart. I realised that the Supreme Spirit (God) was playing the Divine play, assuming the different forms. The children that were under my care were God, indeed!

Chapter 16
Mahatma Gandhi

Mahatma Gandhi visited Ranchi many times. He visited our Yogoda Brahmacharya Vidyalaya and spent some time in our Guest House. During his stay at the Vidyalaya, he used to spin threads from cotton, a bundle of which was preserved in our Yogoda Museum. Several times he visited Nibaranpur, Ranchi where our boys from Yogoda Brahmcharya Vidyalaya used to go as volunteers to control the rush of public visitors.

Mahatma Gandhi was a world reformer and a great political saviour who came on earth to conquer the world with his invincible weapon of love and understanding, and to establish the universal brotherhood with truth as the God in our heart. By his suffering, renunciation and universal love, he made many friends in the world. By the example of his practical life, he taught the people of the world to feel themselves as brothers and the way to harmonize their differences. He used to say that the teachings of Lord Krishna (in Srimad Bhagavad Gita), Christ and Tolstoy exercised a great influence to mould his life.

On 17th December 1945, I visited Mahatma Gandhi in his Saiyadpur Ashram, a few miles away from Calcutta with my friend Kaviraj Jagabandhu Das. We reached the Ashram at about 4 p.m. We first visited the dairy farm, workshop and other places of interest. Then we went to the place at 4-30 pm where Mahatmaji would come to meet people. At that time, thousands of men and women from far and near used to visit him in order to get spiritual counsels directly from him. To keep the people peaceful, songs were played through the record player. One of those songs was the same which, on 16th March 1941, we sang on our return journey from Johna Falls (Gautamdhara) to Yogoda Satsanga, Ranchi at 8 pm. A few lines are:

"Be calm in the performance of religion.
Be hero at the time of doing works.
Don't be afraid and keep your head straight

Forgetting the differences proceed ahead.
God is with us, success is sure to be."

The other songs were from Rabindranath Tagore.

Mahatma Gandhi arrived at the prayer platform at 5.20 p.m. The whispering sounds that were going on stopped completely; our entire attention and eyes were fixed on him. The whole gathering was sanctified with the holy vibration of 'Aum'. The general prayer (daily opening prayer) started; the first verse of Isa Upanishad was read out and explained. Three prayers were said as concluding prayers, one from the Hindu scriptures, one from Bible, and the last one from Koran. During the prayer, the 2nd Chapter of the Srimad Bhagavad Gita was recited and explained.

At the end of the meeting, he requested the public not to travel by illegal means. Reports had reached him that some of the visitors used to travel in trains to visit him without purchasing ticket; some stopped trains by pulling the alarm chain of the train. He intimated us before leaving the prayer platform that he would go to Shantiniketan on 18th December, the next morning.

The salient features of the prayer or the spiritual significance that we experienced was: the moment he arrived at the prayer altar, the life force from the coccyx gradually started rising, and it could not ascend to the top of the head due to the earth connection of my physical body, as we had to sit down on the grassy meadow in front of the prayer altar. My friend, Sri Jagbandhu Kaviraji was a Yogi. He had got his initiation from Swami Bholananda Giri, the founder of Bholananda Sanyas Ashram Laltanbagh, Hardwar. He too, told me that he had the same experience of the upward flow of the life force. He further narrated to me one significant incident of his life:

"Once we were sitting in front of our Gurudeva (Swami Bholananda Giri). At that time, the first political movement of the congress had begun. One of our spiritual brothers, out of curiosity, mentioned the name of Sri Karamchand Gandhi, who had acquired name and fame in that congress movement. On hearing the name, with folded hands, he touched the forehead giving his homage, the way we pay homage to our superiors or God. The spiritual brother was surprised; he asked, 'Gurudeva, why did you salute on hearing the name of an ordinary person?'

Gurudeva replied, 'Whom you are thinking as an ordinary person, to whom I am paying my respect is not an ordinary person. He is the incarnate of 'Ganadevata'. (Ganadevata is the God of success, generally known as 'Ganesha'. Gana means mass, isha or devata means lord, hence Ganesha or Ganadevta is the lord of the masses i.e. the leader of the country)".

My friend now is a 'Swami', a renunciate Yogi, living permanently in his Guru's Ashram at Hardwar.

Once, I had a talk with my Gurudev, Paramahansa Yoganandaji regarding Mahatama Gandhi. He said, "Mahatama Gandhi is a 'Gnana Yogi'. In this life time, he will get full realization of self i.e. Salvation. We too, in the same way pay our respect to him.

Chapter 17

Mandaleswar (108) Sri Sri Mahadevananda Giri Maharaj

On 19th August 1937, I visited Swami Mahadevananda Giri Maharaj, along with our spiritual brother Sri Bhupati Bhattacharya. At 2 p.m., we reached Bholananda Sannyas Ashram, Bhawanipur, Calcutta. He was explaining the Holy Srimad Bhagavad Gita to a gathering. After the Gita Class was over, we took our seats. He said, "If you have any question, please feel free to ask".

I enquired, "How can we get unconditional devotion?" In response, first, he remarked, "There is no way to get it." After a pause, he commented, "Yes, there is a mention of it in Srimad Bhagavad Gita. The unconditional love is also known as 'Para Bhakti', 'Eka Bhakti', 'Nistha Bhakti' and 'Suddha Bhakti'. We have in us the seeds of both good and bad pre-natal tendencies. The bad or evil seeds of the prenatal tendencies grow very quickly. We shall have to destroy those evil seeds and shall have to culture the seeds of the good pre-natal ones. First, we shall have to keep good company and to practise 'Sadhana' under the guidance of a true Guru. Regular control of the senses, that is, self-discipline is very essential in the path of 'Sadhana'. If we can proceed on the path of God in this way, the seed of 'Bhakti' (devotion) will germinate and will grow quickly; and in time, it will be ripe and become 'deep' which is known as 'Suddha Bhakti'. I enquired again,

"How long it takes to get salvation if we practise 'Sadhana' regularly under the guidance of a Guru"? he replied, "Generally, twelve years."

On 8th June 1941, Mandaleswarji, with Swami Iswarananda Giri and Swami Satchidananda Giri (I was then Brahmachari Animananda) arrived at our Yogoda Ashram, Ranchi, at our invitation. We had already arranged a reception for them in our Ashram. Swami Satyananda Giriji requested Mandaleswarji to say (katha bolun) something.

Mandaleswarji explained, "The word 'Katha' is the combination of two letters: 'Ka' and 'tha'. The first alphabet 'Ka' means the ever-joyous Brahma. This blissful Brahma is the purpose or essence of 'Katha'. From the word 'Katha', 'Kathakatha' is created." Regarding the above "Katha", he cited several verses from the Vedas, supporting his statement.

We shall have to achieve the ever-blessed one and ever-joyous one in this world of sorrow. When a man is born, he cries. From that time the troubles start. The man has to come to this world when his virtues are exhausted. He goes to hell if he performs sins in abundance. When the virtuous and sinful works are balanced that man comes back to this world. Though this earth is better in comparison to hell, still it is not free from misery, pain and troubles. It is impossible to get unmixed happiness here on this earth. Happiness is defiled due to the pursuance of malice, envy, jealousy, anger, pride and other vices. Even in Heaven, pure happiness is wanting, which we came to know from the legendary tale of Aristanemi in Yogabasista. The pious Rajarshi Aristanemi, being free from worldly attachments, handed over the responsibility of the kingdom and went to Gandhamadan hill for mediation. The spies of Indra were everywhere. Their duty was to supply Indra the information regarding the religious or pious works of the devotees on earth. If any devotee would perform intense worship by fire ceremonies and deep meditation, the king of heaven would try to test the depth of his devotion and renunciation. The spy furnished the information of the pious deeds of Aristanemi to Indra. Aristanemi was one of the friends of Indra. The king Indra sent one of his spies to Aristanemi to bring his friend to heaven in a plane decorated with the musical party consisting of celestial nymphs, gods, demi-gods like Gandharva, Siddya, Yakshya, Kinnar and full of all sorts of musical instruments and advised the spy to intimate his friend that he need not have to meditate any more for the sake of heaven. On receiving the order from the king, the spy immediately arrived at the Gandhamadan hill and conveyed the words of the king to Aristanemi. The king Aristanemi, being doubtful asked the spy: "Oh good soul, please tell me all about the merits and demerits of heaven". The spy said, "The people can enjoy supreme joy in heaven due to pious work. Of course, it is true there are gradations or durations in joy of heaven according to quantum and intensity of the pious work. During the time of enjoyment in heaven, there are the challenges among equals — envy, jealousy, pride etc. among people at different stages. When the quantum of pious work gets exhausted, people will have to return to the earth." On hearing the spy, the king Aristanemi commented: "I don't like to enjoy such type of heaven, I want unadulterated joy, you may return to your heaven, I bow to you," On receiving the above news, Indra directed his friend to the Sage Valmiki for true knowledge.

The birth itself indicates sorrow. After birth, the individual soul has to suffer various types of pain and sorrow. Gradually, infirmity comes due to old age. The body bends. The man has to walk with a stick in hand. A stage comes when he cannot even walk with the help of a stick. Due to weakness, the body shivers and he falls down. The power of seeing and hearing become weak and one by one all the teeth fall. Gradually, he is tormented with the fear of death. At the end, he is bound to sleep his last sleep. Everybody has to suffer in this way; even great men are no exception.

If you like to acquire happiness, give up all desires and meditate; then the heart will be purified and you will get uninterrupted joy. In order to know how to meditate properly, you will have to go to a God-realised Guru with devotion. It is stated in the scripture : "Awake, arise, sleep no more."

"Oh Divine ones, lead us to Eternal Bliss, so that we can hear the words of God with the ears, we can see His beauty with the eyes and with a calm body and mind, we can get the desired life in order to worship Him. Enjoy the life being unattached, do not covet any other's riches. If you can meditate in this way, your mind will be free from all material desires and you will get Him, the Eternal Joy".

On 11th April, 1946, I visited Mandaleswarji again in Ranchi. He was imparting advice to a group of devotees; mostly women. The instruction was: "Always think that you are doing all the household duties as the service of God. When you will be unable to serve, pray to God, "Why have you deprived me of the ability and the opportunity of service? Please give me the power to serve you."

'God is residing in everybody, as 'Vaiswanar' (Vaiswanar is the God of digestive fire). He is receiving the food, which you cook, residing in every body. During the work of cooking and other house-hold duties, always remember Him and mentally chant His name'.

'On this earth, there can be no final happiness. Birth, disease, infirmity, old age and death are all unhappiness. Due to sins and in order to work out the evil karmas through sufferings, man comes to this earth. There is no real mental peace here on this earth. As for example, look into the lives of so-called happy kings and presidents of different nations. What to speak of the worldly kings, look into the lives of our ideal kings, the saviours of souls, Sri Ramchandra and Sri Krishna, even though by chanting the name of Sri Ramchandra and Sri Krishna our sins are destroyed'.

Let us examine the life history of Sri Ramchandra, whose name has so much power. At the time of coronation, He had to go to the forest for fourteen years. During that time, He had to travel in the forest on foot from one place to another. At that time, His wife was stolen. He had to fight to rescue His wife. After returning to Ayodhya, He could not get peace of mind. Though He had accepted His wife after testing Her chastity, yet for the satisfaction of His subjects, He had to reject His wife. As He used to love Her from the core of His heart, this rejection gave Him unending sorrow. Then, He had to part with His dear brother, Lakshman. At the end, due to the pangs of separation of His dear wife and brother, He committed suicide by drowning in the river Sarayu.

Now let us turn our attention to the life history of Lord Sri Krishna. He was born in prison. He was brought up among the cowboys. He had to roam for the whole day in the meadows with the cows. He could never return home before evening. He had to fight with the demons like Aghasur and Bakasur. When he killed the king Kansa, opposite party attacked him with millions of soldiers and for fear of life, he fled to Dwarka. There, he had to witness the death of his 1,60,000 children and grandchildren in the battle of Musal. How tremendous was the mourning for the children and grand children! Then, there was the spread of false scandal pertaining to theft though He had not taken the Samantak jewel. At the end, he had to leave his mortal coil due to an arrow of hunter. This is the way of world, even for such exalted souls.

No one can boast of happiness, here on this earth. He, who is proud of happiness, gets cheated. But the man who is proud of sorrow is a clever person. To take refuge at the feet of God is the only way to be free from the torments of sorrow. Meditation, japa, kirtan, etc. are also ways to conquer sorrow'. I asked, "Your Holiness commented that the birth of a person is due to pre-natal sins and that this world is devoid of happiness. But the Vedas, the Upanisadas declare otherwise. It is stated in the Upanisadas that creation, preservation and destruction emanate from 'Ananda', that is, joy."

Mandalwswarji replied: 'Matter or inanimate object is not born. The soul or spirit is born. The nature of the spirit is joy. Hence, the declaration that the spirit is joy is right. But what I have expressed, a few minutes before, regarding the existence of sorrow, is apparently visible, but in reality not. Though apparently the individual suffers or feels sorrow, in reality the spirit does not lose the inherent joy. Now take, for example, water. It is a chemical compound and not a mixture. This chemical compound is composed of two parts of hydrogen and one part of oxygen. The nature of hydrogen is inflammable. When ignited, it emits flame. The nature of the oxygen is to help combustion but it does not burn itself. But water is neither a combustible substance nor it helps to burn; rather it extinguishes the fire. Then, we may conclude that in water, both hydrogen and oxygen have lost their inherent nature. Is it not so?" I replied in the affirmative. Mandaleswarji continued: "The nature of water is coolness. Boil it and try to feel it. You won't be able to touch it. It appears that it has lost its own nature but on cooling, it regains its own previous nature."

To segregate the two elements in water, electricity is passed through it. Collect the segregated elements. After examining we will come to know that the two elements are nothing but hydrogen and oxygen. If at the stage of water, hydrogen and oxygen had lost their real nature, then they could not get back their original nature. Thus, the conclusion is this: The gases had lost their nature apparently and not really, when they were in chemical compound, and water apparently had lost its nature at the boiling stage.

Similarly, in the world, the soul apparently loses its joyous nature when tormented by sorrow and pain, but in reality, not. You may argue that a third person was responsible for the creation of a chemical compound and boiling the water. In the case of the world too, mind is the third person responsible for the feeling of pleasure and pain. During the absence of mind, we don't feel pleasure and pain. In deep sleep, the action of mind is absent. During the stage of chloroform too, the action of mind is absent. Hence at that stage, there is no existence of the world. We feel the existence of the world when awake and in dreams. In dreams, there is the apparent existence of the world, though in reality there is no such existence. It is stated in the scriptures that during sleep, the spirit realizes its own glory. Similarly, when awake, the mind realizes its own glory." I said: "I agree, that the spirit realizes its own glory through the instrumentality of mind. But it appears to us that the mind is different, hence, it appears that there are many souls. Please solve the problem."

Mandaleswarji continued: "The spirit is one. The mind too is one but appears many. For example, there is one telescope. The constituent elements of all the lenses are the same, though there are differences in their power. Similarly our mind serves the purpose of the lens residing in the body. It is creating the world."

It is stated in the scriptures, "The Soul Life is Absolute Unity; to appear as the separate and diverse manifestations of the creation He wears a false or unreal veil." At 8.30 p.m., I returned to Yogoda Ashram, Ranchi.

On 14th October, 1947, I met Mandaleswarji, again in Sri Bholananda Sannyas Ashram, Calcutta for full one hour. We discussed religious matters. I enquired: "What is the difference between fate and human effort?"

"Both are unreal, their existence is apparent. There is no existence but Supreme Spirit. If we recognize the individual soul as the doer, then according to Vedanta, it is false. Because soul is Absolute Unity. It is transcendental, unchanged, unruffled, and at rest. Hence, there is no motion in the transcendental unity. How then can we account for His work? If you think that the effort is for the realization of God, it becomes baseless too, because here again arises the question of duality, one is trying to get the other. All the Vedas and Vedanta declare in one voice the existence of One and not two".

I responded citing several verses from the Upanisadas supporting the creation and also quoting some verses from other scriptures supporting my statement.

He commented: "How you will be able to prove the separate and diverse existence? All the four basic laws for proof do not apply here. The first basic law for proving the existence of any substance depends on the eyes. The sight is faulty and, hence, we cannot rely upon it. The eyes cannot see the very small substance, or very near (within the eyes) substance or any object at infinity or in deep darkness or in dazzling light and during sleep. Hence, the proof depending upon sight is untenable. The second proof, inference, also depends upon the object of sight. Hence, in the same way it is also untenable."

"If you argue that Nature coming in contact with the Spirit becomes activated or receives the power of work or like the logic of a lame person sitting on the shoulder of a blind man can walk, both are untenable. Because Nature is inanimate, Matter has no power of work. Spirit is transcendental. He cannot lead the Matter". I told him, "I understand, what you are aiming at. That is our goal, there is no doubt about it. It is true when there is no existence of duality then who will see whom and with what. At that stage, the devotee himself becomes Brahma. So long the devotee does not reach that state of Oneness, we cannot deny the existence of duality".

He commented, "Yes, that's true. That is why the scriptures too, on many occasions, had supported duality but the Supreme Spirit, the Absolute Unity is our aim and goal." After a pause, he said, "Through the power of 'Sadhana' (meditation), we can destroy or burn the accumulated past Karmas (Sanchita Karma) but the pre-natal work that are in action now, cannot be destroyed, they must be worked out. There is no other alternative to it".

My next visit was on 12th October 1954 at Sri Sri Bholananda Sannyas Ashram, Calcutta. At the end of his instructions to the devotees, I ventured one question: "Those emancipated souls, who appear on this earth perform so many works; do they suffer or get in bondage for such actions?"

Mandaleswarji commented, "Whatever they do, is unattached. Their mind is always with God, that is, in tune with the Divine Father. Hence, they are free and unattached while performing their duty. Besides, during their stay in this world, though it appears to the public that they have fallen down from the transcendental state of consciousness, the real nature of the soul is not lost. When the seed is transformed into a tree, it appears to us that the seed has lost its real nature in the tree, but after some time, it reappears in the tree as flowers and seeds.

What is absent in the beginning, and in the end; in the middle too, that is absent. The true nature of the soul, being ever-free before and after; in the middle too, apparent bondage is false. But this apparent bondage, though unreal or false, appears to be real or true, like the dancing of the moon in the water. It is unreal (bondage of the soul) like the movie show. In both, there is no horse or elephant, but in the cinema hall on the projection screen we see them. In the beginning and after (Cinema) projection they were absent, hence, in the middle too, they are unreal. The animals, that are visible in the cinema house, cannot be killed by fire arms or we can't get blood by firing at them. All the shows are played after switching off the electric lights. Similarly, during ignorance, the play of the world is possible. At the advent of knowledge, no play is visible".

I remarked: "The matters of the movie show are taken from some true facts. Hence, at the root there is the truth."

He responded, "Suppose you have seen the play 'Sakuntala'. In the house you may see the figures of Sakuntala and Dusyanta but the players who took the part of the main actor (Dusyanta) and actress (Sakuntala) are not real Sakuntala or Dusyanta. Besides, it is not the same age or time when the real Sakuntala and Dusyanta played. Hence, the root of the show too is unreal".

On 22nd May, 1939 at 5 p.m., I reached our Yogoda Ashram, Puri to spend the summer vacation. On 12th June, 1939, we got intimation that Mandaleswarji would visit our Puri Ashram on 14th June, 1939. I went to the Puri Station to receive him. After our dinner, I had the opportunity to meet him. In course of our conversation, he divulged many incidents of his life to me. While narrating such incidents, he explained how the "Prarabdha Karma" was worked out in his own life. He also explained to me, citing examples form his own life, that "God takes full charge of the life of his devotees, if they have full faith and solely depend on Him".

He said, "Many devotees believe that God is all powerful and that He is omnipresent, but they cannot always believe His benevolent power. Suppose, the only son of a devotee, due to Karmic law, is dead; is it possible for the devotee, to think that God is a well-wisher and that whatever he does, is for our good? But the renunciates should always think that He is the best well-wisher of mankind."

Mandaleswarji commented, "people generally go to cinema for recreation but some discover Vedantic truth out of it". Once he had gone to a cinema at the request of his two friends but he realised the Vedantic truth there. He continued: "In the cinema house, those, who are sitting very near the screen, cannot enjoy the play well due to the reflected light of the screen. It appears to them that the figures are somewhat trembling. But those, who have taken their seats far away from the screen (1st class and box seat), can enjoy the play".

"Similarly the devotees who perform some sort of Yogic techniques regularly and have got the vision of the inner light feel or begin to realize that the world is a sort of Divine play but those who do not perform any technique for God realization think the world as real. During day time, when the cinema hall is full of light (all the doors, windows are open), we cannot see any cinema. Similarly, in Samadhi, when the devotee sees or gets the Astral light, he realizes the world as the diverse manifestation of God. The mirage of the world goes away from a God-realized devotee".

"Some think Brahma, Bishnu and Siva are different gods. But in reality, they are the same power of the Supreme Spirit which appear to be diverse or separate due to different functions of creation, preservation and dissolution".

"You believe many things which you have not seen. As for example, you have not seen the birth of your parents nor your own. But your relations have told you, they are your parents, hence, you believe; such is the case with the Divine Parents. The saints and sages, who have realized the Supreme Spirit as our Divine Parents, have proclaimed the same in the Vedas and, hence, we believe in the glory of our Divine Parents".

On 15th June, 1939, morning, I went to his room. He explained many truths concerning the world. He explained the scripture — "Panchadashi". He explained the true nature of self by self-analysis. "Who am I?", was the first question. "Am I the all-pervading Spirit? Or nature? If we recognize 'self' as 'body' or 'physical matter', then why the dead body cannot move? Then surely this physical body cannot be the doer or enjoyer or sufferer. Is the all-pervading Spirit the doer or sufferer or enjoyer?" The all-pervading Spirit is present in the dead body too, hence, He cannot be the doer.

"The followers of logic think 'self' as the doer. The followers of Sankhya cherish the opinion that self is not the doer or enjoyer but the witness. The followers of Vedanta say, 'self' is unattached; he is not connected with anything. Then 'who' is this doer'? Let us analyze the fact. The visible Sun is an example of the all-pervading Spirit. Though in tropical countries, in summer season, the rays of the sun are very strong; still they do not destroy the combustible substances of the world. With the help of a lens, if we can concentrate the rays of the sun, it can ignite combustible substance. Similarly, the rays of the all-pervading Spirit passing through the lens of 'chitta' or reflecting on the mirror of 'chitta' (we may compare 'chitta' both with lens and mirror), create all the functions of the doer. That is why, during death, when the individual soul ascends to the other world with the Astral body, the 'chitta' too ascends along with the soul. Hence, in other words, 'chitta' can create the functions of the doer".

Chapter 18

A Few Days at Sevayatan[1]

Early morning at 6.30 on the 22nd December, 1947 I reached 'Sevayatan'. The devotees of Y.S.S. from far and near were reaching Sevayatan to participate in the annual function of the institution on 27th. I was happy to meet our old spiritual brothers and to discuss their spiritual progress.

On 23rd, after supper, Swami Satyananda Giriji intimated me: "You and Brahmachari Sadanandaji will be the main speakers for tomorrow's meeting (annual function). Brahmachari Sadanandaji will raise some problem in the meeting. Next day, at 3.30 p.m. the annual function started. Swami Satyananda Giriji presided over the meeting. As arranged, Brahmachari Sadanandaji was the first speaker. He delivered his speech on 'The necessity of religion in the society'. While delivering his speech, he raised some problems pertaining to body and mind. He requested the chair to throw light on the problems.

Swami Satyananda Giriji asked me to speak on "Kriya Yoga" for 10 minutes. Hence I had to curtail and tailor my speech accordingly. In my submission, I tried to respond to the questions raised by Brahmachari Sadanandaji who remarked that man is the combination of body and mind. I agreed with his words in the sense that, so long as the mind is restless it acts as a mind and when it becomes one with the spirit in ecstasy it becomes soul. Hence, mind can be divided into two, one is the ordinary restless mind and the other is soul.

According to statistics, the average longevity of the Indians is only 24 years. Due to the large number of early deaths (Untimely deaths of the babies and children within their 'teens') the average life span becomes so small. If we eliminate the number of the untimely early

---

1. Sevayatan at Jhargram, Medinipur

deaths, the average longevity of Indian will not exceed fifty years. Within these fifty years, the first fifteen years of our lives are practically spent in ignorance. We generally sleep eight hours a day, that is 1/3rd of life (11 to 12 years) is spent in compulsory ignorance.

Now we have nearly 23 years left at our disposal. For the maintenance of the physical body (i.e. taking bath, answering nature's call, eating etc.) we shall have to spend some time. Thus ten to twelve years are spent. Hence, hardly twelve to fourteen years are left at our disposal to solve the triple problems of our life.

The rishis and sages of yesteryears realised that human life is very short and its problems are many. Therefore, we shall accept the cardinals discarding the unnecessary ones.

Our first problem is with this physical body. In order to fight with diseases and to make it strong to face all situations with ease, the rishis had devised many yogic exercises, which are generally known as Yogasana. If we can practise a few yogasanas daily only for a few minutes (say 10-15 minutes) we can combat most of the diseases and can keep the body healthy.

Then the rishis were confronted with the very subtle and diverse problems of the mind. There is always an internal fight going on between the good qualities and evil propensities of the mind. Generally, the individual is defeated in the battle due to the restlessness of the mind. Due to restlessness, the soldiers on the good side cannot fight properly with the infinite soldiers of evil propensities. Hence, after much deliberation they discovered a new way or system, known as "Kriya Yoga" which helps to deploy the soldiers of the good side properly so that they can fight the battle with greater zeal and vigour and be successful at the end. This new system has been tested by millions of devotees and has been proved to be successful in solving the problems of the mind.

Should I ever get another opportunity, I shall explain 'Kriya Yoga' in order to solve the problems of inner soul. Before concluding my speech, let me pray to God so that we may lead our lives properly and at the end may reach His feet.

I had the privilege of visiting Sevayatan again on 24th December 1951. When I reached 'Sevayantan' early morning, the morning general prayer was going on. It was over in a short while, and I was very happy to meet many of my old spiritual brothers. Swamiji told me, 'In the afternoon meeting, you will have to speak. Though we could previously select the subject matter of the speech in the meeting, still considering the present situation of India, you will have to speak on the reasons of present distress and the way out to it."

In the afternoon, the meeting started. National anthem, flag hoisting, opening song and recitations in different languages by the boys of Sevayatan were the attractive features of the meeting. Swami Sarvananda Puri, a disciple of Sri Ramakrishna Mission, was invited to preside over the meeting. The first speaker placed before us a comprehensive picture of the then miserable condition of India. In my presentation, I drew the attention that the subject matter of our discussion is a very vital one and we need to find solution.

First let us try to find out the main reason for the present trouble and distress. The true reason of our suffering, not only in India, but throughout the world is the manifestation of our evil animal nature. The individual soul, while passing through the natural evolution and acquiring the different eighty four lakh of births, different instincts do manifest themselves when coming in contact with the favourable environments from time to time. Nevertheless, it is the animal nature that wants to get everything to its taste. Hence, it is the "animals" that always quarrel among themselves. The true picture of the trouble of the world is nothing but this conflict of interest.

While referring to man, we do not mean only the animal instinct of man but his other side also. It is his divinity. Hence, man is the amalgamation of animalism and divinity in one. By divinity we mean the ascent above the animal nature and to express fully the divine quality in him. But the prenatal animal instincts of many lives come forward to obstruct the expression. So long as we cannot conquer the animal nature in us we cannot remain in the world as brothers. Therefore, in order to rise above the animal nature, we shall have to fight heart and soul. We should learn the process or techniques to fight the animal nature from the great men whom we generally call yogis, as they know the process fully well. He (the yogi) has already been established in divinity by conquering the evil animal nature. If we follow the techniques regularly according to his guidance, we shall surely be able to establish universal brotherhood. In my opinion there is no other way for the elimination of our evil nature and to establish Godhood in us. Aum Santi!

On 25th, there was a group meditation class. The meditation was followed by discussion regarding Kriya Yoga. In that discussion, more than one hundred kriyabans participated. One of the spiritual brothers raised a point: "What is the difference between the 'Aum' technique (listening to the Aum sound) and the 'Jyoti Mudra' (seeing the spiritual light)?"

Another spiritual brother responded: "Where is the difference between these two techniques? Both are the same. The subject matter of realization cannot be explained in words. There may be apparent difference due to the difference of realization, but in essence they are the same because we perceive light both at Kutastha and Aum sound, simultaneously. Another spiritual brother enquired the reasons for not getting good result through Kriya Yoga.

Swami Satyananda Giri replied, "It is due to lack of devotion and faith. Where there is devotion, realization is quickened".

One of our spiritual brothers asked, "If we don't get the opportunity of keeping company of highly advanced spiritual brothers, how can we expect rapid progress in Kriya Yoga?"

I responded, "If there is want of thirst, there comes the question whether the glass is made of gold, silver or any other metal? If there is thirst, there will be hankering for water, and not the debate on the material of the glass. The main reason of lack of progress is due to want of life in Kriya Yoga. Most of the people take initiation into Kriya Yoga at the request of their relatives, or out of curiosity, or to know about it. After a few days, when the curiosity is satisfied, the performance of Kriya becomes lifeless. Further, Kriya that is not performed with devotion regularly according to the guidance of the Guru, cannot produce appreciable result. Where there is devotion, regularity and intensity, there the performance of Kriya becomes perfect. For any doubt, the devotee eagerly visits the advanced Kriya yogi to correct the same. The distance does not stand in the way. The devotee can visit the advanced yogi residing at a long distance, propelled by the heart's desire to keep his company. If the devotee suffers from want of money for the journey, he may travel on foot. According to the degree of intensity of practice, depends the time period for the realization of God. The greater the intensity and the hankering, quicker will be the God contact. I have seen on many occasions that due to the intensity of practice of Kriya Yoga and devotion the wife gets the higher and higher Kriya initiation from her Guru, within a short time whereas the husband, due to want of devotion and intensity or practice, cannot even get the second higher Kriya initiation though both had the Kriya initiation on the same day and at the same time.

It is foolishness to expect good results just after Kriya initiation. Just after sowing seeds, we cannot expect the fruits. After the germination of the seed, the young plant should be protected properly from the goats and cows. For proper growth, the plant requires manure and watering. Then we shall have to wait for the time of fruition. Regular supply of water and manure may accelerate the growth and at the time of flowering we may expect large quantity of flowers and fruits. No one can get B.A. and M.A. degrees within one or two years of study. Years after years we shall have to continue our study patiently. Such is the case with our Kriya Yoga. Patiently we shall have to practice the spiritual exercises regularly with devotion. The senses are the openings in the jar of perception. So, they should be controlled.

Some of us expect the help of the Guru in such a way that he will do everything for the realization of God without doing the necessary labour for themselves. It is true that Guru's help is necessary, But God helps those who help themselves. It is needless to speak more. In short, regular practice of Kriya Yoga with deep devotion under the guidance of our Guru is necessary. We should keep his company from time to time to correct our mistakes. Then in time, God-realization will come. I pray to God for such devotion and perseverance, so that we may all be blessed with Self-realization.

Chapter 19
An Expedition

On 18th December 1939 I visited my parents who were then residing at Dhenkanal State, by train from Ranchi. I reached the place at 8.30 on 19th December. My father was Officer-in-charge of the Bhuban Police Station. In a day or two, I came to know from the local people that there were many saints and yogis living in the "Bharati Hill". It inspired me to visit the hill, but the local people told me that it was impossible to visit the yogis as the hill was full of tigers and other ferocious wild beasts. Further, the yogis used to live in the underground caves not easily traceable for ordinary people.

This gave me further impetus for the expedition. As the Bharati Hill was not so high and as the place was very near our residence, I proposed to visit the place on the 4th of January 1940 and informed my parents. My father ordered three armed policeman to accompany me as body-guards. The doctor-in-charge of the charitable dispensary, Bhuban, was also with me as he was very curious to see the yogis living in the jungle full of ferocious beasts.

After our dinner we started for the Bharati hill at about 1 p.m. The whole region encircling the hill was full of thorny plants and wild jungles. It was very difficult to penetrate the jungle. My body-guards informed me that the hill is forty miles long and few miles wide. At the foot of the hill, we noticed the clear foot-prints of tigers and boars on mud. On seeing the footprints, the guards loaded the rifles with bullets and became alert. One guard was in front of me, the other behind me and the third one by my left side and another ordinary constable with an axe on my right side. The doctor was just behind me, hence one of the guards was practically behind him.

The first problem was how to penetrate the dense thorny jungle encircling the foot of the hill. The in-charge of the armed police commented, "there must be some way through which the water over the hill rushes downwards. Let us search out that way. Due to continuous flow of water during rains the path must be free from thorny plants and we shall be able to climb the hill". After searching for few minutes, we could locate the pathway. As it was the month of January, the course of the water was dry and full of small stones and sand. Lowering our heads, we could penetrate the bush and jungle.

At the height of a few hundred feet, we marked a small plane land full of tall grasses. The grasses were lying low here and there in a circle. I enquired the reason for this and the in-charge of our party said, "There are some wild deers, with branched horns of the size of cow living on this side of the hill. They had spent the night here and it is due to the pressure of their bodies, the grasses had fallen down on the earth in a circular way".

I expressed my doubt. The in-charge remarked, "I shall give you definite proof of it". Then pointing to a tree, he said, "Let us go there for the proof". As we reached the foot of the tree, we noticed that the bark of the tree was torn to pieces at about two feet above the ground. The armed police collected a few furs attached to the bark and explained". The deers rub their horns on the bark; as a result the bark was torn to pieces. The hair near the horn could not stand the pressure of rubbing. That's why they were torn and attached to the torn bark of the tree". We marked large number of circular spots where the flock of deer had spent the night.

Gradually, we proceeded higher and higher up the hill. At about 3-30 p.m., we could reach another plane, where we noticed open caves and the beautiful figures of Gods and Goddesses made of stone within the caves. The friend explained, "It is known as 'Deva Sabha' (A place where the Divine beings meet for their important discussions is known as 'Deva Sabha'). May be the saints and yogis living in the hill met at that particular place for important discussions.

We took rest for a few minutes there. From that side we could see cultivated fields and a river on the other side of the hill. As we had to return to our residence before night-fall, we could not search for more caves where the divine beings were supposed to reside. We started on our return journey. As we came down near the foot of the hill, we could hear the howling of the tigers, here and there. We, however, reached our residence safely.

Chapter 20

My Happiest Days at Lakhanpur Yogoda Ashram

I reached Lakhanpur Yogoda Ashram on 6th October, 1940, where I had a solitary cottage for my meditation. I went there to spend a few days in deep meditation. As I had no work, the whole time was at my disposal, either for the study of scriptures (Upanishads or other such holy books) or meditation. As a member of the Yogoda Satsanga Society, however, it was my duty to attend the weekly (Saturday) religious meetings.

The Yogoda Satsanga K. Vidyapith was at that time a residential M.E. School. On 16th October 1940, the school reopened after the Puja vacation. On 19th October (Saturday) 1940, in the weekly religious meeting all the boys were present. I had to read and explain the meaning and utility of Holy Srimad Bhagavad Gita to the boys.

On 20th, I had a vision of the Goddess of learning, Saraswati Devi. The continuous sound of 'Aum' used to give me such joy and pleasure. The constant ringing of the said sweet and melodious sound made me an introvert and withdraw me 'Inside', especially at night.

On 23rd, at about 2.30 a.m., when I was meditating on the sound of 'Aum', I had the vision of an ocean of light, on which I was floating. When I reached the shore, I was blessed with the vision of Gurudeva. Paramahansaji said, "I am now in America, still I can see you all clearly. Why are you afraid of tigers?" Saying this he transmitted his power in me. From his Christ Eye an electric current (with the accompaniment of light) was transmitted into my Christ eye. In the medulla, I also felt the current strongly electrifying the whole body. He had passed the spiritual light and current for some time. While the current was flowing in my Christ eye, I was also blessed with the vision of Paramaguru Sri Yukteswar Giriji Maharaj and Paramaparamguru Sri Sri Shyamacharan Lahiri Mahasaya. The figure of Sri Sri Shyamacharan Lahiri Mahasaya was that of his old age smiling before me. But the figure of Sri Yuktswarji was very grave who stood before me without speaking any word. The whole night was spent with joy and bliss received from the Gurus of our tradition. On 25th October 1940 I had to deliver a lecture before the staff and students on "the development of memory".

On 26th, Saturday, in the weekly meeting, I spoke about the real meaning of Srimad Bhagavad Gita under the cover of allegory. On 7th October morning, it was decided that the staff and students of the Y.S.S.K.M.E. School would visit the Rakab-Jungle for excursion. Only the top class boys (i.e. 1st class) of the school would be allowed to join our party. Our party consisted of Girinda, Hiralal Babu, Niranjan Babu, Hari Babu and myself, and the 1st class boys of the M.E. School. We started for the excursion in the morning. Near the forest, in the village Keshoreghar, we took some rest for our lunch. After lunch, we started again for the forest. We had penetrated three to four miles inside the forest. We quenched our thirst by drinking water from the river running through the forest. Instead of directly drinking the running water, we removed the sand one foot deep from the surface of the earth at a particular spot by the side of the river where clear water percolated.

The forest was under the Kashipur-Raj estate. Every year, the king of Kashipur used to sell the forest. That year, the king received rupees fifty thousand as sale proceeds of the jungle.

On our return journey we arranged ourselves in two rows. I was the leader of one row and Girinda was the leader of the other. As darkness was fast approaching, and due to fear of the wild ferocious beasts like leopards, panther or other type of tigers, we were walking fast. One local person from Keshoreghar was our guide. We walked more than twenty miles during the excursion, and returned safely to the Ashram late at night.

On another occasion, I visited Lakhanpur Yogoda Ashram on the 4th November, 1947. I followed a daily schedule. I used to sit for meditation from 4 a.m. till 6 a.m. At 6-15 I used to attend the morning general prayer and teach the new students of the Students' Home. From 6-30 a.m. I used to devote my time to the study of scriptures for an hour. After breakfast, I took religious classes from 8 a.m. to 9 a.m. for the inmates of the Ashram and interested persons of the village. The class started from the 6th November 1947 with the first book of the six systems of Indian philosophy (Vaiseshik Darsan).

As I had with me the commentaries of Sri Sri Lahiri Mahasaya on Indian philosophy, I could easily explain the spiritual interpretation of the first book according to his note. On 25th November, 1947, on completion of this book, I started the second book 'Sankhya Philosophy' explaining the same according to the written commentaries of Lahiri Mahasaya. I took a special class with another set of students interested in the real meaning of the Chandi and Srimad Bhagavad Gita from 9 a.m. to 10 a.m. From 10 a.m., I was free to devote my time for my personal study till 11; thereafter I practised meditation for half an hour or so. After meal, I took a short rest and then engaged myself in the study of scriptures or Autobiography of Sri Gurudeva, followed by newspaper reading.

At 4 p.m. the boys of the school would come to me to learn Yogasans till 5 p.m. Thereafter, I used to walk for about forty to forty-five minutes followed by the evening general prayer at 6 p.m. After the general prayer I used to meditate in my own room for two hours. On special occasions, due to special Y.S.S. functions at Lakhanpur some alteration was made in this general routine.

Many of the happiest days were spent in deep meditation and Samadhi at Lakhanpur Yogoda Ashram. I had some of my higher realizations at Lakhanpur. It is difficult, as I have mentioned elsewhere in this book, to record or express the spiritual experiences.

It is like seeing a cinema. The subject matter of the play projected in the show room in one hour may have been a huge volume of printed pages. If the subject matter of say Ramayana or Mahabharata or Srimad Bhagavata is projected through a projector within a few hours, imagine the amount of the subject matter of my realizations that was projected in my mental screen for 21 days (Chapter VIII) continuously without any break. What I had tried to express was a very small portion of total realization. Further, I could not express exactly what I had enjoyed or perceived.

During that Samadhi I had seen the visions of the future of the Yogoda Satsanga Society and also the future events of the world. Most of them had already began to happen.

The subject matter of the realization that I am now going to describe is purely on the physical plane and hence it has no real connection with the self-realization or God contact. But it is unavoidable on the path of Sadhana.

It is written in the scriptures (specially in the Upanishads) that Realization of God or Salvation depends to some extent on the purity of food that we take. "When the food becomes pure, the devotee gets the memory of the past lives, which ultimately leads the yogi to salvation – (Chandyogya Upanishad).

It is also stated in the scriptures that "the yogic perceptions vanish due to impure food". Regarding purity and impurity of food, detailed descriptions are given in the Srimad Bhagavad Gita by Lord Krishna Himself. Regarding the pure food for the yogis, one should consult verse 8, Chapter 17 of the Holy Srimad Bhagavad Gita. Regarding the impure food that the yogis should avoid, one should consult verses 9 and 10 of Chapter 17 of the Holy Gita.

Even the pure food described in the Holy Bhagavad Gita becomes impure within the range of the greedy sight and also on physical touch of the people roaming in gross sex plane. Pure food becomes impure in another way also. As stated in the scriptures, the bodies of the girls or ladies become impure during the period of menstruation. If the girls or ladies during their period of menstruation cook or prepare food, the food becomes impure for the yogis. In India, generally the ladies do not cook or prepare food during the time of menstruation. Of course, it is also true that every girl or lady cannot observe this custom due to lack of assistance in her family, and secondly many do not know the value of the custom; or thirdly due to ignorance of the spiritual law. It is taken for granted that those who are roaming in the gross sex plane, do not understand the real value of such restrictions and hence they ignore the law, and cook or serve the dishes to all the family members. In some families, there is only one woman engaged for cooking and serving the dishes. For such a family, the observation of such spiritual laws is impossible.

As regards my practical experience, I can definitely declare what happens if a yogi violates the strict injunction of the Indian scriptures. On many occasions, I had to accept invitations on social ground. But on rare occasions, it so happened that the food was cooked by the lady or girl whose body was impure due to her natural monthly periods. After taking such food, at night I could realise that the food was impure and the cells of the body did not like to accept the subtle chemical composition of the said food and revolted to throw them off from the body. Due to the revolt of the cells, the blood became heated and as a result of which regular fight ensured between the existing cells of the body on one side and the new chemical composition of the directed food on the other side. The fight continued so long the atomic composition of the new food became favourable to the body. In order to bring under control the new atomic cells, I had to labour hard the whole night. The technique that I used to apply in this: Drawing the life force from the coccyx, I would keep her at the naval centre or at least in the lumber region and then used to practice the Hong-Saw or 'Aum' for sometime. As a result of which tremendous electric current would flow throughout the body with the accompaniment of astral sound and light. When the whole body thus became electrified, the new atomic constitution too became electrified and thereby they became favourable to the body. Till the whole new atomic constitution became favourable to the body, the practice continued spontaneously. The cells of the new chemical composition then were transformed into pure energy. It took the whole night to transform all the new cells into pure energy.

Such incidents used to occur not only at unknown places but also at known places. Such incidents occurred not only at Lakhanpur but also at Ranchi.

Now regarding other higher realizations, let me say a few words. It is about the astral flight. The astral body of yogi is bound to be released from the physical casket and must fly to the astral world at ease if the Kriya Yoga techniques are followed faithfully and regularly according to the guidance of Guru, or the Preceptor.

Chapter 21

My Happy Hours with Sri Sri Sankari Ma

Sri Sri Sankari Ma visited our Yogoda Ashram, Ranchi with one of her disciples Swami Paramanandaji for the first time on 28th March 1941. She arrived at 9 in the morning. I was then teaching class VIII. Brahmachari Sadanandaji knew her; he met her at Kumbha Mela at Hardwar in 1938. He immediately recognised her. Within a few minutes, I finished my class and also joined others. Sri Krishnakalida was fanning her with the hand-made tal-leaf fan. Brahmachari Santanandaji and Brahmachari Sadanandaji presented me before her. After paying due respect, I stood before her. We had conversation for nearly an hour. As the cycle rickshaw was waiting, Ma could not stay in the Ashram for more than an hour. We were still in conversation as she approached the rickshaw. Brahmachari Santanandaji opened the gate. As we all paid our respects, she started for her temporary residence.

On the next day, right from the early morning, Banikantha and I were eager to meet her. As both of us were not familiar with the family members of Dr. Bimala Ray at Ranchi, in whose house Ma was then residing, I decided to accompany Br. Sadanandaji and Sri Krishnakalida. But, Br. Sadanandaji was not interested. He, however, agreed when Krishnakalida requested. Brahmachari Santanandaji was unwell, hence he could not accompany us. At 4 p.m. we reached the place. Sri Sunil Roy, son of Dr. Bimala Roy was a student of our Gymnasium; he used to get regular training from Krishnakalida who was the Physical Education Director of our Gymnasium. When Krishnakalida called Sunil by name, a gentleman came and led us inside the house. Soon, Sunil babu arrived and led us into the room where Sri Sri Sankari Ma was residing. After paying due respect, we took our seats before her. Several ladies were also present in the room.

Brahmachari Sadanandaji enquired: "Ma, have you seen our Sri Sri Shyamacharan Lahiri Mahasaya?" She replied: "Yes, I have seen him". I enquired, "Mother, how many times did you have his darsan?"

She responded, "At Calcutta, Banaras and such other places I had his darsan four times". I asked, "Were all the four darsans in his physical body?" She responded in the affirmative.

"I have heard that you have his darsan in the astral body too. Is it so?" "Yes, I have got the opportunity to meet him in the astral body. Today also I met him in the astral plane."

Banikantha asked, "Is it not a day dream?"

"No".

Brahmachari Sadanandaji asked, "Mother, how many years did you have the fortune of the company of Trailanga Swami?"

"For many years, indeed".

"Mother, if you don't mind, may I ask one question?"

"Yes, you are at liberty to ask any question."

"Following what sort of sadhana did Swamiji (her Guru) get his salvation?"

"At the time of my birth, Swamiji was (200) two hundred years old. He had already got his coveted salvation then and had reached the highest heaven. He had then achieved the stage beyond all the 'gunas' (Trigunatita" - beyond Swattva, Rajas and Tamas). He lived for two hundred and eighty years. From my birth I had never seen him performing any spiritual exercise. Hence, I cannot comment on this. If you like to know the way, how I had got my salvation or the stage of "Turia", I can explain". Then she narrated her own life.

"My parents were the disciples of Swamiji." At that moment, Swami Paramanandaji interrupted the mother and began to tell her life history himself. "From the very childhood, mother used to climb on the shoulder of her Guru (Trailanga Swami). From that time she used to think of him to be his nearest one, being the Guru of her parents. She used to go to take bath with him. One day, Swamiji went into the river with the child on his side, and dived deep. As mother had merged into the water, she got the vision of a beautiful land. Mother enquired, "Papa, what is this?" Swamiji replied, "It is known as 'Goloka', the highest heaven generally known as Hirannyaloka. The people and the things that you have seen are the inhabitants of this Hirannyaloka. From that time, her inner sight opened. On reaching home, Swamiji handed over her a book. She could easily read that book, but couldn't spell the words."

Mother instantly quipped, "Even now I cannot spell the words but can easily read any book".

Brahmachari Sadanandaji enquired: "Mother, will you kindly explain to me how you have conquered the ravage of time and have been able to keep the physical body healthy, stout and strong these one hundred and fifteen years?"

Mother responded, "Time cannot touch him or her who has taken shelter at the feet of the Ruler of the Time ('Mahakala'). Time does not dare to touch untimely to the devotees of 'Mahakala'. Do you see, how the Indians die untimely?" Swami Paramanandaji, interrupting, said, "It is due to her pre-natal very good works that she got Self-Realised souls as parents. Do we possess the pre-natal works that she had, the field (self-realised parents) in which she was born, the rigid performance of Brahmacharya or the strict observance of celibacy she had to endure? It is only possible in such a body." Mother, at that moment, mentioned that she was not allowed to see even the sun and the moon. 'Due to the rays of the sun, our bodies get heated, mind become restless.'

Brahmachari Sadanandaji further enquired, "Mother, Have you acquired the eight 'Siddhis' (spiritual powers)?"

"Eight Siddhis are nothing but conquering eight natures in man. It must be done, otherwise nothing can be achieved. Every devotee must conquer his eight natures. But the devotees should not use the Siddhis without the sanction of his Guru, otherwise, they create trouble in the spiritual path. The spiritual powers come automatically as the devotees proceed on the spiritual path. During the progress, the yogis have to devote some days in a particular spiritual centre. The Gods and Goddesses residing in that particular centre appear before the devotees. The centres generally known as 'Padmas' (astral-centre) can be visible clearly. Thus, the yogis travel from one centre to another, and ultimately ascend at the thousand rayed lotus at the head. When the works at the coccyx goes on, the astral body becomes very heavy. From here, the 'Sadhana' starts. When the works of the sacral centre at the naval takes place, the astral body becomes very light. At this stage, the yogis acquire the power of astral flight. They can easily roam in the sky. When the works of the dorsal (heart) centre are in progress, the yogis can hear the sound of the bell and the astral body becomes very light like the air. In this way, we have to do many works. You are keen about spiritual power. Now, do the works of the coccyx centre".

Banikantha asked, "Ma, are the five elements made of light?" Mother replied: "Yes, they are five different lights."

Sun had set in. It was 7 P.M.; there was darkness all around. We decided to leave so that we could attend the Saturday meeting. We paid our respects and took leave of her. We invited her to Yogoda Ashram next day at 5 p.m.

On 30th, at about 4. P.M., Banikantha and I went to escort Ma from Dr. B. Roy's residence. As soon as we started from Yogoda Ashram, there was a heavy down pour. At 4.25 p.m., we reached our destination. As I called Sunil by name, he opened the door and ushered us into the Mother's room. There was general conversation for a few minutes. The sky had cleared out; Ma intimated her readiness to start. Banikantha was immediately sent to fetch two rickshaws from the town.

Finding her free, I enquired, "Well, Ma, they say that Swamiji (Trailanga Swami) is still alive. Is it so?" Mother said, "At the time of his final departure from the world, he intimated us a fixed date and time. At the appointed date and time, he left the mortal coil in yogasan. While we were making arrangement to immerse his body in water, we could find a few flowers in place of his physical body". On further enquiry, I came to know that Ma had the fortune of the Divine company of her Guru for sixty years.

I enquired, "Ma, during awakening of 'Kula-Kundalini' (life force) what are the signs and symptoms revealed?"

"At the time of awakening of 'Kula-Kundalini', a tremendous sensation ensues at the coccyx. At that time, many yogis are unable to maintain their body in the sitting posture; it falls down. The crawling sensation at the coccyx becomes so strong that it generates tremendous electric current, thereby electrifying the whole body. Sometimes, it appears to the yogi that an ant is moving up through the spine. When it ascends the head, tremendous joy ('Ananda') fills the mind. It is beyond description."

"Do all the yogis realise in the same way?"

"No. The realization differs."

"Does the coiled life force ascend the head directly or by steps?"

"It takes a long time to pass the different centres in the spine. It ascends sometimes a few inches and falls down and sometimes it takes rest in a particular centre. It sometimes ascends and falls down again and again. If the pre-natal karma of the individual is very good, then in a day the coiled life force may ascend the brain."

Mother mentioned the names and addresses of some of her disciples in whom the life force ascended in the head in a day. By that time, Banikantha came back with two rickshaws. Myself and Swami Paramanandaji shared one ricksaw; Ma and Banikantha took the other.

On the way, I collected the information on the time of his first visit to Ma, first initiation and the final initiation in Sannyas. Swamiji told me that he was fortunate to visit whole of India with Ma. I also enquired about the yogic powers that he had witnessed in Sri Sri Ma. Swamiji, too, narrated some of her yogic powers that he had witnessed. As soon as we reached Ashram, the boys of the Y.S.S. Vidyalaya welcomed with affectionate slogans, "Ma has come, Ma has come".

Brahmachari Sadanandaji led us to our old office where Brahmachari Santanandaji was residing. I spread the carpet of the mother on an easy chair. Swami Paramanandaji occupied his seat on another chair. We took our seats on a bench in front of her. Ma first narrated how her Ashram was established. Then she narrated an incident in her life.

"Once, I was down with high fever and delirium. The doctors lost all hope. Sometimes, they could not trace beating of my pulse. I clearly remember that they said, "Let us take her out of the room." I was kept in the Veranda; I used to see many Divine angels, Gods and Goddesses. My Gurudeva Swami Trailanga Swami, Swami Bhaskaranandaji, Lahiri Mahasaya (she said "Lahiri Baba", Baba means father), Swami Vivekananda and other such yogis and saints used to visit me. I would ask people around me to fetch Asanas i.e. seats for them. As these people could not see the saints, they thought I was in delirium. Since no seats were provided, I myself tried to fetch 'Asanas' for them. I could not since they would not allow me to move. Once Gurudeva came, and prepared a medicine for me. After taking that medicine, I was completely cured. Gurudeva advised me to use the little branch of Nim (mergosa) to brush my teeth. But they would not supply me the same. However, by the grace of Gurudeva, now I have a plan to 'die' at Banaras" (The Ashram of Sri Sri Sankari Ma, was at 142, Audh Garbi, Harish Chandra Ghat, Banaras).

At that time, the bell for the general prayer rang and we all entered into the Guru Mandir. As we took our respective seats, the general prayer started. After the prayer was over, Brahmachari Sadanandaji requested Sri Sri Sankari Ma to narrate some of the incidents from the life of Swami Trailanga Swami.

"Today Gurudeva has ordered me to ask the students about the aim of their lives, hence, at first, let me know their aim of life, then I shall narrate incidents".

Kshitishda recorded all our conversation. It was interesting to note that all the students expressed their desire to serve the country although nature of the service was different for different students. Some of the boys expressed their desire to serve the country, remaining as family members. One after another the three boys said, "There is no doubt that I shall serve the country, but I have not yet decided the Ashram from which I shall serve the country". Sri Sri Sankari Ma then turned her head towards me and asked about my aim of life. I said, "You know all, why then ask again?" Then after a pause, I responded, "A renunciate Swami". At that time Swami Paramanandaji jokingly remarked, "there is one facility and that is to remain a Brahmachari. If you like to join the former pre-monastic life, you are at liberty to marry and lead the life of a family member". I instantly replied: "We are confirmed Brahmacharis, we have no time to look backward but to march onward towards the aim". He again remarked jokingly: "Bhowal Swami had reverted to his pre-monastic life".

I humbly submitted, "I am not afraid if I have with me the blessings of you all. You all will protect me at crucial moment".

Then Sri Sri Sankari Ma smilingly said, "The last stage is as a Brahmachari, afterwards you will be a renunciate - a Sannyasi".

Brahmachari Sadanandaji replied that his aim of life was to get the knowledge of Brahma. Kshitishda expressed, "My aim of life is to realise the Infinite Mother". Krishnakalida said, "At present, to serve the country as a Physical Education Director, afterwards to be a "Sannyasi". At last, Banikantha said, "I shall be a Sannyasi". Kshitishda handed over the recorded note on the aim of our lives to Sri Sri Ma. Mother then entertained the boys with many interesting stories from the life of Swami Trailanga Swami.

"Once Swamiji was floating in the Ganges in 'Padmasan' and was being driven by current of the river. The king of Ujjaini at that time was traveling by boat. He met Swamiji near Manikarnika Ghat. The Maharaja had the desire to have his company. Swamiji himself got up in his boat. Maharaja had got one golden sword from the British Government as a presentation. He showed Swamiji the sword. After examining, Swamiji threw away the sword in the Ganges.

The Maharaja was furious; he abused Swamiji, "This Swami is a rogue. I shall put him into jail and expose his roguery".

The boatmen and some other devotees of Swamiji told Maharaja, "Swami is of that type. We shall, however, search out the sword with the help of the divers". Maharaja said, "In that case, he will not get any punishment. I must inflict some punishment on him".

By that time, the Maharaja reached his destination in the river. Swamiji plunged his hand into water and brought back two swords. He then asked Maharaja to identify his own sword. As both the swords were exactly the same, Maharaja could not identify his own. Swamiji commented, "Just now you were shouting, 'my sword', 'my sword'? Why can't you recognise which one is yours? Do you know yourself? First realise yourself, then you will be able to identify your sword". Maharaja felt ashamed. Swamiji gave him one of the two swords and threw the other into the river.

My Gurudeva always stayed completely nude. He was once roaming in the town of Banaras in his usual naked state. The Chief Judge of Banaras passed orders for his arrest. The police could not arrest him due to his miraculous yogic power. The moment they tried to arrest him, they saw him gone away. Swamiji was recognised by the harassed police of Banaras as a baffling problem child. However, observing the harassment of the police, Swamiji, out of pity, himself appeared before the Chief Judge of Banaras. He was imprisoned but the next day he was found outside the jail. The jailor enquired, "Swamiji, I had locked you properly, how have you come out?" Swamiji replied, "If man could be kept under observation, then no one could escape or die".

The jailor said, "When man dies, his physical body is left behind. How have you escaped from the prison with this huge body?" Swamiji remarked, "The physical body is a material substance. It has no power". Saying thus, he disappeared before his presence and reappeared within a few minutes.

On opening the prison the jailor observed knee deep water on the floor. He asked Swamiji, "Wherefrom comes this water?" Swamiji commented: "As you had imprisoned me, last night I had answered the nature's call". The jailor was astonished at the sweet scent of the colourless water.

On another occasion, Swamiji appeared from the sky at a bathing Ghat, at Banaras, meant for ladies. A king and queen with their party had come to visit Banaras. The queen was, at that time, taking her bath. She cried aloud in fear. The people of the king beat him heavily. At night, the king had a vision that Lord Siva of Banaras appeared with His 'Trishul' (three pronged iron spear) on his chest and said, "Look, how you have beaten me today. I shall kill you. Be off from My place". The king ordered his fellow men to leave Banaras; he said that he could not stay there any more since he saw the Trishul on all sides". One of his fellow men advised him to seek apology to the person whom the king had punished. Accordingly, the king prayed for forgiveness and got back his mental peace."

Once a person from the West had come to visit him. Finding him naked, the foreigner hesitated to approach him. When Swamiji directed him to sit by his side, Swamiji remarked, "I am a renunciate, I have nothing to entertain you except these three iron balls". The visitor enquired, "Is it possible to eat?" Swamiji, then prepared his food by putting those three iron balls in his 'Dhuni' (Sacred fire). As the balls became red, one by one, he ate up all the three. The visitor realised his extraordinary yogic power.

On another occasion a person came to test him with a dish full of cooked beef in his hand. He enquired Swamiji, "Is it possible for you to take our meal?" Swamiji replied, "Yes, if you can take my meal". Swamiji then answered the nature's call and offered him the night soil to take. The visitor shuddered at the sight of the excreta but Swamiji took the same. At that time, Anandada (Sri Ananda Mohan Lahiri, the grandson of Sri Sri Shyamacharan Lahiri Mahasaya) commented, "Ma, we have heard all these stories. Please, tell us some of the incidents connected with your life".

Then the Mother narrated the incident how once Swamiji opened her inner Eye at the time of taking bath. "In my early childhood, I used to worship Sri Ram. I had one picture of Sri Ram made of wood. I used to offer flowers, etc. at His feet. But as He could not satisfy my heart's desire, I intended to worship Swami Trailanga Swami in his place. As I was thinking how to invite him, I noticed with great astonishment that Swamiji was sitting next to my wooden Ramji".

I worshipped him with flower garland. By the grace of Swamiji, I entered into Samadhi. On regaining my outward consciousness, I went to Swamiji and was surprised to see the same garland on his neck. I enquired, 'Swamiji where from did you get the garland?' He replied, 'Why, you yourself gave me. Your wooden Ram does not talk with you, and hence you were displeased with him. That's why, I myself had to come to you, I am your Ram".

Then she narrated how she lived in the icy lonely Himalayan caves near Kedarnath, Amarnath, Pasupatinath, Badrinath and such other places for eighteen years. She also narrated how she could visit with her astral body the planets, like the Sun and the Moon. She also described how she visited the temple of 'Mahakal' during Kumbha Mela at Dwaraka. Then with a closing song, our meeting came to an end at 8.30 p.m. We arranged for their departure.

On 10th February 1941 at 5.45 p.m., Kshitishda and myself revisited Sri Sri Sankari Ma. Some of the devotees present there were interested to know about the food that Sankari Ma used to take in such dense forest or cave in the Himalayas. Sri Sri Sankari Ma replied, "We used to get milk from Chamasi type of cows every day. The milk was more white than the ice, hence we did not find any difficulty to collect them. We used to dilute the milk with holy-water to drink". She continued, "There were a special type of fruit of the size of (Marbollum) Haritaki available in the Himalayas. When taken, it tasted very sweet but for six months we did not feel any necessity for food. There were large bread-leaves which when baked resembled 'papad'. We would get salt in the hills and with it we used to take the bread-leaves. Sometimes, Gurudeva used to supply me food".

Just at that moment, the wife of F.N. Aikat (a Government contractor) asked," I have heard from Swami Gyananandaji that there is a special type of leaf available in the Himalayas, which when baked becomes bread. Swamiji had visited the Himalayas several times. Mother, is it so?"

Sri Sri Sankari Ma said, "Try to control the tongue. It looks very small, but mark its terrible nature", pointing to her own tongue. She continued, "What do not the people of the world do for satisfying the tongue? Had it been larger than the usual size, what would happen then?" I replied, "It won't get satisfaction, even if it devoured the world."

The outside visitors left the place, and we were talking with Sri Sri Ma, when Swami Satyanandaji arrived. After exchange of a few words, Ma was partly withdrawn inside. From that withdrawn state of mind, she addressed Satyanandaji, "Well, you said that you won't come, why then have you come?" She then herself divulged the secret of arrival of Swami Satyanandaji. Ma added, "I had a talk with my Gurudeva regarding my visit with Satyanandaji. When I expressed my desire to visit Satyanandaji, Gurudeva told me, 'You may go there. Do you have any difficulty to go there? I said, 'Yes, I can go there, but can you not bring him here?"

Gurudeva remarked, "I am residing in everybody. All those bodies are the different forms of mine. I shall come in that form". Then addressing Swami Satyanandaji, Sri Sri Sankari Ma said, "Love all. Always follow Truth. Purity of heart (Chittasuddhi) is essential. Suppose, I am doing hard labour for Sadhana but if my mind is not purified, will I get anything?"

Swamiji responded in the same way. "No, we won't get anything". The Mother added, "Chitta-suddhi is essential. When the heart becomes pure, you will know everything, even the past lives. I have seen Lahiri Mahasaya. He was very humble, free from all pride or vanity. He remembered all his past lives. He could speak clearly and exactly about all the past lives of other persons too".

I was in Padmasan, in a meditative posture, and attentively listening to her valuable words. Bliss gradually was descending on me as I looked at her. Sri Sri Sankari Ma told me, "Brahmachariji, I am in Divine mood, you may ask any question, whatever you like". As I was in a joyous state, I had not spoken any word. Then Mother asked me, "What type of yoga do you practice? Hatha yoga, or Raja yoga?"

I replied, "I don't know all that, I only practise what Gurudeva had taught me".

She then remarked, "You will get everything from your Guru, but faith and devotion is necessary". She again enquired, "We are practising yoga; but do you love your very own, who is residing in your own body?" Then she added, "Love yourself, the soul, that is living in your body, then you will be able to love all".

As I was deeply absorbing her valuable counsel, looking at her, my mind was withdrawn as if by huge magnet. It was an extraordinary experience. The whole world was floating in my mental sky and felt as if it was a dream. Of course, that experience was only for a short while. When I visited Sri Kumar Nath Sudhakar at Burdwan, I had received similar experience from him. It was his special grace on me. When I came down from that state of mind, Sri Sri Ma enquired, "Where is now Parameswaranandaji?" I replied, "He is now in America. He is now known as Swami Benoyananda Giri". She added, "I love him very much. When you next write him, convey my love and blessings to him". He will one day come to visit me in astral body. Now, he does not know how to fly but very soon he will be able to move with his astral body". Addressing me, she added, "Be Good, then you will be able to realise God. Your birth is for the good of the world. You will have to do lot of work for the world. The whole world will benefit from you".

Pointing to Kshitishda, she commented to Swami Satyanandaji, "The boy is very good". Swami Satyanandaji then enquired, "Mother, have you seen our Babaji?" Mother replied, "Yes, I have seen him. Once as I was sitting by the side of Lahiri Mahasaya, a very young half-naked man with a walking stick in his hand appeared before us. On his arrival, Lahiri Mahasaya bowed his head with reverence and touched his feet. I enquired Lahiri Mahasaya, "Baba, who is this young man?" Lahiri Mahasaya, replied, "He is my Gurudeva". On another occasion, I had visited him at Kumbha Mela.

At 8.40 P.M., we took leave of her after paying our due respects. Ma was to leave Ranchi the next day by the morning train. On 11th, immediately after our breakfast, Sasida and I went to the station to meet Sri Sri Sankari Ma. As we were waiting at the gate for her arrival, she arrived with the family members of Bimal Babu in his motor car. The wife of Bimal Babu, enquired "Well, you have come, are you traveling with Ma?" I responded, "No, I have come to meet her only." By that time Banikantha had arrived. He enquired, "Ma, when will you re-visit Ranchi?" She replied, "I am thinking of establishing an Ashram at Shillong. If I can do that, I may re-visit Ranchi". We all reached the train. The time for departure arrived, and we all paid our due respects. She waved her hand as a gesture of blessing as the train slowly moved out.

On 22nd January, 1942, I had the opportunity of visiting Sri Sri Sankari Ma at Banaras, in her Ashram; and came to know about many holy places she visited.

Chapter 22
A Few Days with My Earthly Mother at Dhenkanal Estate

I reached the Dhenkanal Estate on 9th December, 1939 at 8-30 p.m. to visit my parents. As I was free there, I got ample time for meditation and study of scriptures, specially Upanishad. On the 24th December 1939 at about 2-30 a.m., I had a vivid dream in which I had got the vision of my Gurudev in one of our Yogoda Ashram meetings; he had come and entertained with devotional Kirtan. After the Kirtan was over, he said, "It is good, that you are now alone. Stick to the path of God. Your future is glorious". On awakening with his sweet words, I sat for meditation.

On 29th December, 1939, I meditated the whole night starting from 6-30 p.m. to 7-30 a.m. except half an hour break for supper. I enjoyed the joy beyond description throughout the whole night.

Though there was one cook and one maid servant to help my mother, I used to help her in the domestic chores. At her instance, I would explain to her the Upanishad daily from 3-30 p.m. to 5 p.m.

On 31st December, 1939, I observed partial fast. At night, I slept for three hours only from 8-30 to 11-30 p.m. and spent rest of the night in meditation. I used to spend most of my time in meditation. On 13th January 1940, I returned to Y.S.S. Ranchi.

On 14th December 1940, I was back to Dhenkanal Estate to revisit my parents. Like the previous year, I spent as much time as possible in meditation. On the 19th, I had an opportunity to visit Banchandi, a holy place. It was a very old temple on the foot of a hill. The temple and the image of the goddess, both were made of stone. It was a few miles away from Bhuban Police Station and four miles east to the Bharati hill. It was a very solitary place for deep meditation. On the 25th, I told my mother about the holy places on the Kapilash hill. My mother had visited these places twice earlier, she expressed her desire to revisit those shrines if I could accompany her. I gladly agreed to make those pilgrimages. We decided that we would start on 26th by bullock cart at 10 a.m. As the road through which we had to pass was full of wild beasts like tigers, my father arranged for our bodyguards.

On 26th, my mother and I started by bullock cart for the Kapilash hill. The three armed policemen and two servants followed our cart on foot. The road heading to the Kapilash hill was fairly good. It was only three miles from Bhuban police station. After crossing the Brahmani River, three miles away from our residence, we started for the village 'Day', sixteen to eighteen miles away from our village, where we had to spend the night. In the evening, we reached the State Controlled Bungalow at the village 'Day'. As we had brought our night meals from our house, we were free from the trouble of cooking. I selected a lonely room for my meditation and temporary residence.

On 27th, at 7-30 a.m., we resumed our journey. It appeared to me that the distance from the village 'Day' to Kapilash hill may be two to three miles. Soon we reached our destination. From the foot of the hill, there were two ways leading to the temple on the top of the hill, one encircling the hill and the other though very stiff but shorter one. We selected the shorter route for climbing the hill. On the way, we visited two Ashrams where we observed that monks were performing their penance. As I arrived at the midway ashram, the head monk asked me to sit by his side on a deerskin. After taking some rest in the Ashram, we all resumed our journey and at 9-30 a.m. we reached the Siva temple. Like the system of Jàganath temple at Puri, all sorts of cooked food with clarified butter, Khichri, white rice Paramanna (rice cooked with milk), cakes, curry etc. for our dinner. After performing the usual Puja in the temple, we took our meals. In the temple, there was another image of Siva named Nagewari by the side of Chandra Shekhar Siva. The adjoining places were full of mountains. Half an hour walk up the hill further from the temple, we found a beautiful cave in which there were several images of the goddess, with believers on their laps.

At the top of the hill, there was a plain area where we marked the existence of another image of a god. They say that the gods and goddesses used to meet on special occasion at that place and it was why the plain was termed as 'Deva Sabha".

On our way back from "Deva Sabha", we noticed a spring flowing above another Ashram; the water was pure and digestive. At 3 p.m., we came back to the temple of Chandra Shekhar Siva and purchased our necessary food and tiffin. In the evening, we returned to our previous Bungalow at the Village 'Day'. We visited the local Jagannath temple. At night, we ate the purchased consecrated food. I got two hours for my meditation (2-30 a.m. to 4-30 a.m.).

On 28th December, 1940 at 4-40 a.m., we resumed our journey for our residence at 12 noon.

On 18th September 1941, once more, I visited my parents at Dhenkanal Estate, to enjoy the vacation for Durgapuja. Like previous years, I utilised most of my time in deep meditation. I witnessed the Durgapuja and other local festivals there.

Chapter 23

My Happy Moments with Srimat Kumar Nath Bandopadhyaya (Sudhakar)

Srimat Kumar Nath Sudhakar was a God-realised-soul of our lineage. He received his Kriya Yoga initiation from Srimat Panchanan Bhattacharya, the direct disciple of Sri Sri Shyamacharan Lahiri Mahasaya. Sudhakar won various honorary titles from different educational institutions, like the well known Calcutta University. On 2nd September 1925, he received three titles from Nikhil Bharat Sahitya Sangha (All India Literary Society), Calcutta.

Due to his profound knowledge and deep insight into Indian Philosophy and other scriptures, and specially his yogic powers, people from far and near used to visit him. In order to avoid the rush of the public visitors, he once adopted a trick. He circulated through the well known newspapers about his death, and the death ceremony performed by his relatives and instantly changed his address in a very unknown secluded place at Burdwan. Though he was successful in avoiding the public visitors, he could not cheat Paramahansa Yoganandaji. In 1935, he returned to India from U.S.A. and once visited Srimad Kumar Nath Sudhakar. That's how I too came to know his address. Hence, I intended to visit him and on the 7th July 1938 on my way back to Calcutta from Y.S.S., Ranchi. I visited him at 8 a.m. in the morning.

He first enquired in details all the activities of our society at Ranchi and then entered into deep conversation on spiritual matters. Several times during our conversation, he advised me to practise the "Hongsaa" technique in leisure times. He spoke highly about the value of the technique. He said, "The breath we take, is connected with the Infinite Spirit in such a way that we can never cut off this connection. Following this breath or rather observing the in-going and out-going breath, we can realise that we are not body, but Spirit. This breath is Brahma, and we can realise our own self that is Brahma by following this breath. If you pull one end of a huge mat, the whole mat will move. Similarly, if we could connect our mind with this breath, we can realise that the whole cosmos is moving with it.

While speaking about Paramahansa Yoganandaji, he could not resist his tears. He said, "Swamiji is the second coming of Lahiri Mahasaya. As Mallinath had explained Kalidas, Swamiji has come to explain Lahiri Mahasaya. The people of India do not recognise him. They (Lahiri Mahasaya and Paramhansa Yogananda) are not human beings but Gods, descended on Earth for the good of the world".

Regarding my own life, he advised me: "Don't try to add more University degrees. Your life is not for office work or the so-called service. Don't lose the strength of mind, though the physical body is weak. Within five to ten years of Kriya practice, you will be able to know everything".

Actually I was going back to Calcutta for acquiring further M.A. degree in Sanskrit. He, through his intuitive power being aware of the fact, asked me not to add degree. He predicted, "If you go to the University this time, your life will be in education line as a head of the University. Your life is not for that. Your Guru Paramahansa Yoganandaji is an Avatar. Whatever you desire you will get from him. But you should demand".

As he was predicting, a doubtful thought entered into my mind regarding his highest achievement in the spiritual life. Instantly, receiving my thought current, he stared at my eyes and commanded: "Now your mind will dive deep into the ocean of peace". No sooner he uttered those words that my mind entered into the kingdom of peace and bliss. After a while, he asked, "Come down". Instantly, I regained the normal outward consciousness. I came to realise that the old yogi, who had the power to play with my soul like the child's toy, must have realised God. After paying due respect, I started for Calcutta at 9.30 a.m.

Sri Kumar Nath Sudhakar had written many valuable books for the devotees. Interpretation of Srimad Bhagavad Gita (in our mother tongue Bengali) had been selected as a religious textbook in our Yogoda Satsanga Vidyalaya at Ranchi, Midnapore and such other places.

The followers of the path of God will get spiritual guidance if they read the following books written by Sri Kumar Nath Sudhakar:

1. Madhumayee Chandi
2. Mritubijoya

3. Tapaban
4. Ashokaban
5. Nitya Brindaban
6. Sri Brajangana Gita
7. Sri Gouranga Gita
8. Yogabasistha
9. Amrita
10. Sadhak- Dampati
11. Mriturpare Naba Mahadesh

Chapter 24
The Kumbha Mela

On the 28th December 1941, Swami Dayananda Giri told me that he was going on that day to Allahabad to participate in the Kumbha Mela. I told him, "I am also going within a day or two". On the 31st I started from Ranchi and reached Allahabad Station at 5.30 a.m. on the 1st January 1942. I went to Bholananda Sannyas Ashram, Jamunapatti, Allahabad where Swami Dayananda Giri received me cordially.

Due to the Second World War, the E.I. Railway could not arrange for special trains for the Kumbha Mela. The Railway authorities had circulated a notice that from the 4th January to the 4th February, no ticket would be issued for the Kumbha Mela. Hence, the gathering at Allahabad Kumbha Mela was not so large as was expected.

On the 2nd, early in the morning, I took my bath in the Ganges at Tribeni as it was a very auspicious day for the dip; it was the full moon day. During the month of January 1942, according to the auspicious conjunctions, we had three dips; the first on the 14th January, the second on the 16th and the third on the 21st.

Our Mandaleswar (108) Sri Sri Mahadevananda Giri had informed us that he would join us in time. He arrived at Dwarganj. At 10 a.m. on the 2nd January our party comprising all the monks of "Ananda" sect, accompanied by many elephants, camels, and horses started in a procession to fetch him from Dwarganj.

The 'Naga' (naked sadhus) sect of renunciates was controlling and managing the procession. Mandaleswarji climbed on the decorated elephant meant for him; two boy-attendants spread the ornamented umbrella over his head. The Naga sadhus displaying various feats marched on, some holding gold or silver flags, others scepters or swords along with the elephants, horses and Rajputana camels. We, the monks, followed the long procession in two rows. At 3.30 p.m. we could return to Ashram (temporarily erected huts).

On the 3rd January, at 10 a.m., I had the opportunity to witness the first religious congregation at the (temporarily erected) religious hall. All the Mandaleswars and Mahamandaleswars were sitting in their respective gadis (seats). The devotees, scholars and public were either asking questions or silently listening to their counsels with attention.

A devotee enquired from Mandaleswar Mahadevaji, "Is it possible to live without destroying the lives of others?"

Mandaleswarji replied: "Yes, by taking fallen leaves and fruits - discarding the seeds. If the rice is prepared from the three year old paddy, you can avoid destruction of seeds because such paddy looses the power of germination".

"Does it not hamper the growth or strength of mind or upset the intellect?"

"No. It develops the Satvic nature of the mind. The Rajasik nature is responsible for the upset of the intellect."

"Why do we find difference of intellect in different persons?"

"The same spirit is residing in different bodies. The light of God reflecting on different mirrors appears to be different, creating diversity of intellect".

"Does the world exist?

"No".

"Acharya Shankara has accepted the existence of the world of ours. What is that?"

"It is a sort of dream world. As in dream we feel pleasure and pain, so the existence of it is nothing but a long dream. There is no existence of 'you' and 'I'."

"Is it possible to realize God without passing through the different stages of social and religious orders?"

"Yes. As you can ascend the roof passing over the different steps of the ladder or directly with the help of a bamboo. Every one cannot use the bamboo, for it, one needs the "Sadhan-Chatustaya". (performance of four different sorts of religious acts. For details please consult Vedanta).

"Is the 'Mind' a matter or spirit?"

"It is a material substance. Because it is affected by the material substances like food, medicine, poison and so forth. Spirit cannot be affected by any material substance like food, medicine or poison".

It was time for the midday meal, hence the congregation was dissolved for the time being. After meals, we joined the procession for fetching another Mandaleswar Swami Krishnanandaji of "Nirbani" sect. A procession similar to one mentioned earlier started from Nirbani Akhara. Returning from the procession in the afternoon I took the opportunity to join the previous religious gathering.

I personally put the question before Mandaleswar Mahadevanandaji, "What is difference between Jivatma and Paramatma (individual soul and the Supreme Spirit)?"

"One is transcendental, without attribute, and the other is with attribute. This attribute is called Maya or Prakriti. It is indescribable. As darkness vanishes with the appearance of light, so this Maya is dispelled at the advent of knowledge".

At that time, a few gentlemen came and requested him to impart some instructions. Mandaleswar Mahadevanandaji advised them, "In the body, reside the three 'gunas', may be termed as Sattwa, Rajas and Tamas. The work of Tamas is to sleep, without any protest or excuse it is done. You spend eight hours for this. The work of Rajas is service and all sorts of activities. Without any hesitation you give him his due share. Eight hours are spent in the office or with other activities. Do you give anything to the Sattwa, the giver of peace, bliss and happiness? You should spend eight hours for him. Out of these eight hours, you should devote four hours in meditation, two hours for the study of scriptures and two hours for good company. Then, gradually pay more time to the giver of peace, bliss and joy deducting first two hours from sleep and then further two hours from the unnecessary works. If you can lead your life in this way, you will be owner of real peace, bliss and joy, being free from all the bodily attachments".

On the 4th January, after dinner, I visited "Akshyabat". It was within the fort area, near the underground temple. There were many images of the gods and goddesses within the temple, similar to the gods and goddesses at Puri. In the afternoon, the Mandaleswarji of the 'Udasin' sect (Udasin means renunciate) arrived at the Kumbha Mela. The procession in his honour was a crowded one due to the extraordinary display of various feats by the naga sadhus.

In the evening, I took the opportunity to sit under the feet of our Mandaleswarji in the religious congregation. One gentleman enquired, "How was this world created?"

Mandaleswarji replied, "The Supreme, being above and beyond all attributes, appears to be the world wearing the garb of Maya. Though there is no real existence, still appears to be so. As there is no snake in the rope, it still in darkness appears to be snake. The existence of which is nil in the beginning and in the end, it is taken for granted there is no existence of the same in the middle too".

"As in the Cinema hall, you can see the views of the rivers, oceans and the hills and the appearance of the line of elephants, though the actual existence of which is wanting there. Sitting in the temple during meditation, if you find the droppings of a crow and engage your mind for the search of the nature of the crow, its colour and the direction from which it came and committed the nuisance and such other matters, then you would not be able to meditate. Your duty is to wash the droppings with broomsticks and water of the Ganges, and then dive deep into meditation. Similarly, our duty is to remove the dirt of ignorance with the broomsticks of knowledge and to wash the mind with the Ganges water of devotion and then sit for meditation. Then you will be able to realise the Supreme Truth".

On the 5th January, we arranged for dissemination of the message of our Gurudeva. The day was very auspicious to us as it was his birthday. I delivered a speech on "Raja yoga". Sasida (Sasi Bose Mullick) read out Paramahansaji's writings from Inner-culture Magazine. There were several loudspeakers connected with the mike, so that all present there could hear the speech.

In the afternoon, as usual, I joined the religious congregation. I enquired from Mandaleswar Mahadevanandaji about the real meaning of "Gayatri". He explained, "The word 'Tat' means the Supreme Spirit, who is directing all the minds and intelligence of the universe properly. Dhi means mind and intellect. Citing various Vedic verses and also a few words from Vedanta, he explained the word 'Savita'. In short, Savita means the Creator, Preserver and Destroyer of the cosmos. 'Varenya' means worth worshipping. We meditate on Him".

In the evening, he commented on the query of a person regarding the 'mind': "The all-pervading Spirit is inactive and the mind is inert like the material substance. Hence, all the activities of the mind depend upon the help of other. The mind and intellect become active due to the presence of 'Chit' (Spirit)".

On the 6th morning, as usual, I was present in the religious congregation and enjoyed the religious discourses. In the afternoon, crossing the temporary wooden bridge over the Ganges, I visited the caves in the Jhusi hill in search of highly advanced yogis. All the caves were occupied by renunciate yogis. Avoiding the public, they were meditating all the while in the solitary caves.

On the 7th, I attended the religious conference and very much enjoyed the spiritual discourses. Mandaleswar Mahadevanandaji advised one of the ladies to worship the six "Gs" which interested me the most.

1. First 'G' is the Ganges. You should take bath in the Ganges daily and should drink her water.
2. The second 'G' is "Gita". You should study the Srimad Bhagavad Gita regularly and try to realise the Truth in it.
3. The third "G" is Gayatri. You should count the beads with Gayatri Mantra daily.
4. The fourth 'G' is 'Gau', the 'Cow'. To worship the cow means to maintain her for pure milk in order to keep the body healthy.
5. The fifth 'G' is 'Guru'. You should regularly worship your Guru, follow his words and should practise the Kriya Yoga techniques that you have received from him.
6. The last 'G' is God (Govinda).

You all know 'Govinda' is our Goal. Everything is for (God) Him. If you can serve these six "Gs", regularly, then surely you will realise God in time. The blessings of God and Gurus will shower on your head.

On the 8th, I visited some holy places near the town of Allahabad. First I visited the Bharadwaj Ashram. In the right side temple, resides the five-headed Siva, the king of Prayag; on one side of Him the statues of seven Rishis (Gautam, Viswamitra, Vasishtha, Jamadagni, Atri, Kashyap, Bharadwaj and Arundhati) were there. The image of Lord Krishna also was there. Next I visited the Ashram of Valmiki, where there is the image of Lord Narayana with His four hands — Badri Narayana -the true copy of the image found in the temple of Badrinath in the Himalayas. Narshinga Dewa, Ananta Nag (infinite headed Snake) and Bharadwaj Siva were there. In the 'Vaikuntha Puri', there were two caves, in which small images of Gods and Goddesses were there. In that 'Puri', the most attractive was the image of Goddess Durga with eight hands.

On the 9th, I participated in the religious conference in the evening. Out of many discourses by Mandaleswar Mahadevanandaji, existence of the world deserves to be mentioned. Mandaleswarji explained,

"Practically, there is no existence of this world. The mind, in the dream, creates the world, rather visualizes the world. During a dream, the eyes remain closed. While visualising the world, though the eyes are open, still the reports of the eyes are untenable as the eyes cannot see the objects at a long distance or the objects within the eyes. They cannot see the objects in the darkness or in very strong light. The furnishing of wrong reports in scanty light is like the vision of mirage. Though the dreams are untrue, temporarily they appear to be true and influence the body and mind to the extent that people become afraid at the sight of snake, feel pleasure and pain and so on.

In the same way, the conceptions of the world are long dreams. This world is like the child of a barren lady. Our Divine Mother Goddess Durga was a barren Mother. She had the child 'Ganesh' as the outcome of "Narayana-Vrata". (special form of worshipping Lord Narayana, the Lord of the Universe, by the ladies). When she was to pay Lord Siva the sacerdotal fee, she heard the cry of Ganesh in her sleeping room. She had received Kartika in the Kusha-grass field. This world is the outcome of imagination. The imagination of one person differs from the other. The ordinary flower that cannot create sensation or influence the general public may be the instrument of a beautiful poetry for a poet. This active world of sorrows cannot come out of inactive, ever-blissful, ever-joyous Brahma. That's why the sage Kapil had imagined a third person, "Trigunamoyee Prakriti" (nature with three qualities) as the creator of the world. Three gunas are Sattwa, Rajas, Tamas. This needs to be realised at heart", Mandaleswarji concluded.

On the 11th, I enquired, from Mandaleswar Mahadevanandaji during the religious conference, "Is it possible to realize the Infinite? If he were the subject matter of realization, then will He not be finite? Further, if we study carefully the six systems of Indian Philosophy, we find that different schools of Philosophies widely differ in their views. From these, should we not conclude that He is incomprehensible?"

Mandaleswarji commented: "No, He is not incomprehensible. He who realizes Him becomes Brahma himself. The commentators of different systems of Indian Philosophy were all truely realised-souls. They had equally realised God at heart. But due to the difference of calibre of consciousness among their disciples, they expressed the Supreme Spirit differently. Charvak tried to draw the attention of his disciples to the Truth above and beyond the physical body. The logicians, through the logic, expressed the existence of soul as above the physical entity. He is both the doer and the enjoyer or sufferer of good and evil actions. Afterwards, in the Sankhya Philosophy, he has been described as the enjoyer or sufferer, but not the doer of actions. When the disciples, through regular meditation, become advanced, they realise the Supreme Being as the Absolute Unity. He is neither the doer nor the receiver of the fruits of the actions. He is transcendental. Practically, all the scriptures declare and describe the One Infinite, but the true meaning of the scriptures should be realised with the help of the God-realised-persons. It is impossible to solve the riddles in the scriptures without the help of the knower of Truth."

In the Kumbha Mela, every Mandaleswar invites all the monks under other Mandaleswars at least for a day in his Ashram for dinner, generally known as 'Bhandara'. It is not the ordinary feast but a special one, in which at the specific time, the Mandaleswars with their monks in a queue enter into the cordon through the special entrance. This cordon is a spacious enclosure where at least ten thousand people could be accommodated for the dinner. At the gate, one monk is placed to receive the invited monks along with their Mandaleswars and to eliminate the un-invited persons. It is interesting to note the method of elimination of the un-invited persons. The gatekeeper monk stands at the narrow entrance with a silver stick in his hand. The Secretary of the Ashram, also stands just in front of the gatekeeper to identify the persons not belonging to his group. At the time of entry, the Secretary points out the undesirable person, and instantly the gatekeeper closes the entrance by placing the silver stick in between the bars of the gate. He then politely requests the intruder to come with his own party and Mandaleswar. After all the members have entered, the Secretary himself steps in. The Mandaleswars are accommodated and entertained in a special room, in a special way. Their seats are also special. After the entertainment, the host donates with devotion silken clothing and money not less than one hundred rupees per head. The secretaries and spiritual ministers are also entertained in a special way; generally they are accommodated with the Mandaleswars. They too receive donations of money and clothing but little less than the Mandaleswars.

The sadhus and renunciates sit on their own seats of blanket or kusa- grass or on seats supplied by the host. It is amazing that though thousands of monks dine together at a place, yet no one from outside can understand what is going on inside. The monks do not speak at all; very silently they take their meals. In each line, several inspectors are placed to look after the arrangement. Once, I had seen that, in a line, some of the monks had been supplied sweet-meats for a number of times while others did not get even once; but without any grievance, they were taking their meals. Of course, when it was pointed out by the inspector to the suppliers of the sweets, the deficiency was made up.

In the Kumbha Mela, I had to take the Bhandara daily and had to accept clothings and money on each occasion. The supervisors in the 'Bhandara' used to start the function with the utterance of the usual words of signal "Namah Parvatipataya Har". So long as the different items of the meals were served on the leaf plates, we used to recite the 15th Chapter of the holy Srimad Bhagavad Gita. If within that time, different items could not be served, the monks, one after another, would recite verse or verses from the Upanishada or other scriptures. When all the items were served for the first time, we were directed to start eating by the supervisor, generally known as "Kothari Maharaj"; the direction being the usual signal. The function came to an end when all were fully satisfied and the words of signal expressed by the Swamiji Maharaj (Kothari Maharaj). Then in rows we would go to the place of washing and one by one clean our hands and mouth with water. This, in short, is the description of our Bhandara.

The main Kumbha dip was scheduled on the 14th January. The executive committee of ours had fixed the time for starting the different processions of different Mandaleswar. At 5-45 a.m., the procession of the Nirvani Akhara started. At 6-45 a.m., our Ananda Akhara, along with Niranjan Akhara, started for the dip. At 7.45 a.m., the procession of the Juna Akhara started. After an interval of every one hour, other processions started. There were two roads, side by side, from the heart of the Mela to the junction of Ganga, Jamuna and Saraswati. One road was meant for those incoming to the Sangam (confluence of the three rivers) and the other for outgoing. No one was allowed to enter into the cordoned main two roads during the time of processions. The main roads were protected by a number of civil police. On the two sides of the road leading to the Sangam, men, women and children stood paying their respects. Many people devotionally scattered their offerings (flowers, sweets, money, etc.) at the feet of the monks as the procession was moving slowly towards the Ganges. The policemen kept their vigilant eyes on the beggars so that they may not enter into the road to collect the money, thereby causing disturbances to the procession. There were many volunteers helping the policemen, either on horses or on foot, to protect the procession. On both the sides of the roads, there were temporary wooden posts and thick ropes were fastened throughout, thus making the cordon. By 12:00 noon, all the processions returned safely after taking dips in the Sangam.

At 1 o'clock, we all assembled for the 'Bhandara'. After taking Bhandara, we returned to our respective Ashrams. Sasida (Sasi Bose Mullick - our spiritual brother) informed me that he was going to visit a mysterious yogi residing in a solitary cave at Jushi, who was always in ecstasy. Swami Dayananda Giri, our spiritual brother and I became very enthusiastic to have his darshan (sacred glance). At the time of starting, five more renunciates accompanied us. Sasida took his loaded camera to take the yogi's photos. The cave was dark. The yogi was in samadhi (ecstasy) in a cross-legged posture (Padmasana) on a pile of straw in that cave. His eyes were fixed at the point between the eyebrows without any winking. A fly was moving over his eyelids but could not disturb the yogi who was above and beyond body consciousness. It was afternoon, when we reached the grotto. The shivering cold of the winter could not create any sensation to the naked body of the yogi. The age of the yogi appeared to be 20 to 21 years, but it was not possible to ascertain the correct age of the yogi as he had already conquered the ravage of the time. It may be possible that he was living for centuries like Babaji. Sasida did not know how to take his snaps as the cave was dark and as he had no light arrangement with his camera; the diffused light of the sun was not sufficient for the snap shot.

However, the monks decided to take him out of his grotto for camera exposure. We had one blanket with us which had been spread outside the cave. Sasida, applied his physical strength to carry the yogi out of his cave and placed the physical body in a posture according to Sasida's choice for good snaps. As Sasida took several pictures, the yogi smiled a while; the reason of which we could not understand then.

Sasida sent the film to a studio for washing. When the pictures were supplied by the company, we all were wonderstruck to see the picture of the yogi missing, though the cave, meadows, trees, blanket and all were clear in the photos. It is beyond the jurisdiction of our modern science, how the yogi could trick the camera. The meaning of the smiling face of the yogi was clear then. Sasida could realise then that without permission no one could "steal" his image or pictures.

However, a few days later, Sasida alone went to the yogi and with folded hands begged permission for taking a single snap and thus succeeded to get his picture.

On the 16th January, 1942, we had another dip. For several days it was raining heavily - but the inclement weather could not disturb the processions of the monks. On the 19th, our Mandaleswarji invited all other Mandaleswars in our Ashram for the Bhandara.

Swami Dayananda Giri and I decided to leave Allahabad on the 20th January as after the last dip on the 21st everyone would be anxious to leave. It would be nearly impossible to get Railway tickets. Accordingly, on the 20th January, 1942, Swami Dayanandaji and I started from Allahabad for Y.S.S., Ranchi via Banaras. On the way to Ranchi, we also visited Vindhachal, old Nalanda University, Gaya and Rajgir. On the 27th January, 1942, I reached Y.S.S. Ranchi.

So far, I described the Religious Conferences and the procession of the monks for the dip. Among thousands of yogis, sadhus, renunciates I mentioned about visit to a single yogi. Now let me mention about other yogis and renunciates. From time to time, I used to visit the monks, sadhus and renunciates of different orders in search of real yogis or God-realised-Souls. Of course, finding God-realised Souls is impossible unless and until they themselves very kindly expose themselves. On both the sides of the Ganges, thousands of sadhus, Brahmacharis and renunciates were living on the open bank; most of them had no clothings at all. A few Brahmacharis had loincloth as their only possession, reducing the demand of the body to the minimum. Those who want to see the happy and unattached lives of the Indian monks and renunciates must visit the Indian Kumbha Mela — thousands of renunciates, free from the material entanglements, free from clothing problems, free from handling money, living under the natural canopy of ever-compassionate God. Many of the sadhus and saints had high university degrees or Sanskrit titles like Vedanta Tirtha, Shastri and so on.

As I was walking along the bank of the Ganges or through the areas thickly (temporarily) populated by renunciates, my eyes were attracted by a woman saint sitting on a tiger skin. She appeared to be the head of an Ashram or an institution as she was encircled by a number of devotees or disciples. Succumbing to the spiritual charm, a number of persons were either standing or sitting in front of her, with folded hands, begging her motherly blessings, the only treasure she had to bestow on others. She appeared to be the Mother of the Mela. She was distributing fruits to every devotee who was approaching her with devotion. She had only one "ornament" in her physical body which was nothing but ash besmeared all over her body to protect it from heat and cold. From her motherly eyes, emanated the spiritual aura, that naturally charmed all the devotees seeking spiritual treasure.

Various kinds of renunciates enrich the Kumbha Mela. Those, who want to meet the highly advanced souls or God-realised ones, must visit the 'Sangam' at dead of night between 12-30 a.m. to 3 a.m. when they would take their bath. Many of them would travel through the air as they had acquired the power of materialization and dematerialization of the bodies. I came to know of this fact from some of our renunciate friends.

To quote from Autobiography of a Yogi by Paramhansa Yogananda, Chapter 42:

"Anchorites wearing loin cloths sat quickly in little groups, their bodies besmeared with ashes that protect them from heat and cold. The spiritual eye was vividly represented on their foreheads by a single spot of sandal wood paste. Shaven headed Swamis appeared by the thousands, ochre robed, carrying their bamboo staff and begging bowl. Their faces beamed with the renunciate's peace as they walked about or held philosophical discussions with disciples. Here and there, under the trees around, huge piles of burning logs, were picturesque sadhus, their hair braided and massed in coils on top of their heads. Some wore beards several feet in length, curled and tied in a knot. They meditated quietly or extended their hands in blessing to the passing throng beggars, maharajas on elephants, fakirs with their arms held grotesquely aloft, brahmacharis carrying meditation elbow-props, humble sages whose solemnity had an inner bliss. High above the din, we heard the ceaseless summons of the temple bells".

"Our temporary dwelling huts were made up of mud, bamboo and straw, the walls being temporarily erected with bamboo-mats. Inside of which we had a pair of blankets, one for the protection from cold and the other spread on the piles of straw for our beds."

Some sadhus, due to want of straw, bamboo and rope, had dug the earth and their very modest dwelling caves attracted me most. I would like to relate the events pertaining to my visit to Kumbha Mela at Allahabad in the year 1954.

On the 16th January 1954, a devotee, who was a resident of Allahabad visited me at Y.S.S., Ranchi and took Kriya Yoga initiation from me. He said, "Swamiji I am going to Allahabad by car, will you kindly accompany me to visit Kumbha Mela?"

I said, "I am busy with some urgent works of Y.S.S. Ranchi. Shortly I shall start for the Kumbha Mela and I wish to stay at the Bholananda Sannyas Ashram there".

He requested me to intimate him the date and time of my arrival there. I agreed and I did so accordingly. On the 28th January 1954, the train reached Allahabad station at 11-15 a.m. At the station, I was received by the devotee. Hence, I had to go to his residence first.

I had intimated Swami Vishweshwarananda Giriji, the Secretary of the Bholananda Sannyas Ashram regarding the date and time of my arrival there. Accordingly a room had been reserved for me. On the 30th January, 1954, in the afternoon, I reached Bholananda Sannyas Ashram. Swami Vishweshwaranandaji said, "Swamiji, I have reserved a room for you. Why did you not come here on the appointed day?" I humbly intimated him the real reason. Swamiji commented, "Why then are you anxious to come here. In my opinion, you will get much better comfort there. So you need not come here". Though my attraction was always for staying amidst the monks, but God's will was otherwise. I had to stay at the house of the devotee.

I had hired one new bicycle with the help of the devotee. On this bicycle I used to visit Kumbha Mela and used to take my bath in the 'Triveni' (Sangam) daily. I also would visit the town from time to time on the bicycle.

On the 2nd February, a monk from the native land of the devotee arrived at his house. He expressed his desire to help him to visit the Kumbha Mela. Two sons of the devotee also joined us. We all reached the Kumbha Mela at 9 a.m. First, I intended to visit our Bholananda Sannyas Ashram, and accordingly as we were going to cross the Ganges by the temporary bridge No. 4, we were informed at the gate, that the bridge was broken and fourteen lives were lost. We returned to the gate of Bridge No. 2, but due to the heavy pressure of the crowd, we could not penetrate the people. Hence, instead of attempting to cross the river, we directly approached the Sangam. I alone took my dip at Triveni. After visiting the places of interest, we came back to our residence at 12.30 p.m.

The 3rd February, 1954 was the day for the main dip for the Kumbha Yoga at Tribeni Sangam at Allahabad. Hence, finishing my morning Kriya Yoga earlier than the scheduled hour, I went out on a bicycle at 5.20 a.m. As I was nearing the place, the crowd became thicker and thicker. Luckily a police van carrying 15 to 20 policemen was going ahead of me clearing the road. I had the help of the van from Thorn Hill Road to Jawaharlal Nehru Road. Then it turned in another direction. Hence, I had to push through the crowd alone. First, I thought of going directly to the Bholananda Sannyas Ashram, but due to many red tapes I could not cross bridge No. 4 with my bicycle. Hence, I had to come back to the Cantonment Executive Officers' Camp by the side of the Ganges where I kept my bicycle and crossed bridge No. 4 on foot. Due to the very thick crowd of the devotees, it took me an hour to cross the bridge. I could not reach the Ashram in time to join the procession. However, as I crossed the river, I noticed that our Mandaleswarji was sitting on the elephant and the procession was moving slowly. I knew from my previous experience of the Kumbha Mela of the 1942 that if I could not join our own procession, it would be impossible to join any other procession or to go to the place of Sangam alone for the dip in time. But ahead was the huge multitude of devotees. Further, if I could not join our procession at the start, I would not be allowed to join the procession in the middle. According to the convention of the Kumbha Mela procession for the holy dip, the monks should march in pairs and a band of Naga Sadhus used to march on both sides of the procession in order to protect it from intruders. At the time of the start, if the number of the monks becomes odd, then there must be one left after making up the marching pairs; but if the number becomes even, then there will be no one left after making up the pair. However, pushing, elbowing, jumping, I soon entered into the procession and after searching I realised that there was one "needed" for making one pair. I had filled up the void and happily proceeded onwards with the same rhythmic steps. Crossing bridge No. 3, within half an hour, we reached the Tribeni Sangam.

I had a mind to go back with my party to our Ashram, but as I reached the shore after the dip, three ladies requested me to help them reach their destination, Bharat Sevashram. While I was directing them to the road leading to their destination, the old lady among the group fervently requested me holding my hands, "My son, please guide us upto the destination". Hence, I could not return with our party to our Ashram. I had to lead them to the Bharat Sevashram and from there I returned to our camp (Cantonment Executive Officer" camp).

On the 2nd, another devotee and his wife came to the place where I was staying. These devotees also had their Kriya Yoga initiation from me. They fervently requested me to accompany them to Ranchi via Banaras and Patna by their car. I joined them on my return journey.

This time, the Kumbha Mela had seen one of the most severe tragedies in memorable history. Due to the arrangement of extra trains for the Kumbha Mela, millions of people got the opportunity to come to Allahabad for the dip. About five million people had assembled for the holy dip. At the appointed time, all the five million people were trying to go to the Triveni Sangam for the holy dip. Hence, gradually the pressure of incoming devotees was increasing and at 10 a.m., it became maximum, when incoming and outgoing throngs met. Though there were separate roads for the incoming and outgoing devotees, due to high pressure the separation was lost. If anyone by chance, would fall down, there was no hope for his life as thousands of people would walk over his body.

Though I was going through a place, far away from the public road, still, in my presence, several persons had fallen down and I, with the help of others, had protected their lives. On reaching the camp, I came to know that during the dip, 350 persons had died and several thousands persons were injured. Gradually, the number of the dead and injured increased. Soon the entrance was closed and the protecting forces got busy in protecting the injured ones and collecting the dead bodies as well as their belongings. In the office of the protection force, heaps of clothings, shoes, sticks and various other belongings of the dead and seriously injured persons were lying.

Next day, all the leading newspapers in India were full of the description of pathetic incidents of the Kumbha Mela. Several thousand had died and all the nearby hospitals were full with the injured persons.

By that time, Kumbha Mela was over. I left Allahabad on 5th February, 1954 for Banaras as arranged earlier, but this time with a painful remembrance of the tragic incident.

At Banaras, I, along with the party, enjoyed a dip in the Ganges; travelled by boat, performed Siva Puja in the temple and so on. We left Banaras for Patna on the way to Ranchi and reached Y.S.S. Ashram, Ranchi at 8.45 p.m. on 6th February, 1954.

Let me conclude with some more quotes from Autobiography of a Yogi by Paramhansa Yogananda; Chapter 42, regarding the importance of Kumbha Mela.

"Our party reached the Kumbha Mela on January 23, 1936 at Allahabad. The surging crowd of nearly two million persons was an impressive sight, even an overwhelming one. The peculiar genius of the Indians is the reverence innate in even the lowliest peasant for the worth of the spirit and for the monks and sadhus that have forsaken worldly ties to seek a diviner anchorage. Impostors and hypocrites there are indeed; but India respects all for the sake of the few that illumine the land with supernal blessings. Westerners that were viewing the vast spectacle had a unique opportunity to feel the pulse of the nation, the spiritual odour to which India owes her quenchless vitality under the blows of time".

Chapter 25

Ananda Moyi Ma in Dakshineswar

Sri Sri Ananda Moyi Ma intimated us that she would visit our Y.S.S., Dakshineswar on 9th May, 1958. Accordingly, Swami Atmananda Giriji instructed me to make all arrangements for her reception. He further intimated that I should receive her on behalf of the Society at Yogoda Math, Dakshineswar. I made all arrangements in time including purchase of flowers and garlands.

Sri Sri Ananda Moyi Ma arrived at 6 p.m. A meeting had also been arranged for her reception. In the meeting, I garlanded her and offered a few flowers at her feet. After visiting the Math (Press, Guru Mandir, etc.) she came back to the Guru Mandir, where a special meeting had been arranged in her honour.

In the meeting I requested her to impart us some instructions. She commented: "Try to follow the instructions that Paramahansa Yoganandaji imparted to you". Then she concluded: "God is the only real substance and all other things in the world are transitory, hence, unreal. Keep this thought always alive in your heart".

From Yogoda Math, Dakshineswar, we led her to Tulsi Yogoda Ashram, Calcutta. From there Sri Sri Ananda Moyi Ma returned to her Ashram and we came back to our Yogoda Math, Dakshineswar.

I had visited Sri Sri Ananda Moyi Ma many times. On 30th December 1953, a devotee informed me of the arrival of Sri Sri Ananda Moyi Ma at Ranchi. I sent him to her Ashram to request for the time when I could meet her. At 10 a.m., we bicycled to her Ashram. At the gate, I noticed the large crowd. However, a Brahmachari disciple of the mother came forward and led us to the mother. Mother was then busy replying to the questions of the devotees. I was listening to those questions and answers. At 11 a.m., I returned with the 'Prasad' received from Ma.

At 4-00 p.m., I revisited the Ashram of Sri Sri Ananda Moyi Ma. Sweet Kirtan was going on. It ended shortly thereafter. A devotee stood up and intimated us, "Mother is ready now. You are at liberty to ask any question you like. She will give reply". Then one after another, the devotees started asking questions. Mother replied. A few such questions were:

"Is it possible to pray to God and work out the pre-natal works (Prarabdha Bhoga) simultaneously"?

Mother replied: "Both are works. You are doing both the works, as both are actions of the body. That which is always demanding ("Dehi, Dehi") is the body (Deha). Man is always simultaneously praying and either enjoying or suffering. To pray means expression of desires. A school-boy is praying for passing the school examination. Someone is praying for the re-dressal of sorrow or relief from disease, etc. Prayer also means want. Hence, due to want man prays.

Simultaneous performance of prayer and working out of "Prarabdha" is possible from material standpoint. But real prayer, which means 'we don't want anything but God', is not possible during the working out of "Prarabdha Karma" because there is always a pull at the back. During the various kinds of sufferings prayer comes automatically for the way out of them. Prayer for Him alone comes when the "Prarabdha Bhoga" is nearly complete. Such thoughts like 'You are my all, I can't move without you' come as waves after working out "Prarabdha Bhoga". As the waves are infinite, the prayers too are infinite. It is why the prayer will continue for eternity".

"Wave is an individual soul. When he gets salvation, does he not then become free from prayer?"

Sri Sri Ma responded: "When the individual soul gets salvation, it becomes the Ocean. Hence, he is still in the bosom of the ocean. How can we say that the wave becomes free. It is His 'Lila'."

The devotee enquired: "Can Lila be applied to human beings?"

"In the scriptures, we find the mention of Lila of Him and not of any individual soul. For the human beings, no Lila is possible. It is his suffering".

Then another devotee requested mother to speak about 'Kripa' i.e., grace of God. Mother commented: "His grace is unconditional".

I enquired: "It is written in the scriptures that one gets God when He accepts him. Is there any condition for this acceptance? Because we see He does not accept all, that is, everybody does not get salvation."

Mother replied: "His grace is unconditional. Due to His grace man performs 'Sadhana'. When he is advanced, his mind becomes purified and he reaches a stage where from he feels the pull of His unconditional grace. Suppose you are going towards the ocean, you may reach and may try to swim; but you are drifted to the shore by the waves. Still you are trying to swim. A time will come when you will be able to swim. A time will come when you will feel the pull from inside of the ocean".

A young girl enquired, "Why can't I put faith on Him fully? I believe and the next moment disbelief comes".

Mother replied: "Once full faith really comes, it cannot be shaken. There is no doubt about it. When the mind is concentrated on Him, He is always before the eyes, then how the faith can be flickered?"

Another devotee enquired: "How can we realize Him?"

Mother:

"If you dig here and there, you won't get water. Dig in a place, go on digging to the level where the water is flowing. You must reach that level, otherwise you won't get. Water is everywhere, unless you reach that level how can you expect water. Similarly, God is everywhere, when you are doing 'Sadhana' but you have not reached that stage where He may be experienced fully."

The first devotee again enquired: "Some of the scriptures declare that there is no 'Prarabdha' for a God-realised soul and in others, we find that even the God realised should have to work out the 'Prarabdha'. What is the truth?"

Mother:

"You see the fan is moving; it may be recognised as its 'Prarabdha'. Now switch off the electric current; still for a short time the fan willcontinue to move. Looking at this movement you may say that the fan is working out its 'Prarabdha'. But if you think of the absence of the current, you may declare, it has no 'Prarabdha'.

The meeting ended. I bicycled back to Yogoda Ashram.

Chapter 26
In the Holy Himalayas

From my early childhood I cherished the desire to go to the Himalayas for solitary meditation. It was 1947. I expressed my desire to Paramhansa Yoganandaji in U.S.A. seeking his blessings and asking for his permission for visiting the holy places in the Himalayas. He simply commented, "If you wish to go on a trip, it is better too". On receiving the letter, I requested the office of the Y.S.S., Ranchi for the necessary travelling expenses. I was then the Headmaster of Yogoda Satsanga Branch Vidyalaya, Ranchi. The Secretary relieved me of my responsibilities and duties, and sanctioned money for the tour.

I left Ranchi on the 3rd May 1947. First, I went to Y.S.S., Lakhanpur and informed Girinda of my proposed trip to the Himalayas. He offered to accompany me. On 12th May 1947, I started from Howrah station. Girinda, now known as Swami Bidyananda Giri, joined me at Hardwar. We stayed at Sri Sri Bholananda Sannyas Ashram, Laltarabagh, Hardwar. Swami Bishudhananda Giriji, a disciple of Swami Sri Yukteswar Giriji Maharaj was a very influential and popular monk at Sri Sri Bholananda Sannyas Ashram. He was happy to learn about our intended pilgrimage. He gave me two introductory letters, one for Mandaleswar Sri Sri (108) Swami Jagadiswarananda Bharati and the other addressed to Srimat Swami Paramanandaji at Kailash Ashram, Hrishikesh (Kothari Maharaj) for facilitating our Himalayan journey.

On the 16th evening, we reached Kailash Ashram, Hrishikesh by bus. On 17th morning, I visited Mandaleswar Sri Sri (108) Swami Bishudhananda Giriji, he was then at Kailash Ashram. Kailash Ashram was very solitary and beautiful, situated on the bank of the Ganges; indeed, fit for deep meditation of the renunciates. Later, on the same day, I called on Mandaleswar Sri Sri (108) Swami Jagadiswarananda Bharatiji. I paid my respects. He told me that the office of Kali Kambali had sent our free-ration tickets for visiting all the four 'Dhamas', namely

Jamunotry, Gangotry, Kedarnath and Badrinath. He asked, "When do you intend to start? I replied: "Tomorrow". He handed over all the tickets. I told him, "We intended to visit only Kedarnath and Badrinath". He commented: "You are young men. This is the time for visiting the holy places. So many old men and women are visiting all the four 'Dhamas'. You are young and cannot visit them?"

I humbly replied: "Yes, we shall visit all the four Dhamas". He was very pleased. We decided to visit first the temple of Goddess Jamuna, situated at the source of river Jamuna. One Hatha Yogi, Brahamachari Hariharanandaji joined us. In the afternoon, we went to the sub-office, and reserved three seats for Tihiri, 56 miles away from Hrishikesh. On the 18th at 6 a.m., we revisited Mandaleswarji for his blessings before starting for the pilgrimage. We visited Kothari Maharaj and deposited our extra luggage in his office. The bus for Tihiri started at 9.30 a.m. from Hrishikesh. There were stiff ups and downs with sharp bends in the hilly track. The landscape was beautiful. There were small villages and very small towns; small brooks and rivers flowing at great speed descending from stiff hills. Nine miles from Hrishikesh was the small town Narendra Nagar, and 18 miles from Narendra Nagar was another town 'Chamba'. As we proceeded further and were descending, a new vista opened up; the small villages and towns looked like a garland on the neck of the river a few thousand feet below, as if we were viewing the scenes through the window of an aeroplane. On one side was the stiff hill and on the other was the river flowing few thousand feet below. Thousands, nay millions, of ever green trees, mostly ferns and among the bush Phyloclades and Cladodes, were ever beautifying the hills and mountains. From an elevation of 6 thousand feet, the bus descended for 12 miles negotiating many sharp bends to reach Tihiri bus stand at 7 p.m. Tihiri town in the Garhwal State was 2278 ft. above the sea level. We decided to take rest for a day at Tihiri town for visiting the holy places and temples in the town. We spent the night at the Sikh Gurudwara.

On the 19th at 4 p.m., we went out to visit the places of interest. We first visited the temple of Sri Ramji. There were several round stones aptly called 'Salagram Narayanas", symbolising the deep blue round balls visible during meditation. Inside the temple, there were stone images of Sri Ramachandra and Sri Lakshmana with Goddess Sita in the middle. By the side of this temple was the temple of Mahabir, and nearby was the temple of Sri Badrinathji housing the stone image of

Lord Badrinarayan with (the images of) Sri Sri Lakshmi Devi and Goddess Srinaga Devi on both sides. In front of the temple of Sri Ramchandra was the temple of Goddess Durga (Sri Sri Bhagabati), with (the stone image of) the Divine Mother.

I was pleasantly surprised to see Mandaleswar Sri Sri (108) Bishnudevananda Giriji in the temple of Sri Badrinathji whom we had met at Kailash Ashram in Hrishikesh. He was on his way to Uttar Kashi. I had some conversation with him. I enquired about the origin or source of the river Ganga. He said: "One of the many names of the Ganga is 'Tripathaga'. When Sri Sri Bhagirath brought her on the earth, she flowed through three ways. One of her courses was through the hill, the name of which was Alakananda, the other through the heaven for the gods and goddesses, known as Mandakini and the third on earth known as Bhagirathi or 'Ganga' (Ganges)". The source of the river Mandakini was from the Kedarnath hill, Alakananda from the Badrinath hill and the Ganges from the "Gomukh".

Generally, the meeting places of two rivers are considered as holy places, and hence we find various temples at such places. At Tihiri, near the temple of Sri Badrinathji, the river Bilangana met the river Ganges. The local people called the river Bilangana as 'Alakananda'.

Since there was no transport beyond Tihiri, we had to walk about 71 miles to reach Jamunotry, the first place of our pilgrimage and the origin of the river Jamuna. In absence of mile-stones, it was very difficult to ascertain the actual distances between various halting stations which we collected from local people which may or may not be accurate. At 5.20 p.m., we started from Tihiri and reached the first halting place, Gadisarai five miles away at 7.15 p.m. On the 20th May 1947 at 4 a.m. we left Gadisarai and reached Bharnala at 9 a.m. Mandaleswar Srimat (108) Paramahansa Bishnudevanandaji joined us at Bharnala. It took five hours to cover a distance of just six miles due to the difficulty in trekking the hilly track. We began our journey again in the afternoon to reach the third resting place, 'Cham' the same evening. Mandaleswar Maharaj reached there a few minutes before us.

We got our free ration tickets from the office of the Kali Kambali, who had ration shops at each halting place throughout the Himalayan journey. Accordingly we used to get our ration and fuel, etc. free of cost from each ration shop, plus the required quantity of salt, spices and the necessary utensils for cooking and for taking meals. We had, however, to carry our necessary warm clothings and blankets and also other necessary articles, like torchlight, notebook, fountain pen, cotton, iodine, etc.

On the 21st, we started from 'Cham' at 4.45 a.m. and reached 'Nagun' at 7 a.m. on the way to Dharasu junction where roads from Jamunotry, Uttarkashi, Kathgodam and other places met. The fifteen miles journey from Bharnala to 'Dharasu' junction was comparatively easy due to absence of steep ascending and descending. We took our breakfast at 'Nagun' and resumed our journey at 7.35 a.m. reaching Dharasu at 9.30 am. After travelling 26 miles from Tihiri to Dharasu with all our belongings, we were so tired that we could not walk with all the belongings on our shoulders. Travelling in the Himalayan mountains with load on shoulders proved to be difficult as we were not used to travelling with goods on shoulder even in the plains. Hence, we decided to hire a cooly for carrying our luggage. I got a young man, 'Jivananda', for a cooly. He belonged to the priestly class and not a cooly by profession. He was intending to visit the holy places in the Himalayas. For want of money, his desire could not materialise. However, it was settled with him that he would carry all our belongings so long as we don't get bus for our return journey. Besides, he would cook our meals twice daily. In return, he would get meals twice and breakfast. As regards cash money, he demanded rupees forty in advance and rupees one hundred at the end of the journey.

On 22nd, at 5 a.m. we started for Jamunotry, and at 8.55 a.m. we reached the first halting place, Kumbha Ara or Chati. Chati was the general name for all resting places where all sorts of arrangements were available for proper rest for cash money. At Chati, there were many ration shops, hotels and rest rooms free of cost available for all. As we were free from the burden of our luggage, we walked faster. After making proper arrangements for our rest, Jivananda went in for cooking our food.

There were several halting places from Dharasu to Jamunotry at varying distances of about four to nine miles - Kumbha Ara (9miles), Silkera (5 miles), Dandalgao (7 miles), Gangani (4 miles), Jamuna (7 miles), Hanuman(5 miles), Janaki Ma (4 miles) and Jamunotry (4 miles). In these halting places, we took rest during day or night as the case may be. The beginning of our journey was very good, steep uphills and down-slopes were negligible. The first nine miles from Dharasu to Kumbha Ara were beautiful; small villages on both sides, with the greenery of paddy, wheat, cabbage, radish, potatoes, sugarcane, etc. Near the springs or by the side of the Ganges, there were innumerable banana plants.

In the afternoon, we started at 4 p.m. and reached Silkera at 6.30 p.m. Due to the presence of large number of pilgrims beyond the capacity of the resting houses, we had to spend our night in the open within the jungle. We felt the Himalayan cold keenly. Next morning at 5 a.m., we started from Silkera to climb the steep hill. For about four miles, the journey was continuously upward and then for a few yards downwards. At an interval of 30 to 40 yards, there were sharp bends. We took rest at Gangani after climbing eleven miles.

On the 24th May 1947, we started from Gangani at 5 a.m. and reached Jamuna at 8.30 a.m. The road, by the side of the river Jamuna, was very rough with broken stones. On both the sides, there were hilly fruits and flower trees; many were unknown. Among known trees were pomegranate roses. The range from Gangani to Jamunotry was known as "Gandhmadan Hill", associated with the search for the medicinal herbs, Visallakarani by Mahavir Hanuman for saving the life of Sri Lakshmana.

There were millions of Visallakarani herbs on both the sides of the way. Through the 'Gandhamadan Hill', as we proceeded towards Hanuman Chati, we crossed several bridges. The path was very rough, full of undulations. We proceeded onward through heavy showers and storms. At 7 p.m., we could reach the 'Hanuman Chati'.

On the 25 th, we started from Hanuman Chati at 5.45 a.m., and reached Janaki Ma, the next halting place, at 9 a.m. It was nearly inaccessible. Sometimes, we had to make our way through dense forest and sometimes by the side of the very steep cliff. After taking rest for a while, we resumed our journey.

Opposite Janaki Ma was the village Kharsali where many priests resided. The land was very fertile. The fields were full of grains and vegetables. The houses were all made of wood. The image of the Goddess Jamuna is shifted to Kharsali when the Jamuna temple remained covered with snow for six months. From Janaki Ma to Jamunotry was a difficult journey since the path was very narrow, just about a foot, and ran across the thick jungle that encircled the very steep hill. The distance was only four miles, still, we could reach only after 1.30 p.m.

Jamunotry (10,800 ft. high)

The ranges of Jamunotry remain covered with snow throughout the year. In the bosom of the Himalayan mountains, the snow covered ranges look very beautiful. After reaching an altitude of about 11,500 feet through that dense forest encircling the 'Bhairav' temple we descended to a height of 10,800 ft. to reach Jamunotry. On one side of the river Jamuna was the resting place and on the other side was the temple of Goddess Jamuna. The water in Jamuna was very cold as the melting snow joined the river. But there were many hot springs by the side of the temple. There were several small tanks to collect the water from the hot springs. According to the temperature of the water, the tanks were differentiated by different names.

The small tank attached to the temple of Goddess Jamuna was called "Brahma Kundu". The next to Brahma Kunda was Bishnu Kunda. The third one was Gouri Kunda and then Surya Kunda and Gupta Muni, adjacent to one another. Then there were several very hot springs. The hot spring where water came out with force like the water from a huge syringe, was known as the 'Face of Jamuna'. Our guiding priest told me that the real source of Jamuna was Jambudwip, a mountain attached to Jamunotry. Both the mountains were nearly inaccessible due to their slippery steep slope covered with snow throughout the year.

By the side of "Face of Jamuna", there was a similar hot spring with water coming out with force was known as Vasudhara. Next was another very hot spring, almost at the boiling temperature coming out of a narrow fissure with high pressure. No one could approach it. Priests called this 8th spring as Goutam Rishi. Most interesting was the Chasm by the side of a perpendicular rock near the 8th spring through which steam came out continuously. It was known as Agni Kunda. No one could approach Agni Kunda due to its perpendicular position and tremendous heat.

All the springs and tanks mentioned above were on the right side when one faces the temple. There were three hot springs on the left side too. The first spring that came out of a heap of rocks with force was known as Gomukhi. Next to it was the second spring, Gouri, and the third towards the resting house was Suryamukhi. All the stones in touch with springs were very hot.

The temple of Goddess Jamuna was made of black stone. On the left of Goddess Jamuna, there was white stone image of the Goddess

Ganga. In front of Goddess Ganga and Jamuna were the images of Mahabir and Lord Sri Krishna, respectively.

After resting a while in the rest house, we took bath in the hot spring. Not only we were refreshed but also the body pain mysteriously disappeared. We engaged a priest for the puja of the Goddess Jamuna and took the prasad (consecrated food). In the afternoon at 3 p.m., I spoke with the priest, "After so much hardship, we reached this holy place. We are disappointed not to find any Himalayan yogi about whom we have heard so many miraculous stories".

The priest said, "Yes, there are many highly advanced yogis in the Himalayas. They generally do not come to the common holy temples or places. They live in the inaccessible caves, enjoying uninterrupted ecstasy as longs they please". Then he narrated one of his "eye witness" incidents, "A yogi used to live in the cave in this mountain in front of the temple a few yards away from us. But since the cave was by the side of the slippery perpendicular snow covered mountain, no one could approach him. The naked yogi used to remain in the cave most of the time, in Samadhi, on the show. As the door was in front of us, we could observe his movements. Once, he remained in ecstasy for seventeen days at a stretch. On the 18th day, he came down before us and requested us to arrange a Bhandara (feast) for him. As I was thinking about the materials for the Bhandara as well as for the men whom we could entertain, the yogi being aware of my thought said, 'Don't worry about the materials and the men. Both the materials and men are coming. You will have to manage the Bhandara. While he was still speaking, a group of people arrived carrying various kinds of materials for the feast — flour, milk, ghee (clarified butter), sugar and various kinds of sweetmeats, etc. Most probably the yogi had ordered, in a vision, the local king for the same. However, we cooked the food and managed for the distribution of the meal to the people present on that day. The yogi was happily looking after the Bhandara, at the end of which he expressed his last desire. 'The work, for which I had come in this world, has come to an end. Now please, arrange for my funeral'. Nearly all the people present fled, afraid of burning a living yogi. I thought, unless and until the yogi was above and beyond the body consciousness, he could not dare order us to arrange for the burning of his living body. Thinking thus, I approached for the arrangement of woods for the funeral in order to receive the blessings of the yogi. As I approached some of our fellow brothers (priests) joined me. At that time, a rich man arrived at the place with large quantity of sandal wood for the purpose of a funeral as he was directed to do so in a dream. As the arrangement were complete, the yogi blessed us all. Slowly, he climbed and sat on the funeral pyre in a cross-legged posture. Ordering us to set the wood on fire, he entered into deep Samadhi. We poured clarified butter on the wood and ignited the same. The flame of fire soon spread in all directions and consumed the motionless physical body of the yogi".

In the afternoon at 5 p.m., I sat for meditation. The atmosphere was saturated with the thought of renunciation and holy vibrations; hence, my mind was withdrawn instantly, and I was absorbed in deep meditation. After the meditation was over, I was thinking about the yogis of the Himalayan caves — renouncing all worldly desires, how they were enjoying the bliss of God-contact. Naturally, their thoughts of renunciation filled my mind. I thought that renouncing everything I would remain there and would spend the rest of my life in deep meditation. The desire for travelling the other holy places was gone, what to speak of returning to Yogoda Ashram, Ranchi. Due to association of ideas, the thought of Gurudeva came over my mind and how his flight toward the Himalayas was interrupted. Then gradually the most valuable words of Sri Yukteswarji to my Guru came to my mind. As Paramhansa Yoganandaji wanted permission to go to the Himalayas in the hope of achieving continuous divine communion in the unbroken solicitude, Sri Yukteswar Giriji said, "Many hillmen live in the Himalayas, yet possess no God-perception. Wisdom is better sought from a man of realization than from an inert mountain". And the subsequent valuable words of Sri Ram Gopal Mazumdar, "Young yogi, I see you are running away from your master. He has everything you need; you should return to him. Mountains cannot be your guru". All these thoughts changed my desire to reside in the Himalayan cave for God-contact.

On 26th May 1947 at 6 a.m., we started for the next holy place, 'Uttar Kashi', 39 miles from Jamunotry. For twenty miles we had to retrace our journey upto Gangani. By 11 a.m., we could cover a distance of 8 miles and reached the Hanuman Chati. On our return journey, we came through the path running along the back of the river Jamuna. From 2 p.m., it was raining heavily. Hence, we could not leave the resting place. The devotees or the pilgrims from both up and down journeys rushed for shelter, and Hanuman Chati became over crowded.

Incessantly it was raining for hours together, and the devotees too were performing their spiritual duties. Some were meditating, while others were either singing the hymns of God or reciting hymns from the Vedas or other scriptures; some were reciting the name (Japa) of the Divine Father or Mother. We performed our Kriya Yoga exercises as usual.

On the 27th at 5 a.m., we resumed our journey, and reached the halting place, Jamuna at 10 a.m. After taking meals and rest, we started for Gangani and reached there in the afternoon.

On the 28th May at 5.30 a.m. we started from Gangani for Uttarkashi through the dense forest. There were various kinds of flowering plants with sweet fragrance on both sides of the path. Probably we had climbed twelve to thirteen thousand feet high, passing through the most dense forest when we heard the howling of the tiger from our left side within a few feet.

At noon, we reached the resting place Singotta. After meals and some rest, we resumed our journey and at 6 p.m., we found a very small forlorn room by the side of our path, which could hardly accommodate 5 to 6 persons only. Finding no other alternative, we had to take shelter there, as it was impossible to reach Uttarkashi before night fall, five miles ahead.

Uttarkashi – Kashi of the North

Similar to Banaras, there was a bathing ghat by the name "Manikarnika" in the Ganges. Like the old Siva temple of the Banaras, the Siva temple in the 'Himalayan Banaras' was also very old. The image of the "Siva Linga" was very big. In front of it was the thick and tall 'Trisul' (Three pointed iron spear) and the image of Sri Ganesh.

There was a temple for the eleven Rudras, in front of which was the famous temple of Goddess Durga, Mahishasura Mardini by name. There were twelve Siva Lingas in the temple. Then, the temple of the Divine Mother "Annapurna" could be seen next to the huge holy tree, "Ashawattha". Next to the Annapurna temple was the brass statue of the Rishi Dattatreya, and temple of Sri Ramji. There was also the old Gopeshwar temple of Lord Sri Krishna housing the image of Sivalinga. I was surprised as I could not trace its historical background.

After visiting all these temples, we visited the temple of Jagatguru Srimat Shankaracharya. On the left of His statue, was the statue of Sri (108) Swami Totakacharya. Both the statues were made of marble.

Then we visited the Ashram of Sri Sri Anandamoyee Ma. Srimat Mahananda Brahmachariji was, at that time, engaged in worshipping the Divine Mother Kali. We had a short conversation with him. Besides, these temples and ashram, there were many small temples of antiquity, mathas and ashrams. There were two large resting houses and two institutions engaged in free distribution of both cooked and uncooked food to the Sadhus and renunciates. However, in the morning, after arriving at the holy places, we first performed our spiritual duties such as bathing in the Ganges at Manikarnika Ghat and Pujas in the temples.

Towards Gangotri

On the 30th, we started for the next holy place Gangotri — fifty-six miles from Uttarkashi. On the way there were 10 halting places at different distances, beginning with Manari (9 miles), then Bhatbari (9 miles), Ganganani (9 miles), Luharinag (4 miles), Sukhigao (3 miles), Jhala (2.5 miles), Harasila (3 miles), Dharali (4.5 miles), Bharab Chati (6 miles), and finally Gangotri (6 miles).

On the 30th May, we could travel 18 miles. Hence, we took night shelter at Bhatbari, where there was the old temple of 'Bhaskareswar' Siva established by Jagatguru Shankara. On the 31st, we could not cover more than 13 miles; for there were many bridges on the Ganges. At short distances, we found natural orchards on both the sides of the path. Fruit-trees like mangoes, and strawberries were in abundance. The Himalayan strawberries were sweeter and thicker than the strawberries of our Y.S.S., Ranchi. There were several hot springs on the way. We took bath in the hot spring near the resting place Ganganani, where we had arranged for midday meal and rest. At night, we took rest at Luharinag.

On the 1st June, we could cover only about 13 miles due to rains. We had to cross many springs and several times the Ganges over the bridges. There were many fruits orchards on both sides. Among the fruits, apples and nuts of several kinds were in large quantities. Near Harasila halt, there was a temple of Divine Parents Lakshmi-Narayan. We moved on to Dharali. Dharali was famous for two reasons. Rishi Markanda realised the ultimate Truth at Dharali. When the temple at Gangotri remains covered with snow from October to March, worship of the Goddess Ganga is done at Dharali.

In the jungles, we saw Himalayan pine, some of them were very old, probably more than five hundred years. Among the cattle, Chamari type of cows, goats and rams were common. The huge tuft tails, full of thick and long furs of the Chamari cows are generally used in Indian temples. The necks of the Chamari cows were like the neck of the buffalos. The bodies of the goats and rams had long and dense furs.

The main local business was fur clothing. The local goats had larger horns than those in the plains. Large number of Bhutanese had settled at Dharali. There was a Siva temple at the junction of the rivers Ganges and Dudhaganga.

On 2nd June, we had to cover very carefully the last 12 miles. We were entertained by natural sweet fragrance of thousands of flowering plants, particularly Chameli on both sides; some of them were very tall. At Jangula village, three miles from Dharali, the path was bifurcated - one, along the Ganges leading to Gangotri, and the other over the high mountains. The path over the mountain was for Tibet through Nilong at an altitude of 18,500 feet, twenty miles from Gangla junction. The Nilong pass proceeded to connect to Lake Manas (Manas Sarovar).

Though I was very careful, I was about to fall a few thousand feet below in the Ganges; due to the grace of Gurudeva I was protected with the aid of the stick in my hand. Girinda followed the circular path used by general public; I had taken the hill men's path. Bhairav was situated at the junction of the rivers Bhagirathi and Janhavi, flowing from Sri Kailash. At the junction of the rivers, there was a temple dedicated to Lord Bhairav (one of the many names of Lord Siva). At 4.30 p.m., we reached Gangotri and sheltered ourselves at the rest house.

Gangotri

The main temple was the beautiful temple of Goddess Ganga. In the centre of the temple was the beautiful image of Goddess Ganga, made of white marble stone. On Her left was the image of the Goddess Jamuna and on the right was the attractive image of Goddess Lakshmi (Goddess of Wealth). A little below, in front of the temple, were the images of the Goddess Annapurna, King Bhagirath, Jagatguru Shankaracharya and Saraswati Devi (Goddess of Learning). All the images were very beautiful and attractive. On the right side, there was the temple of Lord Siva. On the rear side of the Siva temple, there were some inscriptions in Sanskrit on a copper plate — Acharya Shankar had established these three temples and in 1700 A.D., Sri Amar Sinha Jana repaired the temples.

There was a huge stone called Bhagirath Sila on which the king Bhagirath used to meditate. Afterwards two fire ceremonies were performed on that stone, and subsequently two altars were erected on that famous stone as Siva and Sakti. There was Surya Kund, a lake, by the side of Bhagirath Sila which had been swept away by strong flood at mid-day in the year 159 A.D. We learnt from the local people that there were sixty temples at Dharali at one stage; save and except one, all other temples had been washed away by the Ganges.

Just opposite the temple of Gangadevi, there were many cottages for the monks. There were two bridges, one in front of the main temple and the other by the side of the Gouri tank. The distance between the main temple and Gouri Tank was two furlongs only. In front of the Gouri Tank there was a beautiful cave where Swami Shashwatiananda Giri of Govardhan Math, Puri used to live. There were two other caves. Since the doors were closed, I could not contact them. I visited Swami Krishanashrana, Swami Tapoban and Swami Pragyanath in their cottages. Swami Krishanashrana remained naked, always silent. His only belonging was a mat of jute for meditation. Swami Tapoban was a very famous monk in the Himalayas, a veteran Gyana yogi. He spoke highly of Mandaleswar Swami Bishnudwanandaji. Swamiji told me, "Now a days, our attention is not within but with the outward garbs. That's why there are so many quarrels with different sects of the renunciates or monks. Now we need to reverse our attention from outside to inside". Swami Pragyanathji was a Bengali monk. He was the disciple of Swami Gambhiranandaji. He has Ashrams, Maths and caves at Uttarkashi, Badrinath and such other places. In the evening, he used to entertain all the monks present in that holy place. Brahmachari Hariharanandaji had left us long before in order to complete the Himalayan tour quickly. In the afternoon, I had some conversation with him. I enquired, "What are the first realizations on the path of Sadhana"? He said, "They differ according to the pre-natal deeds or tendencies and also according to the path of Sadhana followed. The paths of God are different and many. Hence, only the devotee can describe the path through which he has gone. Generally, the devotees get that sort of realization first which their Guru, observing their trend of mind or nature, bestows on them. You are the follower of yoga. Hence, I believe, you will be able to explain questions on the path of yoga. What are the main realizations at the time of 'Kundalini Awakening?" I replied, "By Gayatri Japa or such other mantras and through the practice of Pranayama when the Kundalini awakes, the life force ascends through the spine and the crawling sensation is felt. At different spinal centres, the feelings or realizations are different. When the life force ascends at the heart centre, wonderful 'Anahata' sounds are heard. The devotees remain attached with that beautiful sound for a long time. We shall have to pass that stage and to rise higher. If the yogi cannot come down from the brain centre, he becomes mad. At that time, the yogi Guru helps his disciple".

I enquired, "What is difference between travelling with the Astral body and roaming in dreams?" He replied, "Astral body is a body made of light. It is quite different and separate from the physical body. Hence, yogi travels with this body as Acharya Shankar entered with his astral body into another body. But during dreams, the man realizes various glories of his soul within the body. During awakening, the soul resides at the eyes, in dreams at the cervical centre, and in deep sleep it remains at heart. Hence, during dreams the individual realizes the glories of the cervical centre".

We, thus, spent the whole day of the 3rd June. 4th was Lunar Eclipse. From the very early morning, all the pilgrims, from far and near, took bath in the Ganges, performed spiritual rites such as puja, fire ceremony, reading of the scriptures like Vedas, Gita and Chandi, recited various hymns specially the hymns composed by Acharya Shankara for the Goddess Ganga, and above all meditation. It was an interesting and wonderful experience of divine vibrations of devotion everywhere. Indeed, it was a holy place. We, too, performed puja after taking bath in the Ganges spending most of the time mainly in meditation.

On the same day, we started our return journey and could walk 12 miles before noon. We took rest at Dharali and reached Jhala in the afternoon. Hence, we could cover 17 1/2 miles towards Boodha Kedarnath.

Boodha Kedarnath

To reach Sri Sri Old Kedarnath, one must come back to Bhatbari. On the 5th we did not cover much distance. We took rest at Ganganani. On the 6th, at 9 a.m., we could return to Bhatbari (9 miles) within 4 hours. It was difficult to make out the actual distance between two halting places as there were no milestones. We collected such information from local people. Since these were largely guesses, there are differences in different guide books. It was also impossible to guess the approximate distance from the rate of walking as the speed of walking varied from one spot to another due to the topography of the place. After lunch, we took rest for some time and resumed our journey at 2.30 p.m. reaching Dogada halt in the evening, six miles away from Bhatbari. From Bhatbari to Old Kedar, there were five halts at different distances from one another - Bhatbari to Dogada (6 miles), Chuna (3 miles), Belog (4 miles), Pangrala (about 5 miles), Jhala (about 5 miles), and Old Kedar (5 miles).

On the way to Sri Sri Kedarnath Dham

On the 8th June 1947 at 8 a.m., we reached the Old Kedar, at the base of the Sri Kailash ranges. On the 9th morning, we started for the Sri Kedarnath Dham, one of the four most holy places where fifty thousand pilgrims visit every year. At distances of two or three miles, there were halting places with a few exceptions. The names and the approximate distances of the halting places were Bura Kedar to Binodbahal (2 miles), Binodbahal to Rampur (2 miles), Rampur to Kalna (2 miles), Kalna to Bhairav (3 miles), Bhairav to Bhot (3 miles), Bhot to Raipur via Gotu (4 miles), Raipur to Dophanda (2 miles), Dophanda to Pawali (2 miles), Pawali to Taliposala (4 miles), Taliposala to Mungu (4 miles), Mungu to Triyuginarayan (5 miles), Triyuginarayan to Jangal (7 miles) and Jangal to Sri Sri Kedarnath (5 miles).

From Bura Kedar to Sri Sri Kedarnath, the pathway was difficult due to continuous steep climbing up and down for miles together. The path over the ranges of the Sri Kailash (Pawali is the local name) was between 14 to 18 thousand feet high. Sometimes, we could see the lightening of the thunderstorms a few thousand feet below. Sometimes we had to walk through the snow-covered path. The thing that attracted me most was the vast expanse of natural flowerbeds of seasonal flowers of different colours where only flowers, not leaves, just about 9 inches above the ground could be seen. Only rarely, a few plants were as tall as 18 inches. At some places, the Lilly variety of flowers pierced up through the snow. Only after Mungu, there were regular flower plants like rose and jasmine. We collected some rose and jasmine for our worship at Triyuginarayan temple.

The stone image of Triyuginarayan (Image of Lord Bishnu) was placed on a spring that bifurcated the flow, one falling in the Bishnu tank and the other in the Saraswat tank; the overflows collecting at Rudra Kunda and latter's overflow passed through Brahmakunda. People took bath in the Brahmakunda. We had performed our spiritual duties according to the direction of the local priest at Triyuginarayan on the 12th June 1947.

From Triyuginarayan to Kedarnath, the path had been transformed into road with regular milestones throughout. We took rest at Bura Kedar on the 8th June at Bhot on the 9th, at Dophanda on the 10th and at Mungu on the 11th June. There were several temples on the way from Triyuginarayan to Sri Kedarnath. The temple of Goddess Sakambhari, Lord Ganesha (God of success) and Divine Mother Gouri deserve mention.

Holy Kedarnath

On the 13th June 1947, we reached Sri Sri Kedarnath, 11,753 feet high from the sea level. It was situated at the junction of the three rivers, Ganga, Saraswati and Mandakini. The Ganga flowed towards the west, the Saraswati towards the East and Mandakini towards the south. In the centre of the 1st floor of the temple was the huge stone image of Kedar- linga. On the left of Him was the image of Goddess Gouri, and on the right was the image of the Lord Ganesha; in the ground floor, at the centre, the servants of Lord Siva (Nandis), on the right the five Pandavas along with Draupadi, and on the left Naranarayana; on the rear side of the temple, there was the image of Mahadeva and Isan tank; on the eastern side of the temple were Hanga and Reta tanks. The water of the river Saraswati flowed through the Saraswati tank slowly, and with force through the Reta tank.

On the eastern side, there was the temple of Satyanarayana and the mountain Bhairav. On the Bhairav plateau, nearly two and half miles away from Kedarnath, there was the natural flower garden of pristine beauty. On the southern side, there were images of Goddess Naba Kota Durga, Annapurna and the river Mandakini. On the northern side, there was the feeble flow of the Ganges following which the Pandavas had gone away for good.

The northern summit of the visible mountain peak was known as Bhrigu peak where from Yudhisthir, the eldest Pandava ascended the Heaven. That's why Bhrigu peak was also known as peak for ascending heaven. The folk belief is that Draupadi, the wife of the Pandavas, died at that place. On the 14th, we started for Guptakashi, 24 miles from Kedarnath, and reached there on the 15th morning.

Gupta Kashi

Guptakashi means hidden Banaras. In the centre of the temple of Lord Siva (Baba Biswanath) were the images of Sivalinga, Goddess Parvati, Ganesha, Nandiswar, and Lakshminarayan. On its side was the temple of Gourisankara. At the centre of the Gourisankar temple, there was the white marble statue of the Siva and Sakti in one - right side was the form of Lord Siva and the left was Goddess Durga. On the right side of the combined form were the forms of Lord Sri Krishna with four hands and Ganeshji, and on the left Goddess Annapurna and Goddess Kali with four hands. The place was very calm and quiet, one of the finest places for meditation in the Himalayas. There were market and post office for the public in that holy place.

On the way to Badrinath

On the 15th after midday meal, we started for the last coveted holy place, Sri Sri Badrinath, 78 miles from Guptakashi. At a distance of two miles and three furlongs from Guptakashi, we visited the Usha Math, one of the most interesting Maths in the Himalayas. There were various temples and stone images of innumerable gods and goddesses. On the way, we visited the temples of Gopeswar Mahadeva and Bishnuprayag. On the 17th morning at 7 a.m., we visited Gopeswar temple. It was like all other temples full of several images of gods and goddesses. On the 18th, we visited our Joshi Math, famous temple for the monks of Giri order, founded by Acharya Shankara, 32 miles from the Gopeswar temple. The distance from Joshi Math to Vishnuprayag was only two miles. It was situated at the junction of the rivers Alakananda and Dhabaliganga. At the centre of the main temple was the image of Lord Vishnu and at the left of Him was Sri Sri Lakshmi Devi, on the right was Garuda and in front was the image of Lord Narayana. On the 20th, we reached the holy place Sri Sri Badrikashram at 8 a.m., 17 miles away from Bishnuprayag.

Holy Place Badarikashrama

Badarikashrama, at an altitude of 10,400 feet, was situated between the two mountains, Nara on the east and Narayan at the west. Some of the local people called the mountains as Krishnarjuna — Narayan as Mt. Krishna and Mt. Nara as Mt. Arjuna. At the junction of the two holy rivers Saraswati and Alakananda was the holy place Badari. Two miles away towards the north in the village Managram was the meeting place of those two holy rivers. Two miles away from the meeting place was the famous Vasundhara. There were five holy rocks and five lakes:

1. Narad-rock - Where Rishi Narada used to meditate. It was inside the river Alakananda, and a little below was the lake Narada.
2. Varaha rock - by the side of the Narad rock in the Alakananda.
3. Markendya rock - where the Rishi Markandya used to meditate.
4. Narasimha rock - They say that Narasimha Narayan was residing in the Ganges as Rock.
5. Garuda rock - The carrier of Narayan once took rest on that rock.

Main Badrinath Temple

At the entrance, there were the stone image of Mahavir and Garuda. On the right side is the temple of Goddess Lakshmi (Goddess of riches) and on the left of Ghanta Karna. At the centre, stood the stone image of Narayana, nearly 15 feet high, decorated with various gold ornaments set with diamond, ruby, emerald and such other jewels. His dress was yellow; on the neck was the garland of wild Himalayan flowers; and on the head signed the golden crown, set with all sorts of most valuable jewels, specially big diamonds. Above the crown was the umbrella made of gold border with jewels. At the right side of Narayana was Cubera, Udhav, Garuda, and Ganesh. On His left were Narada and Lakshmi. All were richly decorated. The feet of Narayana were covered with devotional offerings, specially flowers that did not allow me to see the ornaments in the feet.

At Badarikashrama, there were several hot springs, among which only one was used by the public for bath, the water of which was collected in a tank. Just opposite the temple, on the other side of the Ganges, there were many small cottages for the monks and yogis. In the afternoon, I visited some of the inmates. The whole atmosphere of the holy place Badarikashrama was full of spiritual vibration. We spent more than two days in that place performing our spiritual works.

On the 22nd at 2.15 p.m., we commenced our return journey and reached Pandukeshwar in the evening, 11 miles from Badarikashrama. On our return journey, we visited several other holy places, like Sri Sri Nandaprayag, Sri Sri Rudraprayag, Sri Sri Devaprayag. Sri Nandaprayag was 54 miles from Badrinath situated at the junction of the rivers Nanda and Alakananda, which we visited on the 25th June 1947. Sri Rudrapryag was 36 miles away from Nandaprayag, situated at the junction of the rivers Alakananda and Mandakini, which we visited on the 26th June 1947. The river Alakananda was flowing from Sri Badrinarayana, the river Mandakini was flowing from Sri Kedarnath. The distance from Kedarnath to Rudraprayag was 48 miles. From Sri Badrinath to Rudraprayag was nearly 90 miles.

On the 28th June, we reached Kritinagar, a town 21 miles from Rudraprayag where we booked our seats on a bus for Devaprayag. On the 29th, we reached Devaprayag; two hours and fifteen minutes journey by bus. After performing our puja, etc., we returned to Hrishikesh by bus -about five and half hours' journey by bus. After paying return visit to Kailash Ashrama, we returned to Sri Sri Bholananda Sannyas Ashram, Hardwar.

Chapter 27
Visiting the Son of Gandha Baba

I had an opportunity of visiting the son of Gandha Baba in Burdwan at his residence. When he came before me, a very sweet and most attractive perfume was emanating from his body. Realizing the heavenly and unusually strong fragrance, I thought it might be coming from his inner body. Hence, I asked, "Is this perfume coming from your navel centre?" He replied in the affirmation.

During our conversation, I came to know that he had acquired some of the yogic powers of his father. The yogis have the power to transmit their knowledge to their students or their disciples through some secret yogic way. In some way or the other, Gandha Baba had transmitted his knowledge to his son, whose intuitive channels were ready to accept the same at that time through the regular practice of yogic techniques. Natural question is the science behind the display and transfer of perfumes either in one's own body or in others or to any substance. His real name was Vishudhananda, who had learnt many astonishing yoga secrets from a Tibetan yogi who used to display the same publicly.

While explaining the science behind all those displays, Paramhansa Yogananda said, "Years later, I understood by inner realization, how Gandha Baba accomplished his materializations. The method, alas, is beyond the reach of the world's hungry hordes". "The different sensory stimuli to which man reacts namely tactual, visual, gustatory, auditory, and Olfactory - are produced by vibratory variations in electrons and protons. The vibrations in turn are regulated by prana, "lifetrons", subtle life forces or finer-than-atomic energies intelligently charged with the five distinctive sensory idea substances.

"Gandha Baba, tuning himself with the pranic force by certain yoga practice, was able to guide the lifetrons to rearrange their vibratory structure and to objectify the desired result. His perfume, fruit, and other miracles were actual materializations of mundane vibrations, and were not inner sensations hypnotically produced".

In the foot-note, Paramahansaji further added: "Laymen scarcely realize the vast strides of twentieth-century science. Transmutation of metals and other alchemical dreams are seeing fulfillment every day in centres of scientific research over the world. The eminent French chemist, M. Georges Claude, performed "miracles" at Fontainebleau in 1928 through his demonstrations of oxygen transformations. The Associated Press reported that M. Claude, at a scientific gathering, "turned a handful of sand into precious stones, iron into a state resembling melted chocolate, and, after depriving flowers of their tents, turned them to the consistency of glass".

There is interesting meaning of Sutras of Bibhutipada in Patanjali.

1. In the Sutra 26, of the said 'pada' it was written, "We can get the knowledge of the Great Cosmos, concentrating our mind on the sun".
2. "We can get the knowledge of the stars, concentrating our mind on the moon". (Sutra 27)
3. "We can get the knowledge of the 'Dhruba' star (Pole Star), fixing our mind on it". (Sutra 28)
4. "We can get the full knowledge of the whole body system along with its functions, fixing our attention on the naval centre. (Sutra-29)

During my usual meditation, the above thoughts disturbed me much. Then at the end I got a vision. In that vision I clearly perceived how due to the variations of vibrations of the lifetronic forces in my body, the sun, the moon, etc. were created in my Christ eye. Then I came to know also the meaning of the words, "The moon is located at the root of the palate". Hence, we should bear in mind that the book of Patanjali is a book written on yoga. The sun, moon, etc. mentioned in his book are the formulated laws pertaining to yoga. The sun, the moon, the 'Dhruba' star, etc. are not heavenly astronomical bodies.

On another occasion, while I was reading the Bible, I found what Lord Jesus Christ tried to convey to His disciples. At one place, it is written, "If, therefore, thine eye be single, thy whole body shall be full of light". Mathew 6-22.

During meditation, I could not avoid the thought. At last, at dead of night, I got the vision. I saw a large auditorium where a divine angel was delivering a lecture to a large gathering sitting in rows. I was sitting in the front row very near the divine angel. He was explaining the Bible and those words of Lord Christ, in a scientific manner. After explaining once, he enquired from me, whether I could follow the explanation. I replied in the negative. Then he explained to me again. Again he asked me, about the perception of the meaning. This time I replied in the affirmative. Then he ordered me to explain the scientific meaning of the 'words' to the audience. At his direction, I approached the black board and explained the same to the audience. As I came to the end of my explanation, the vision terminated.

On another occasion while I was writing the spiritual interpretation of the Holy Vedas (Rig Vedas), I was struggling with the real meaning of a particular verse. At night during my meditation I got the vision, which gave me the clear insight of that particular verse.

However, such yogic powers of the yogis may be used for beneficial purposes only like mitigation of sorrows of the afflicted persons, curing of the diseases and so forth. But if the yogic powers are utilised for personal gain or for name and fame, it is very bad. It is a sort of misuse of power. At the end the yogis have to suffer for misuse of power. Put God first, then everything will follow automatically. Of course, it is true that many highly advanced yogis fall from their elevated position due to the transgression of spiritual laws for name, fame and personal gain.

Paramahansa Yoganandaji had narrated in detail why a yogi had fallen from his elevated position and had lost all his yogic powers. His main purpose to describe that fall of a yogi may be to give warning to the students who are following the path of God. If we follow the dictates of the evil propensities and do not care to observe the spiritual laws rigidly, we are sure to fall down from the path of God.

Paramahansa Yoganandaji in His autobiography wrote:

> *"I never saw Afzal after that day, but a few years later Babu came to my home to show me a newspaper report of the Mohammedan's public confession. From it, I learned the fact I have just told you about Afzal's early initiation from a Hindu Guru".*

The gist of the latter part of the published document, as recalled by Sri Yukteshwarji, was as follows: "I, Afzal Khan, am writing these words as an act of penance and as a warning to those who seek the possession of miraculous powers. For years, I have been misusing the wondrous abilities imparted to me through the grace of God and my master. I became drunk with egotism, feeling that I was beyond the ordinary laws of morality. My day of reckoning finally arrived.

Recently I met an old man on a road outside Calcutta. He limped along painfully, carrying a shining object that looked like gold. I addressed him with greed in my heart.

"I am Afzal Khan, the great Fakir. What have you there?"

"This ball of gold is my sole material wealth; it can be of no interest to a fakir. I implore you, Sir, to heal my limp". I touched the ball and walked away without reply. The old man hobbled after me. He soon raised an outcry. "My gold is gone". As I paid no attention, he suddenly spoke in a stern voice that issued oddly from his frail body. "Do you not recognize me?"

I stood speechless, aghast at the belated discovery that this unimpressive old cripple was none other than the great saint who, long ago, had initiated me into yoga. He straightened himself; his body instantly became strong and youthful.

My guru's glance was fiery. "I see with my own eyes that you use your powers, not to help suffering humanity, but to prey on it like a common thief. I withdraw your occult powers; Hazrat is now freed from you. No longer shall you be a terror in Bengal."

I called on Hazrat in anguished tones; for the first time, he did not appear in my inner sight. But a dark veil suddenly lifted; I saw clearly the blasphemy of my life.

"My guru, I thank you for banishing my long delusion". I was sobbing at his feet. "I promise to forsake my worldly ambitions. I will retire to the mountains for lonely meditation on God, hoping to atone for my evil past".

My master treated me with silent compassion. 'I feel your sincerity', he said finally. Because of your earlier years of strict obedience, and because of your present repentance, I shall grant you one boon. Your other powers are now gone, but whenever food and clothing are needed, you may still call successfully on Hazrat to supply them. Devote yourself whole-heatedly to divine understanding in the mountain solitudes". My guru then vanished. I was left to my tears and reflections. Farewell, world. I go to seek the forgiveness of the Cosmic Beloved.

However, such yogic powers may be utilised for mitigation of the sufferings of the bewildered people of the world, specially for curing the diseases which visit nearly every house in the world. What is the science behind such cure? How the yogis cure the ailments of the patients instantaneously, which puzzle the general public and the doctors of the hospitals alike?

In order to understand the science behind such instantaneous cure, we should know the relation of thought, life force, and the body. The body is the frozen thought and frozen energy of God. The yogis not only know the truth, but also realise at heart that the thought is frozen into energy and energy is frozen into the physical body of man. The body is made of invisible (invisible to the ordinary eye and also to ordinary compound microscope) electrons, and the electrons are made of invisible (invisible to the electron microscope) lifetrons which too are made of the invisible thought of God. Therefore, we can say thought is the brain of the cells and units of lifetrons are present in every atom of the body. Hence, the thought of a disease upset the entire functions of the life-force in the cells of the body, whereas a strong or powerful thought of health corrects any disorder in the tissue system. The thought of a highly advanced yogi is not the thought of an ordinary man. It is impregnated with the omnipresent Divine will of God. This Divinely tuned willpower of the yogi can change any atomic constitution of the body in order to correct the disorder in the tissue system. This Divinely tuned willpower of the yogis may be termed as Soul Force, acquired through regular and faithful practice of yoga system under the guidance of a true yogi. The yogi can cure a disease from a distance without touching the body of the afflicted person. The yogi transmits his Soul Force in the ether. This all accomplishing will power can produce the desired result in patient's body. Ordinary songs and speeches received through the transistor or radio produce some mental effect upon the listener, but the words of a true yogi, impregnated with the Soul Force being transmitted through the ether, produce the desired result.

In my book, "The Laws of Pre-natal Karma", I have explained certain fundamental laws that are responsible for the sufferings of man, which may be skillfully adjusted by various means. A few points that deserves mention here are:

1. For every action, there must be a counter-action or reaction. Where there are many actions, the resultant action is the final action. Good works produce good results — name, fame, health, money and so on. Evil works produce defame, ill-name, loss of money, diseases and various kinds of sufferings.

2. What we have done, that we can undo either directly sufferings, by astrological means, by auto-suggestion, by the interference of the yogi and various other means.
3. There are certain karmic laws which cannot be avoided and must be worked out either partly or wholly. While interfering with such karmic sufferings, the yogis in question have to transfer the diseases or such other sufferings of the persons in question to their own bodies. By certain secret yogic process, the yogis unite their minds and astral bodies with those of the suffering individuals, the diseases are conveyed whole or partly to the yogi's bodies. Though the yogis suffer in that way, still their minds are not affected due to their Self-realization.

Chapter 28
We Visit France

On 15th May 1969, along with my spiritual assistant, Paramahansa Haridashi Mata, I started for France by Air India as Spiritual Director of Atma Bodha Satsanga to give initiation to a number of students of the society. There we had to stay for nearly twenty days for initiation and public lectures. The report of our activities had been published by the President of the Atma Bodha Satsanga, in France and also by Sri Dwarika Nath Chatterjee, Ambassador, Embassy of India, France.

By appointments, the public used to visit us to solve their various problems. During their visits either the President of the Society or his wife used to serve as an interpreter. My spiritual assistant also used to sit by my side. Once, a woman came to me to solve her problem. She enquired: "How can I get peace of mind?" while I was advising her, my spiritual assistant wanted to explain in her own way to get the peace of mind. I allowed her to do so.

Paramahansa Haridashi Mata, without any hesitation, told her: "You can't get peace of mind by serving five husbands".

"Oh! they are not my real husbands".

"Well, then forsake them and serve the Divine Beloved, who is the Husband of us all". Then she asked the interpreter: "Is she a Goddess or a human being?". Anusua Mata was at that time working as an interpreter. As she asked her question, I replied: "Well, she is both".

On another occasion, a lady came to me to solve her problem. I granted her five minutes. Within that time, she also wanted to speak to my spiritual assistant. Paramahansa Haridashi Mata said: "I don't like to speak to a film star".

Rishi Atri, the President of the Society was acting as an interpreter. He enquired from her: "Are you a film actress?" She affirmed happily. By then her scheduled time expired and she left the place making room for the next visitor.

On another occasion, Haridashi Mata said to me: "Well, Swamiji, in this Chapel, a few years ago a lady had died. Due to her unnatural death, she is now residing here as a ghost". The day she divulged the above fact to me was the day for weekly meeting of the society in the Chapel. Though the meeting was over, still all the members were within the hall, downstairs for refreshment (Prasad). I enquired about the fact from Anusua Mata. She, in turn, after proper enquiry, came to know the fact to be true.

How could Paramahansa Haridashi Mata know life history of the public woman or the film star or the presence of a ghost who was once the resident of the house? What is the science behind all such miracles?

If a person, through practice of yoga, can still need his or her mind for a long time and if the mind of such a yogi becomes absolutely free from all restless thoughts, he or she can reflect within himself or herself, the thoughts that pass through the consciousness of another person. Of course, this is only possible when he or she can remain in that thought-free state for any length of time. When this stage of mind is attained, then on that clear unexposed plate of his or her mind he or she can photograph any thought or any question.

There is another process by which a yogi can know the life history of an individual. As is by faithful and regular practice of yoga techniques, a yogi can go into the realm of his or her subconscious mind without being intruded upon by the thought of his or her own conscious mind. By consciously projecting subconscious mind into the subconscious mind of another, one can know the thoughts and experiences of the person in question.

The third is the best way of all. When a highly advanced yogi can go into the deepest region of Bliss of the super conscious mind at will, and can transfer his consciousness there, then the yogi, through the God-given omniscient power of intuition, can know all the present, past and future thoughts of an individual. Through this all seeing intuitive power, the yogi can know all the pre-natal actions hidden dormant in the mind of another person, and hence all the present and past history of any person. The super conscious mind hides behind the restlessness of conscious life and also of the subconscious mind. Regarding the highest attainment of Paramahansa Haridashi Mata, I have already written separately in this book.

We visited various places of interest in France and returned to India on the 6th June 1969 via London by Air India.

Chapter 29

We Do Not Visit Australia and South Africa

Mysterious are the ways of Providence. We cannot understand or fathom the subtle ways of God and Gurus. Hence, it is very difficult to explain the apparent dislodge of our fixed plan.

The people of S.R.F. (Sydney), Australia, especially Mr. C. I. Tenuket, the Secretary of the Society, were trying their level best to get me in their midst for spiritual guidance and initiation of the deserving ones. In this they had passed one resolution in their meeting with the top-ranking members and had sent the copy to our Western Headquarters for approval. It is a matter of great interest that even individual prayers were sent to Sri Sri Daya Mata, who was in Australia for at least three months, which I came to know from various individual letters sent to me from S.R.F., Australia. Intuitively, I could understand that my journey to Australia would be interrupted by some invisible hand. A plan had also been chalked out by the adjacent countries to have me in their midst when my work in Australia would be over.

By that time Sri Sri Daya Mata had arrived in India and was residing at Dakshineswar in our midst. My visit to S.R.F., Sydney had been discussed in the urgent meeting of the Board of Directors. They passed a resolution that the Board of Directors could not spare me even for a month as India needed me so urgently. But the reasons which frustrated all the plans of the people of Sydney (S.R.F.), Australia and the adjacent countries were different.

On the 1st January 1961, at Y.S.S., Dakshineswar at dead of night, my Guru Paramahansa Yoganandaji appeared before me and told me: "I had gone to Babaji Maharaj on the 27th December 1960 at Kailash to discuss about you. I had come back on the 28 th December. On my arrival there, Babaji Maharaj commented, "You have come to discuss about Animananda. Well, he should not go to Australia now." The Gurus, until now used to call me most of the times as 'Anima', on rare occasions 'Animananda'.

Paramahansa Yoganandaji then explained to me the reason why I should not go to Australia: 'If you go to Australia now, Haridashi Devi would leave her mortal coil. She is now trying to leave this world and fly to the Highest Heaven for good. She has one desire to die at Banaras. Hence, don't allow her to go to Banaras. If she can any how go to Banaras, she will never come back, and will die there on the day of her arrival.

"Secondly, if she does not get permission to go to Banaras from you, she is contemplating to go to Kamakshya. She has got one companion, who will bear all her expenses including the journey to the holy place. If she gets a chance to go to that holy place, Kamakshya, she will discard her physical body there and would be one with Divine Mother in the temple".

"Thirdly, if you do not allow her to go to Kamakshya too, she will try to leave her body by hunger strike. On going to Ranchi, please drop a letter to her requesting her not to go either to Banaras or to Kamakshya. You should also write requesting her to take regular meals daily. If she goes away now, you won't be able to do the works of the world alone. My desire also will not be fulfilled."

"Now, you will have to do the works in India. Those works are not yet finished, and hence, I don't think it is advisable to go to Australia now. The people of Australia are trying their best to take you there now".

It was the silent wish of Babaji which worked in the minds of the Board of Directors in India, not to allow me to go to Australia. But how did the silent wish work in the minds of all the members of the Board of Directors? Let me quote one similar instance from the Autobiography of Paramahansa Yoganandaji:

"Lahiri, do you remember that seat", the yogi pointed to a folded blanket in one corner.

"No, Sir". Somewhat dazed at the strangeness of my adventure, I added "I must leave now, before nightfall. I have business in the morning at my office".

The mysterious saint replied in English, "The office was brought for you, and not you for the office".

I was dumbfounded that this forest ascetic should not only speak English but also paraphrase the words of Christ ('The Sabbath was made for man, and not man for the Sabbath' - Mark 2/27).

"I see my telegram took effect". The yogi's remark was incomprehensible to me; I asked its meaning.

"I refer to the telegram that summoned you to these isolated parts. It was I who silently suggested to the mind of your superior officer that you be transferred to Ranikhet. When one feels unity with mankind, all minds become transmitting stations through which he can work at will".

As Babaji's being was one with the Divine Father, he felt his unity with the mankind. He could silently transmit his wish to the minds of the members of the Board of Directors in India.

There was a subtle Divine hand's work behind my aborted journey to South Africa. When the people of South Africa were trying to get me there for their initiation, I wrote a personal letter to Shri N.R.Mukherjee, Under-Secretary (Com.) regarding the possibility of visiting South Africa, as I had come to know from the Manager N. Jamnadas and Co., Calcutta, that the Government of India are not issuing any passport to any one for visiting Pakistan and South Africa. In reply to my letter, I received the following letter from Sri K.B. Bala, Under Secretary (PV), Government of India, Ministry of External Affairs No. VI/405/7/63/69 dated New Delhi (11), the 8th October, 1969:

Dear Sir,

I am directed to refer to your letter No. 873 of September 28, 1969 addressed to Shri N.R.Mukherjee, Under Secretary (Com.), regarding passport facilities for visit to South Africa for purposes. Other than tourism and business, you should apply for a passport on a prescribed form to the Regional Passport Officer, Calcutta.

As regards grant of visa etc., you may please write to the British High Commission, Shantipath, Chanakyapuri, New Delhi - 11.

Yours faithfully, (K.B. Bala) Under Secretary (PV)

On receipt of the letter, I got extra endorsements made for visiting South Africa, Kenya, Uganda, Republic of Tanzania and Rhodesia in my existing Passport. I had stated all these here, even though not very relevant, only to show that there was no obstruction from the human side notwithstanding the then political situation. But the Divine Hand interrupted our plans.

A few days ago, Paramahansa Yoganandaji told me, "Anima, very soon people from Africa will come to take you in their country. Now, everywhere in the world fire is blazing. You should not go to Africa now. Who knows fire may fall on whose head".

Previously, Paramahansa Haridashi Mata too, had come to know through her intuition regarding the future happenings (war, flood and so forth) and had intimated me accordingly before I received this message from my Guru. The warning from my Guru came when I had already got extra endorsements made for trip to South Africa in my existing Passport.

Due to this "universal fire", we did not go to South Africa. The Gurus also diverted the minds of the people who were scheduled to arrive in India to take me to their land and had managed to send them to other parts of the world.

Epilogue

Swamiji was born in 1915. He met Paramhansa Yoganandaji on 25 September, 1935 for the first time when Paramhansa Yoganandaji was in Calcutta to deliver a lecture on Pranayama in the Albert Hall. Swamiji, then Sri Anil Basu, was just 20 year old. His spiritual journey that had started years ago came to the mainstream scientific way of self realization after he met Paramhansa Yoganandaji.

Swamiji maintained meticulous diary ever since; not only date and year but also the time of the day and the night. The diaries that Swamiji gave me to prepare this book, he documented episodes till May 1969 when Swamiji visited France. Another half story is dated to October 1969 when Swamiji did not visit Australia and South Africa under divine guidance and instruction exemplifying the oft quoted maxim, "Man proposes, God disposes". Swamiji was in his physical body for another 36 years till he left for the heavenly abode in 2005.

Swamiji had set up an Ashram in Sarasbediya, a village near Salboni – an obscure place deep in Medinipur district of West Bengal that later became an active hub of extremist activists. The Ashram in Sarasbediya was established somewhere in mid 1960's. Swami Abhayanandaji of Golkunda Ashram in Purulia was initiated by Swamiji in Sarasbediya Ashram in 1968 when Abhayanandaji was just 14 years old and a student of class 8.

Swamiji withdrew himself to Sarasbediya in isolation for deep meditation away from his previous work sites of SRF. The Ashram was named Sri Sri Yogoda Ashram Centre. He lived here alone, except one village boy to assist him in day to day chores.

As Abhayanandaji grew up and refused to marry and decided to take to spiritual life, Swamiji advised him to set up an Ashram and leave the family life. Abhayanandaji and Swamiji inspected many sites, but final choice fell upon the plot, rather field, where Golkunda Ashram is located now. This Ashram too is at an obscure corner of Purulia. It was set up in 1985. Swamiji used to share his time between Sarasbediya and Golkunda Ashrams, especially after 1985. He would occasionally visit his disciples in Kolkata for a few days. I met Swamiji in 2000.

'When the disciple is ready, the Guru will come', they say. So true it is for me when Swamiji appeared, rather reappeared in our life 48 years after I first met him as a child in our village home.

I was at a conference in Ramakrishna Mission, Coimbatore in 2000. I shared a few experiences with Swamiji Maharaj there. He advised me to take initiation. Clueless, I did not know how to go about the process. Swamiji Maharaj was kind enough to organize everything on phone and a date, after about two months, was fixed for me to be initiated at the Ramakrishna Mission, Belur Math. After the Conference, I returned back to Delhi.

My sisters who were initiated by Brahmachari Animanandaji have been searching for their Guru desperately. On my return to Delhi, I received a message from my sisters in Uttarpara and Udang that they have been able to trace Animanandaji. He has an Ashram in Sarasbediya, Salboni in Medinipur.

Animanandaji had initiated my parents, sisters, sister-in-law and a few other neighbours when he visited our village probably in 1952 – some 48 years ago. Correspondence between my father and Animanandaji went on for several years. Then they got disconnected. In the meanwhile, both our parents and eldest brother left for the heavenly abode.

I knew my sisters were desperate to trace their Guru. I called them up to say that in a few days, I would come to Kolkata and Udang; we'll visit Sarasbediya and see Animanandaji. I reached Udang. We hired a cab and started early in the morning for Sarasbediya (Salboni) Ashram. We reached just before noon. It took us some time to hunt the Ashram. It was a small campus surrounded by high walled boundaries. Inside there were a few mango and other fruit trees, a water pump, and a small Kutia (cottage) where Animanandaji lived. As we knocked at the gate that was closed, a young man came and opened the gate. He informed Animanandaji about our arrival. Animanandaji came out of his Kutia. We touched his feet one by one.

He looked so different that I was not sure that we were at the right place and with the right person. Our lasting impression was of a beaming young Brahmachari Animanandaji (then 37 year old) clad in spotless white dress. Whom we now meet is a serene saint of 85 years in saffron. I asked him, "Sir, Are you Animanandaji?" The saint responded, "Baba, that was my previous name. I am now in the Swami order. I am now Swami Satchidananda Giri."

He asked, "What is your name? Where are you from?" As I told about myself and introduced my sisters, Swamiji went inside and brought a diary. He flipped through the pages and traced every name he had initiated in Udang 48 years ago. We felt comfortable, we were at the right place. My sisters were thrilled to find their Guru again.

We had lunch at the Ashram. I thought for a while, what would have my father or eldest brother done if they were here at this moment. Sure, they would invite Swamiji to visit our home at Udang. I decided to invite Swamiji to Udang. I requested him to come to Udang. He readily agreed and also gave us the date of his visit. We planned to pick him up from Salboni and take him to Udang on the decided date.

As we were ready to leave, something happened that I must share with all of you. Swamiji asked us to take a few mangoes from the Ashram. The Ashram boy got some mangoes – real big size and a plastic bag. Swamiji himself started putting the mangoes in the bag. He was trying to push as many mangoes as he can in that small bag. He was so happy like a child to give, he kept on pushing and asking for more mangoes. He exclaimed, 'see how such a small bag is taking so many mangoes!" I could not resist my amusement; but quietly drew his attention that the other side of the plastic bag had already given way, and actually mangoes were going out of the other end. My sisters were amused as Swamiji's child like joy and later embarrassment. I have experienced this pure child in Swamiji time and again later.

On the appointed date, I picked up Swamiji from the Ashram and took him to Udang. Swamiji graced our village home. After some initial hospitality, Swamiji called me and told me, "I'll give you initiation day after tomorrow at ten in the morning." I was shaken with surprise; that was the date and time fixed for my initiation at the Ramakrishna Mission, Belur Math. I recollected my reading, "When the disciple is ready, the Guru will come". Here comes my Guru! I was initiated. What a divine grace to be disciple of a saint!

Later, Gurudev graced our village home. He visited Delhi and stayed with us at my official staff quarter in NIEPA. We had a separate room for the Goddess. Gurudev preferred to stay there. He liked NIEPA accommodation for the garden that had lots of different flowers.

However, his first preference was our flat in West Delhi that he will mark as Delhi-34. It was vacant and reserved as our post retirement rendezvous. Here, he was totally to himself. My sister used to come and stay whenever Gurudev came to stay with us in Delhi. Whenever she could not, we got a boy from the village to stay. I would visit for few hours after my office during the week days and spend the weekend in the divine company of Gurudev. It was a duplex flat with two rooms at the fourth floor and two at the third floor. Gurudev stayed in one room at the top floor; other room in the same floor was our temple.

Let me share a few episodes that we keep remembering and enjoying. Gurudev used to maintain diaries and write letters to his disciples. Indeed, a lot of writing. One day, he asked me 'Baba, would you please get me a pen.' I bought four pens – ordinary ball point pens – blue, black, green and red on my way back to the flat. When I handed over the pens, he was so thrilled that he rushed down to the third floor and shouted for my sister, "Ma, Ma, see Baba has bought four pens for me'. Joy in his face and the entire being was so obvious. My sister, Chhordi smiled the way a mother smiles at her son's innocence.

Delhi becomes very cold. It touches 4 degree centigrade. Forgetting a saint's capability of overcoming dualities of hot and cold, I bought a set of thermals and a cap for Gurudev. First he was not sure whether he should put on those thermals. He asked Chhordi who readily permitted with her flowing motherly affection. He immediately, like an obedient child put on the thermal and the cap. He started perspiring, but sat quietly admiring how I was able to buy the pieces that fitted him so well. Chhordi noticed his perspiration and asked him to take off the cap and the thermal. He readily obeyed like a child, again.

Swamiji visited our home at Udang, NIEPA quarters and 'Delhi-34' on several occasions and stayed for few weeks at one stretch especially when he stayed at Delhi -34 till 2003. He used to travel from Purulia Ashram. It is during his stay in Delhi -34, he handed over the diaries that contained the manuscript of this book.

Swamiji spent last few years of life in his Purulia Ashram. His constant company and care giver was his disciple Swami Abhayanandaji and his younger brother Gopal. Other disciples from Purulia, Kolkata and other places trickled down visiting the Ashram for Guru Darshan from time to time. I was also one of them. I visited Purulia Ashram on several occasions with my sisters and other relatives who were also disciples of Swamiji.

Swamiji stopped visiting other Ashrams including Sarasbediya, Rangamati and Lakhanpur where he spent long time of his life. Swami Abhayanandaji who was his only constant company noticed some change in Swamiji. He remained in his trance for long hours, occasionally being non-communicative. When Abhayanandaji used to pursue Swamiji, he would reluctantly reveal his will to take Samadhi and join his Guru, Paramhansa Yoganandaji.

In 2004, Swamiji visited a few of his disciples in Kolkata. Ever since he came back, he withdrew himself much more into his inner world. He never shared his experiences in Kolkata. Sometimes he expressed his wish of *Atmagopan* (going underground) or to isolate himself completely from people.

Swami Abhayanandaji probably perceived Swamiji's determined wish. He decided not to leave Swamiji alone lest he leaves his physical body. He asked Swamiji if he has some wish to fulfil. Swamiji expressed his wish to visit Narmada once again for the last time- Amarkantak, Onkareswar, and Ujjain. According to Swami Abhayananda, "Swamiji probably wished to take Samadhi at Onkareswar". Abhayanandaji and Mr. Daga, another disciple took the lead. A group of 13 devotees and Swamiji left for Narmada in early March, 2005 and returned back to Purulia Ashram by mid-March (1st *Falguna*). Not to leave Swamiji alone in a room, Abhayanandaji with two other disciples slept in the same room with Swamiji.

Ever since Swamiji came back from Narmada, he seemed lost in some thought occasionally expressing his will to leave the body. As told by Swami Abhayanandaji, on one night in Golkunda Ashram, Swamiji sat on prayer at eleven in the night with the wish to leave the body in Samadhi. Perceiving his intention, Abhayanandaji broke his Samadhi at 2.00 a.m. Swamiji refused to leave the position and posture. Abhayanandaji insisted and won over his Guru.

In December, Swamiji developed some breathing trouble. On 24th December, 2005 the breathing problem was little more and became a matter of concern. Abhayanandaji and a few local disciples decided to move him to a Nursing Home in Purulia town in the care of doctors. Ambulance was called. Sri Ashish Paramanik, Sri Dhiren Haldar and Sri Brahmananda accompanied Swamiji in the ambulance. Swamiji advised Abhayanandaji to come on his bike. Swamiji was fully aware that, by dint of the spiritual power given to his disciple, Swamiji would not be able to leave the body as long as Abhayanandaji was with him.

Thus, he separated Abhayanandaji from his proximity. Swamiji rested his head on the lap of Sri Ashish Paramanik and left for his heavenly abode on the way to the nursing home to merge with his Guru.

Thus came the end of an illustrious life of a saint who uplifted many lives in various parts of India and the world.

Swami Satchidananda Giri

Swamiji in the Ashram (Purulia)

Bhai Animanandaji (Before Sanithood)

Swamiji with Swami Vidyananda Giri at the
Guru Mandir in Purulia Ashram

Swamiji, Then Bhai Animanandaji in Different
Yoga Asanas

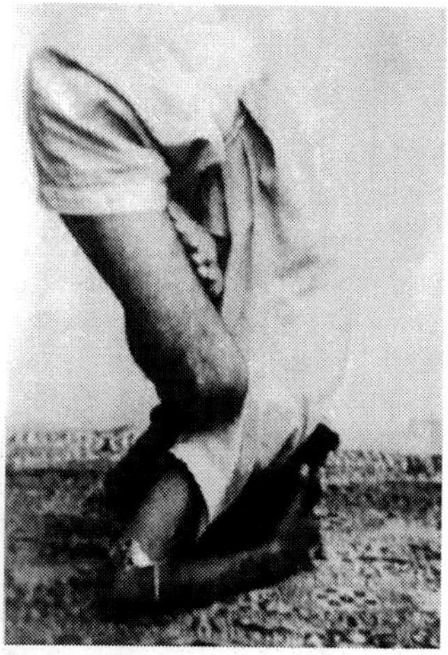

Swamiji with Disciples

Garva Griha at Purulia Ashrama

Swamiji at Guru Mandir in Purulia Ashrama

Swamiji Samadhi Mandir